THIRD EDITION

Vocabulary for the College-Bound Student

Vocabulary books by the authors

Vocabulary and Composition Through Pleasurable Reading, Books I–VI
Vocabulary for Enjoyment, Books I–III
Vocabulary for the High School Student, Books A, B
Vocabulary for the High School Student
Vocabulary for the College-Bound Student
The Joy of Vocabulary

THIRD EDITION

Vocabulary for the College-Bound Student

HAROLD LEVINE
Chairman Emeritus of English,
Benjamin Cardozo High School, New York

NORMAN LEVINE
Associate Professor of English,
City College of the City University of New York

ROBERT T. LEVINE
Professor of English,
North Carolina A & T State University

Dedicated to serving

our nation's youth

AMSCO SCHOOL PUBLICATIONS, INC.

315 Hudson Street / New York, N.Y. 10013

When ordering this book, please specify:
either **R 573 S** or
VOCABULARY FOR THE COLLEGE-BOUND STUDENT
SOFTBOUND

ISBN 0-87720-758-5

Printed in the United States of America

2 3 4 5 6 7 8 9 10   99 98 97 96 95 94

PREFACE

The aim of this updated and enlarged edition is to help high school students build a superior vocabulary and use it effectively. About two hundred new lesson words have been incorporated into the text. The exercises, to an even greater extent than in the previous edition, teach close reading and concise writing at the same time as vocabulary. Some exercises ask students to write "minicompositions" of no more than three sentences, in which they not only use their new lesson words, but also learn an important composition skill, like stating an opinion and supporting it with reasons or examples.

Except for the above changes, the vocabulary-building procedures of the previous edition have been retained.

Learning New Words From the Context (Chapter 2) is an adventure in critical thinking. It presents eighty short passages in which possibly unfamiliar words can be defined with help from clues in the context. By teaching students how to interpret such clues, this chapter provides them with a lifelong tool for vocabulary growth, *and at the same time, it makes them better readers.*

Building Vocabulary Through Central Ideas (Chapter 3) involves students in studying twenty-five groups of related words. In the FLATTERY group, they will learn *adulation, cajole, obsequious,* etc.—and in the REASONING group, *analogy, axiomatic, specious,* etc.

Words Derived From Greek (Chapter 4) teaches derivatives from twenty-five Ancient Greek word elements. For example, from EU, meaning "good," we get *euphemism, euphoria, euthanasia,* etc.—and from DYS, meaning "bad," *dysfunction, dyspepsia, dystrophy,* etc.

Words Derived From Latin (Chapter 5), the largest source of English words, teaches derivatives from thirty Latin roots. The root VOR, for example, meaning "eat," gives us *carnivorous, frugivorous, voracious,* etc.—and the root FRACT, meaning "break," yields *fractious, infraction, refractory,* etc.

Words From Classical Mythology and History (Chapter 6) teaches not only derivatives from the myths of the Ancient Greeks and Romans, like *amazon, hector, narcissistic,* etc. It also teaches derivatives from classical history, like *Draconian, Lucullan, marathon,* etc.

Anglo-Saxon Vocabulary (Chapter 7) teaches derivatives from prefixes like WITH, meaning "back,": *withdraw, withhold*, etc.—and suffixes like LING, meaning "little,": *sapling, stripling*, etc. It also pairs some Anglo-Saxon words with nearly synonymous Latin-derived words—for example, *flay* with *excoriate*—to help students enrich their vocabularies.

French Words in English (Chapter 8) teaches about one hundred fifty loanwords integrated into English from French—*clairvoyant, canard, concierge, martinet, nonpareil*, etc.

Italian Words in English (Chapter 9) teaches similar borrowings from Italian—*alfresco, crescendo, diva, imbroglio, impresario*, etc.

Spanish Words in English (Chapter 10) teaches such loanwords from Spanish as *aficionado, barrio, bodega, bonanza, macho*, etc.

Sample Vocabulary Questions in Pre-College Tests (Chapter 11) reprints, with permission, a total of sixty-three sentence completion, antonym, and word analogy questions intended to acquaint students with the following pre-college tests:

1. PSAT/NMSQT (The Preliminary Scholastic Aptitude Test/ National Merit Scholarship Qualifying Test)
2. SAT (The Scholastic Aptitude Test)

Of the reprinted questions, twenty-one are sample questions with accompanying explanations, and forty-two are practice-test questions, for which the official answer keys are provided.

Dictionary of Words Taught in This Text (Chapter 12) is appended for ease of reference and review.

Students should be encouraged to use their newly learned words whenever appropriate in their writing and classroom discussions. Only through actual use will they be able to incorporate such words into their vocabularies. They should also be encouraged to own a good dictionary and to develop the dictionary habit.

The Authors

CONTENTS

Chapter 4   Words Derived From Greek   99

Chapter 5 Words Derived From Latin 136

LATIN PREFIXES 1–15 137; **16–30** 140

LATIN ROOTS

Chapter 6   Words From Classical Mythology and
              History   187

Chapter 7   Anglo-Saxon Vocabulary   199

CHAPTER 1

The Importance of Vocabulary to You

Vocabulary and thinking

Words stand for ideas. Words are the tools of thought. If your word power is limited, your ability to think will also be limited, since you can neither receive ideas nor communicate with others except within the confines of an inadequate vocabulary. But if you broaden your vocabulary, you will find it easier to do the thinking that success in life often demands.

Vocabulary and college admission

College admissions officers will be interested in the extent of your vocabulary, for a good vocabulary will suggest that you are likely to do well in college. It will suggest, too, that you have done wide reading, since reading is the principal way of developing a good vocabulary. In the college entrance and scholarship tests you are likely to take, you will find vocabulary a major ingredient.

Vocabulary growth through reading

Persons who read widely gradually build up extensive vocabularies, especially if they have a curiosity about words. This curiosity, compelling them to regard every unfamiliar word as a breakdown in communication between author and reader, sends them thumbing through the dictionary. Should you, too, develop such word curiosity, you will be assured a lifetime of vocabulary growth.

1

Though reading is the basic means of vocabulary growth, it is a relatively slow means. For the college-bound student who has not yet achieved a superior vocabulary, reading needs to be supplemented by a direct attack that will yield comparatively rapid growth—and that is the purpose of this book.

Vocabulary growth through this book

This book will involve you in a five-pronged attack on vocabulary.

Attack #1: Learning New Words From the Context

Often, we can discover the meaning of an unfamiliar word from its *context*—the other words with which it is used. Note, for example, how we can determine the meaning of *parsimonious* in the following sentence:

People vary in their tipping habits from the very generous to the very *parsimonious*.

Obviously, from the above context, *parsimonious* is the opposite of *generous*; *parsimonious* means "stingy."

Chapter II will teach you the various clues for learning the meaning of a possibly unfamiliar word, like *parsimonious*, from its context. As you learn to use these clues, you will be broadening your vocabulary and—what is even more important—becoming a more skillful reader.

Attack #2: Learning Vocabulary in Groups of Related Words

Vocabulary growth that evolves from a day's reading has one serious disadvantage: it is poorly organized. The new words you encounter as you read usually bear little relationship to one another. This, of course, does not mean that you should think any the less of reading as a means of vocabulary building. It does, however, suggest that you may achieve relatively rapid vocabulary growth by studying *groups of related words*.

In the "central-ideas" chapter you will find twenty-five groups of related words. Each group presents words revolving about one idea—*joy, sadness, flattery, age, relatives, reasoning,* etc. The new words are further explained in hundreds of illustrative sentences that have one feature in common: they present new vocabulary in such context as will make the meaning obvious and easy to remember.

Attack #3: Learning Vocabulary Derived From Greek and Latin

The principle of the lever has enabled humans, using relatively little effort, to do a great amount of work. You can apply the same principle to learning vocabulary. If you study certain productive Greek and Latin prefixes and roots, you can gain word leverage. Each prefix or root adequately understood will help you learn the meanings of the many English words it has produced. In the Greek and Latin chapters, you will meet important prefixes and roots, each with numerous English offspring.

Rounding out the attack on Greek and Latin are two briefer chapters. One will teach you useful English words derived from classical (Latin and Greek) mythology and history. The other, dealing with the interplay of Latin and Anglo-Saxon, will contribute further to your word hoard.

Attack #4: Learning Vocabulary Borrowed From French, Italian, and Spanish

Since English has borrowed heavily from French, you are sure to encounter adopted French words in books, newspapers, and magazines. Such words are considered a part of our English vocabulary and are often key words in the passages in which they occur. Not to know the meanings of common French borrowings is therefore a serious vocabulary deficiency.

The French chapter presents more than one hundred fifty commonly used loanwords, divided into small, easy-to-learn groups. To give you confidence in your understanding of each word, care has been taken to make the definitions and illustrative sentences as helpful as possible. You will find similar treatment in the briefer chapters on important Italian and Spanish loanwords.

"Exercising" new vocabulary

Muscular exercise is essential, especially during your years of physical growth. Vocabulary exercise, too, is essential in your periods of word growth.

To learn new words effectively, you must put them to use early and often. The challenging drills and tests in this book will give you abundant opportunities for varied vocabulary exercise. But you should do more.

In your reading and listening experiences, be conscious of vocabulary. In your speaking and writing, take the initiative on suitable occasions to use new vocabulary. Such follow-up is a *must* if you are to make new words securely yours.

CHAPTER 2

Learning New Words From the Context

What is the context?

Most of the time, a word is used not by itself but with other words. These other words are its **context**. The meaning of a word is often found in its context—the other words with which it is used.

Suppose, for example, we were asked for the meaning of *strike*. We would not be able to give a definite answer because *strike*, as presented to us, is all by itself; it has no context.

But if we were asked to define *strike* in one of the following sentences, we would have no trouble telling its meaning from its *context*—the other words with which it is used.

1. *Strike* three! You're out!
   (*Strike* means "a ball pitched over the plate between a batter's knees and shoulders.")

2. There were no milk deliveries because of a *strike*.
   (*Strike* means "a work stoppage because of a labor dispute.")

3. He made a fist as if to *strike* me.
   (*Strike* means "hit.")

How can the context help you expand your vocabulary?

Here is an amazing fact: the context can often give you the meaning not only of common words like *strike*, **but also of unfamiliar words, including words you have never before seen or heard!**

''What,'' asks a friend, ''is *xenophobic*?''
''How should I know?'' you say. ''I never heard of it.''
''It's in today's paper,'' says the friend.
''Here it is.''

You take the newspaper and read the sentence with the strange word: ''The new ruler is *xenophobic*; he has ordered all foreigners to leave the country.''

''Aha!'' you say. ''Now I know: *xenophobic* means '*afraid or distrustful of foreigners.*' The context gives us the meaning.''

Of course, you are right.

What can this chapter do for you?

This chapter will teach you how to use the context to get the meaning of unfamiliar words. Once you learn this skill, it will serve you for the rest of your life in two important ways: (1) it will keep enlarging your vocabulary; and (2) it will make you an ever better reader.

Part 1.
Contexts With Contrasting Words

Each passage below contains a word in italics. If you read the passage carefully, you will find a clue to the meaning of this word in an opposite word (**antonym**) or a contrasting idea.

For each passage, enter on your paper (*a*) the clue that led you to the meaning, and (*b*) the meaning itself. The answers for the first two passages have been given for you as examples.

1. "That you, Joe?" he asked . . .
   "Who else could it be?" I *retorted*.—William R. Scott
   a. CLUE: *Retorted* is the opposite of "asked."
   b. MEANING: *Retorted* means "answered."

2. Some substances that cause cancer were once regarded as *noncarcinogenic*.
   a. CLUE: *Noncarcinogenic* is in contrast with "that cause cancer."
   b. MEANING: *Noncarcinogenic* means "not cancer-causing."

3. At this stage we cannot tell whether the new regulations will be to our advantage or *detriment*.

4. If his health *ameliorates*, he will stay on the job; if it becomes worse, he will have to resign.

5. In this firm the industrious are promoted and the *indolent* are encouraged to leave.

6. Parents, I suppose, were as much a problem *formerly* as they are today.—Gretchen Finletter

7. If you are going to get up before dawn tomorrow, you had better *retire* by 11 P.M.

8. Evidence presented at the trials of the two public officials showed that they had *subverted* the laws they were supposed to uphold.

9. Many who used to waste fuel are *conserving* it, now that it has become so much more expensive.

10. Only one lower wing and the landing gear had been completely demolished. The rest of the machine was virtually *intact*.—Edwin Way Teale

11. Those who volunteered to help turned out to be more of an *impediment* than an aid.

12. The Sullivan home, which used to stand on this corner, was erected in 1929 and *razed* in 1992.

13. Time has proved that Seward's purchase of Alaska from Russia in 1967 for $7,200,000 was wisdom, not *folly*.

14. When millions face starvation, we cannot be *parsimonious* in doling out aid; we must be generous.

15. . . . A wave of rebelliousness ran through the countryside. Bulls which had always been *tractable* suddenly turned savage, sheep broke down hedges and devoured clover, cows kicked the pail over . . .—George Orwell

16. Children will tell how old they are, but older people are inclined to be *reticent* about their age.

17. The organization is trying to put on a show of *harmony* though there is deep conflict within its ranks.

18. Those who heeded our advice did well; those who *ignored* it did not.

19. Her learner's permit is still in effect but mine is *invalid*.

20. There once was a society in Hawaii for the special purpose of introducing *exotic* birds. Today when you go to the islands, you see, instead of the exquisite native birds that greeted Captain Cook, mynas from India, cardinals from the United States or Brazil, doves from Asia . . .

—Rachel Carson

Study Your New Words, Group 1

You have just defined twenty new words simply by contrasting them with other words or expressions in the context. Now, to reinforce your grasp of these words and make them a part of your active vocabulary, study the following:

WORD	MEANING AND TYPICAL USE
ameliorate (*v.*) ə-'mēl-yə-ˌrāt	become better; make better; improve (*ant.* **worsen**) 　　We expected business conditions to *ameliorate*, but they grew worse.

*amelioration (*n.*)
ə-'mēl-yə-'rā-shən

improvement

conserve (*v.*)
kən-'sərv

keep from waste, loss, or decay; save (*ant.* **waste**)
    One way to *conserve* water is to repair leaking faucets.

conservation (*n.*)
ˌkän-sər-'vā-shən

preservation from loss, injury, or waste

conservationist (*n.*)
ˌkän-sər-'vā-shə-nəst

one who advocates the conservation of natural resources

detriment (*n.*)
'de-trə-mənt

injury, damage, or something that causes it; disadvantage (*ant.* **advantage**)
    Skipping meals can be a *detriment* to your health.

detrimental (*adj.*)
ˌde-trə-'ment-'l

harmful; damaging

exotic (*adj.*)
ig-'zät-ik

1. introduced from another country; foreign (*ant.* **native**)
    The chrysanthemum is an *exotic* plant; it was introduced from the Orient.

2. strikingly unusual; strange
    This wallpaper has an *exotic* charm.

folly (*n.*)
'fäl-ē

lack of good sense; foolish action or undertaking (*ant.* **wisdom**)
    It is *folly* to go on a long drive with a nearly empty gas tank.

formerly (*adv.*)
'fȯr-mər-lē

in an earlier period; previously (*ant.* **now**)
    Our physics instructor was *formerly* an engineer.

former (*adj.*)
'fȯr-mər

preceding; previous (*ant.* **latter**)

harmony (*n.*)
'här-mə-nē

peaceable or friendly relations; accord; agreement; tranquillity (*ant.* **conflict; disharmony**)
    A boundary dispute is making it impossible for the neighbors to live in *harmony*.

---

*Note that *amelioration* is a bonus word—you can understand it instantly if you know *ameliorate*. Useful bonus words, like *amelioration*, will be introduced from now on.

harmonious (*adj.*) här-'mō-nē-əs	friendly; amicable
ignore (*v.*) ig-'no(ə)r	refuse to take notice of; disregard (*ant.* **heed**) You may get into a serious accident if you *ignore* a full-stop sign.
ignoramus (*n.*) ˌig-nə-'rā-məs	ignorant, stupid person; dunce
impediment (*n.*) im-'ped-ə-mənt	something that hinders or obstructs; hindrance; obstacle (*ant.* **aid**) A person's lack of education is often an *impediment* to advancement.
impede (*v.*) im-pēd	interfere with or slow the progress of; hinder; obstruct
indolent (*adj.*) 'in-də-lənt	disposed to avoid exertion; lazy; idle; lethargic (*ant.* **industrious**) I was so comfortable in the reclining chair that I became *indolent* and did not feel like studying.
indolence (*n.*) 'in-də-ləns	idleness; laziness
intact (*adj.*) in-'takt	untouched by anything that damages or diminishes; left complete or entire; uninjured (*ant.* **imperfect**) The tornado demolished the barn but left the farmhouse *intact*.
invalid (*adj.*) in-'val-əd	not valid; having no force or effect; void (*ant.* **valid**, binding in law) The courts have ruled that a forced confession is *invalid* and cannot be introduced as evidence.
invalidate (*v.*) in-'val-ə-ˌdāt	abolish; annul
invalid (*n.*) 'in-və-ləd	sickly or disabled person
noncarcinogenic (*adj.*) 'nän-ˌkär-sə-nō-'jen-ik	not producing, or tending to produce, cancer (*ant.* **carcinogenic**) Cancer-causing ingredients must be replaced by others that are *noncarcinogenic*.
parsimonious (*adj.*) ˌpär-sə-'mō-nē-əs	unduly sparing in the spending of money; stingy (*ant.* **generous**)

Some accuse the government of being too *generous* in funding road improvement and too *parsimonious* in financing education.

parsimony (*n.*)
'pär-sə-ˌmō-nē

stinginess; parsimoniousness (*ant.* **generosity**)

raze (*v.*)
'rāz

destroy utterly by tearing down; demolish; level to the ground (*ant.* **erect**)
The building was so badly damaged in the fire that it had to be *razed*.

reticent (*adj.*)
'ret-ə-sənt

inclined to be silent or secretive; uncommunicative (*ant.* **frank**)
Have you noticed that people who boast about their successes are *reticent* about their failures?

reticence (*n.*)
'ret-ə-səns

restraint in communicating (*ant.* **frankness**)

retire (*v.*)
ri-'tī(ə)r

1. withdraw from active duty or business
Does your grandfather plan to *retire* at 65 or continue to work?
2. go to bed (*ant.* **rise**)
Please do not phone after 10 P.M. because my folks *retire* early.

retort (*v.*)
ri-'tort

answer; reply sharply or angrily (*ant.* **ask**)
"Giving up?" she asked.
"Absolutely not!" I *retorted*.

retort (*n.*)
ri-'tort

quick, witty, or sharp reply; answer

subvert (*v.*)
səb-'vərt

overturn or overthrow from the foundation; undermine (*ant.* **uphold**)
We are *subverting* our fuel-conservation efforts when we heat rooms that are not occupied.

subversion (*n.*)
səb-'vər-zhən

sabotage; undermining

tractable (*adj.*)
'trak-tə-bəl

easily led, taught, or controlled; yielding; docile (*ant.* **unruly; intractable**)
A child who misbehaves may be more *tractable* in a small group than in a large one.

tractability (*n.*)
ˌtrak-tə-'bil-ət-ē

obedience

Apply What You Have Learned

EXERCISE 2.1: SENTENCE COMPLETION

Which choice, A or B, makes the sentence correct? Enter the *letter* of your choice on your answer page.

1. When I heard the noise, I ignored it. I went __?__ .
   (A) on with my work   (B) to investigate
2. The more we conserve heat, the __?__ fuel we have for future use.
   (A) more   (B) less
3. It is folly to __?__ .
   (A) apply your brakes suddenly on an icy road
   (B) reduce your speed drastically in a thick fog
4. The reticent witness provided __?__ details.
   (A) few   (B) abundant
5. I like __?__ food, but I also have a craving for exotic dishes.
   (A) foreign   (B) American
6. You would not expect parsimonious persons to __?__ .
   (A) collect bits of string   (B) spend freely
7. Because of __?__ , the company is doing its utmost to ameliorate service.
   (A) a shortage of raw materials   (B) customer complaints
8. The stolen jewels were found intact; __?__ was missing.
   (A) nothing   (B) a diamond ring
9. Most of the listeners were tractable; they __?__ the speaker's instructions.
   (A) readily followed   (B) totally disregarded
10. Carcinogenic materials __?__ to our health.
    (A) are a threat   (B) pose no danger

EXERCISE 2.2: CONCISE WRITING

Express the thought of each sentence below in no more than four words. The first two sentences have been rewritten as examples.

1. "Wait outside!" he replied in a sharp and angry tone of voice.
   "Wait outside!" he retorted.
2. We are opposed to the waste, mismanagement, and destruction of our natural resources.
   We are conservationists.

3. The advice that they have been giving is doing more harm than good.
4. His inclination to exert himself as little as possible is self-defeating.
5. Is there a possibility that friendly relations can be restored?
6. The house that they lived in was leveled to the ground.
7. All the things that belonged to her arrived with nothing missing or damaged.
8. At an earlier period of time, land could be bought for very little money.
9. Wills that have not been signed are not binding in law.
10. What time was it when you went to bed for the night?

EXERCISE 2.3: CLOSE READING

Carefully read the statements below and answer the questions.

STATEMENTS

A fallen tree was blocking traffic on Bainbridge Road.

The Z Company had a disastrous year but decided to stay in business.

Russ has said very little about what had happened.

Angela's motto was "Take it easy." She could have done much more if she had wanted, but she kept saying, "Why kill myself?"

Our new storm door has reduced heat loss.

The ABC Company's employees had never gone on strike.

Billy refused to remain in his seat, despite the pleas of his parents and the usher.

While the rest of us were trying to sell tickets, one member of the cast was privately telling people that the play was not worth seeing.

Despite her large income, Alicia bought only the barest necessities.

The refugees perished in the avalanche, but the inn from which they had fled suffered no damage.

QUESTIONS

1. What was impeding something?
2. Who was intractable?
3. Who seemed indolent?
4. Who was reticent?
5. Who appeared to be parsimonious?

6. What was helping to conserve something?
7. Who probably expected some amelioration?
8. Who was subversive?
9. Who seemed to be enjoying harmony?
10. What was left intact?

EXERCISE 2.4: ANTONYMS

Complete the sentence by writing, on your answer paper, the antonym of the italicized word. Select your antonyms from pages 7–10.

1. Truly, I do not care whether you *heed* my suggestion or _?_ it.
2. Now that the *conflict* is over, _?_ may soon be restored.
3. As an officer of the club, you should *uphold* the constitution, not _?_ it.
4. I cannot see the *wisdom* of your actions; they are pure _?_ .
5. Usually I *rise* at 6:45 A.M. and _?_ by 11 P.M.
6. The newcomer, *unruly* at first, is becoming more _?_ .
7. Not all the trees on the school grounds are *native* to our soil. Some are _?_ .
8. An early start, we thought, would work to our *advantage*, but it turned out to be to our _?_ .
9. _?_ , she worked as a bookkeeper. *Now* she is studying for a law degree.
10. Did the medicine _?_ your condition or *worsen* it?

EXERCISE 2.5: COMPOSITION

Answer in a sentence or two.

1. What is one way to conserve energy that many people ignore?
2. Is it always folly to raze a structurally sound building? Explain.
3. Why do conservationists want to prevent even the most exotic plants and animals from disappearing from the face of the earth?
4. Give an example of how a reticent witness can subvert the process of justice.
5. Would you rather have a parsimonious friend or an indolent one? Why?

EXERCISE 2.6: BRAINTEASERS

As clues to the complete word, you are given some of the letters and the number of missing letters. On your answer paper, write the complete word.

He knows math, but in art and literature he is a(n) (4)**ram**(2).
(Answer: **ignoramus**)

1. Skipping breakfast may be (5)**men**(3) to your health.
2. Please step aside. You are **imp**(5) our progress.
3. Turn off that noise. Let's have some peace and (6)**ill**(3).
4. When its own crops fail, a nation must buy food from (3)**tic** sources.
5. A license that expired yesterday is no longer (2)**lid**.
6. (6)**vat**(3) can help prevent future shortages.
7. Though formerly enemies, they are now on (1)**arm**(6) terms.
8. Our sugar is (2)**dig**(5), but our tea is imported.
9. Did he tell you anything, or is he still (9)**cat**(3)?
10. (2)**dust**(5) workers deserve higher pay than indolent ones.

Part 2.
Contexts With Similar Words

Often you can learn the meaning of an unfamiliar word from a *similar* word or expression in the context. Do you know what *castigated* means? If not, you should be able to find out from the following:

> The candidate denounced his opponent for her views on foreign policy, and she *castigated* him for his attitude toward education.

Here, the meaning of *castigated* is given to us by a similar word in the context, *denounced*.

Do you know what *remote* means? If not, you can learn it from the following passage:

> There lay a young man, fast asleep—sleeping so soundly, so deeply, that he was far, far away from them both. Oh, so *remote* . . .—Katherine Mansfield

The context teaches us that *remote* means "far."

Let's try one more. Find the meaning of *reluctantly* in the next passage.

> My mother scolded me for my thoughtlessness and bade me say good-bye to them. *Reluctantly* I obeyed her, wishing that I did not have to do so.—Richard Wright

The clue here is in the words *wishing that I did not have to do so.* They suggest that *reluctantly* means "unwillingly."

Pretest 2

Write the meaning of the italicized word. (Hint: Look for a *similar* word or expression in the context.)

1. Mr. Smith had already become acquainted with British *cinemas* in small towns. Also, he was a Southern Californian and had that familiarity with movies that belongs to all Southern Californians.

> —Eric Knight

15

2. Burke tossed the circular into the wastebasket without *perusing* it. He never reads junk mail.

3. The dealer asked for $1200. He *spurned* my offer of $1100, and when I went to $1150, he refused that too.

4. Your whistling *galls* me. In fact, your entire behavior irritates me.

5. I said the water was *tepid*. She didn't believe me. She tested it herself to see if it was lukewarm.

6. Eileen and I hated the book [*Bird Life for Children*], so we were quite prepared to *despise* birds when we started off that morning on our first bird walk.—Ruth McKenney

7. Everyone brimmed with enthusiasm. Carl was particularly *ebullient*.

8. She is eager to bet me she will win the match, but I told her I do not *wager*.

9. A fight started between two of the opposing athletes. Several of their teammates joined in. It was quite a *scuffle*.

10. . . . the picture changed and sport began to *wane*.
    A good many factors contributed to the decline of sport.—E. B. White

11. Later I realized I had made some *inane* remarks, and I was ashamed of myself for having been so silly.

12. She was supposed to be *indemnified*—the repair bill came to $180—but she has not yet been repaid.

13. Dorene is quite *finicky* about her penmanship. I am much less fussy.

14. The fact is, we have all been a good deal puzzled because the affair is so simple, and yet *baffles* us altogether.—Edgar Allan Poe

15. Though the starting salary is only $300 a week, Roberta has been promised an early promotion and a higher *stipend*.

16. They *exhorted* us to join them for dinner, but we resisted their urging and thanked them very much.

17. When an Englishman has anything surprising to tell he never *exaggerates* it, never overstates it . . .

    —Stephen B. Leacock

18. I know how to change a tire, but tuning an engine is beyond my *expertise*.

19. Asians who have never been to the *Occident* learn much about Western culture from films and television.

20. Gerald suspected we were being watched. "Really?" I asked. "What makes you think we are under *surveillance*?"

Study Your New Words, *Group 2*

You have just tried to define twenty new words with the help of similar words or expressions in the context. To strengthen your grasp of these new words, study the following:

WORD	MEANING AND TYPICAL USE
baffle (*v.*) 'baf-əl	bewilder; perplex; fill with confusion; puzzle; frustrate At last, we have found a solution to a problem that has been *baffling* us.
baffling (*adj.*) 'baf-liŋ	frustrating; bewildering
cinema (*n.*) 'sin-ə-mə	movies; motion picture industry Which do you like better, TV or the *cinema*?
cinematography (*n.*) ˌsin-ə-mə-'täg-rə-fē	art of making motion pictures
despise (*v.*) di-'spīz	look down on with contempt or disgust; loathe; regard as inferior (*ant.* **admire**) The world *admires* heroes and *despises* cowards.
despicable (*adj.*) 'des-pik-ə-bəl	worthy of contempt; contemptible (*ant.* **laudable**)
ebullient (*adj.*) i-'bül-yənt	overflowing with enthusiasm; exuberant Hundreds of *ebullient* fans thronged the airport to greet the new champions.
ebullience (*n.*) i-'bül-yəns	exuberance
exaggerate (*v.*) ig-'zaj-ə-ˌrāt	overstate; go beyond the limits of the actual truth (*ant.* **minimize**) You *exaggerated* when you called me an excellent cook. I can't make anything except chocolate pudding.
exaggeration (*n.*) ig-ˌzaj-ə-'rā-shən	overstatement (*ant.* **understatement**)

exhort (*v.*)
ig-'zȯrt

arouse by words; advise strongly; urge
The newscaster *exhorted* drivers to leave their cars at home because of the slippery roads.

exhortation (*n.*)
ˌeks-ˌȯr-'tā-shən

urgent recommendation or advice

expertise (*n.*)
ˌek-spər-'tēz

specialized skill or technical knowledge; know-how; expertness
The Waldos hire an accountant to prepare their tax return because they lack the *expertise* to do it themselves.

finicky (*adj.*)
'fin-i-kē

excessively concerned with trifles or details; hard to please; fussy; particular
Abe showed me I had forgotten to dot one of my i's. He is very *finicky* about such matters.

gall (*v.*)
'gȯl

make sore; irritate mentally; annoy; vex
Why are you in such a bad mood? What is *galling* you?

gall (*n.*)
'gȯl

brazen boldness; nerve (*ant.* **meekness**)

inane (*adj.*)
in-'ān

lacking significance or sense; pointless; silly; insipid (*ant.* **deep; profound**)
I asked him how the water was, and he said "wet." Now isn't that *inane*?

inanity (*n.*)
in-'an-ət-ē

foolishness; shallowness

indemnify (*v.*)
in-'dem-nə-ˌfī

compensate for loss, damage, or injury; reimburse; repay
Some of the tenants were not *indemnified* for their losses in the fire, as they carried no insurance.

Occident (*n.*)
'äk-sə-dənt

west; countries of America and Europe (*ant.* **Orient**)
The plane that landed in Shanghai brought tourists from the United States, Canada, Brazil, Italy, and other countries in the *Occident*.

occidental (*adj.*)
ˌäk-sə-'dent'l

western (*ant.* **oriental**)

peruse (*v.*)
pə-'rüz

read; look at fairly attentively; study
Before signing a contract, you should *peruse* its contents and discuss any questions you may have with your attorney.

perusal (*n.*)
pə-'rü-zəl

reading; study

scuffle (*v.*)
'skəf-əl

struggle at close quarters in a rough and confused manner; wrestle; grapple
The players who *scuffled* with the umpires were suspended and heavily fined.

scuffle (*n.*)
'skəf-əl

brawl; fight

spurn (*v.*)
'spərn

thrust aside with disdain or contempt; reject (*ant.* **accept**)
We wanted to assist, but they *spurned* all offers of aid.

stipend (*n.*)
'stī-ˌpend

fixed pay for services; salary; regular allowance awarded a scholarship winner
My sister's scholarship will pay her an annual *stipend* of $1000 for four years.

surveillance (*n.*)
sər-'vā-ləns

close watch over a person, group, or area; supervision
The patients in the intensive care ward are under continuous *surveillance*.

tepid (*adj.*)
'tep-əd

moderately warm; lukewarm
The soup was served hot, but I didn't get to it for about five minutes, and by then it was *tepid*.

tepidly (*adv.*)
'tep-əd-lē

unenthusiastically; lukewarmly

wager (*v.*)
'wā-jər

risk (something) on the outcome of a contest or uncertain event; gamble; bet
Those who had *wagered* we would win are out of some money; we lost the game.

wager (*n.*)
'wā-jər

bet

wane (*v.*)
'wān

decrease in power or size; dwindle; decline; sink
The senator may not be reelected. His popularity is *waning*.

Apply What You Have Learned

EXERCISE 2.7: SENTENCE COMPLETION

Which choice, A or B, makes the sentence correct? Enter the *letter* of your choice on your answer page.

1. They spurned my suggestion and did as __?__ .
   (A) they pleased   (B) I advised
2. To send someone a birthday card __?__ her or his birthday is absolutely inane.
   (A) six months after   (B) three days before
3. The Independents have just __?__ two more seats; their influence is waning.
   (A) won   (B) lost
4. After four years of service in the American embassy in __?__ , Williams is longing to return to the Occident.
   (A) Tokyo   (B) Madrid
5. Our guests are not finicky; they are __?__ to please.
   (A) hard   (B) easy
6. Asked if she were coming to Class Night, an ebullient senior answered: __?__ .
   (A) "I guess so."   (B) "I wouldn't miss it for the world!"
7. The __?__ provides live entertainment.
   (A) theater   (B) cinema
8. He is just under five eleven, and when he gives his height, he says: __?__ . He does not exaggerate.
   (A) "six feet"   (B) "five ten"
9. We are keeping __?__ the suspects; they are under surveillance.
   (A) a lookout for   (B) an eye on
10. Surely you would not want to __?__ someone you despise.
    (A) ignore   (B) associate with

EXERCISE 2.8: CONCISE WRITING

Express the thought of each sentence below in no more than four words.

1. Stephanie sometimes makes a statement that goes beyond the limits of the actual truth.

2. We were greeted in a manner that was lacking in enthusiasm.
3. Those who hold insurance policies will be compensated for their losses.
4. A close watch is being kept over our comings and goings.
5. We pay no attention to remarks that have no sense or significance.
6. He does not have the specialized skills that she has.
7. Don't be so overly concerned with trifles and minor details.
8. They were seen struggling at close quarters in a rough and confused manner.
9. Michael looks down with contempt on people who are inclined to avoid exertion.
10. People from the United States visit the countries of Asia.

EXERCISE 2.9: CLOSE READING

Carefully read the statements below and answer the questions.

STATEMENTS

A closed-circuit TV screen enabled the security guard to watch the three visitors as they rode up in the elevator.

Joyce was dissatisfied with the way George had set the table because some of the spoons and forks were not exactly parallel.

It took five minutes for Armand to replace the washer of the leaking faucet.

Dan's insurance company paid in full for the damage to Barbara's car.

Roger urged the audience to contribute generously for the relief of the earthquake victims.

The producer said the play had opened to a full house, but Emily, who attended the performance, recalls seeing a number of vacant seats.

Susan protested that Denny's conclusions made no sense at all.

Many residents enthusiastically supported the mayor's program.

The pushing and shoving began when a latecomer tried to get in at the head of the line. Two people were hurt.

Before the match, both rivals had agreed that the loser would pay for the refreshments.

QUESTIONS

1. Who detected an exaggeration?
2. Who was finicky?
3. Who made a wager?
4. Who indemnified someone?
5. Who started a scuffle?
6. Who was under surveillance?
7. Who was ebullient?
8. Who was exhorted?
9. Who demonstrated mechanical expertise?
10. Who stated that something was inane?

EXERCISE 2.10: SYNONYMS AND ANTONYMS

A. Find a SYNONYM on pages 17–19 for the italicized word.

1. These bills *annoy* me.
2. Charlie Chaplin was a star of the silent *movies*.
3. The crowd was *exuberant*.
4. The water was *lukewarm*.
5. You are acquiring *know-how* in carpentry.

B. Find an ANTONYM on pages 17–19 for the italicized word.

6. Do not *minimize* your achievements.
7. The freighter is bound for the *Orient*.
8. Their behavior was *admirable*.
9. She said something very *profound*.
10. The winner will probably *accept* the award.

EXERCISE 2.11: COMPOSITION

Answer in a sentence or two.

1. What is one thing that might baffle a visitor from the Orient. Why?
2. Why should a bank maintain surveillance over an employee with an excessive fondness for wagering?

3. What would you say to someone who exaggerates the damage you did to his or her property and asks to be indemnified?
4. If you are hurt in an accident, why would it be inane to minimize your injury?
5. Does a married employee deserve a higher stipend than an unmarried one with the same expertise? Explain.

EXERCISE 2.12: BRAINTEASERS

As clues to the complete word, you are given some of the letters and the number of missing letters. On your answer paper, write the complete word.

1. Infants learning to walk need continuous (3)**v e i l**(5).
2. The problem baffles us. We are bewildered and (1)**r u s t**(5).
3. I noticed the article, but I had no time to (3)**u s e** it.
4. Marco Polo's travels led to trade between China and the (4)**d e n**(1).
5. If the offer had been reasonable, it would not have been (2)**u r n**(2).
6. We cannot praise what you have done because it is not (4)**a b l e**.
7. The unemployed watched their savings (1)**w i n**(3).
8. Making a movie requires some (2)**p e r**(4) in cinematography.
9. Many remained in their homes, despite repeated (5)**t a t**(3)s that they leave for higher ground.
10. Stop fussing over petty details. Don't be so (1)**a r t**(6).

Part 3.
"Commonsense" Contexts

Do you know what *reel* means in the following sentence?

> It weighs a ton, and strong porters *reel* under its weight.
> —W. Somerset Maugham

Note that the context contains neither a contrasting nor a similar word to help with the meaning of *reel*. Yet you can tell what it means just by using a bit of **common sense.** You ask yourself:

> "How would I behave if I were to carry, or try to carry, something that feels like a ton?"

You realize that you would "sway dizzily," or "stagger." That is exactly what *reel* means.

Can you give a definition of *severed*? Do you know what *pinioned* means? If not, you should be able to discover their meanings from the following context by applying common sense.

> ". . . I whirled about, grabbing the razor-sharp knife from my belt sheath, and slashed three or four times with a full sweep of my arms in the direction of the touch. By luck I *severed* two of the lassoing arms that were gripping me; in another instant the octopus would have had my two arms *pinioned* and I should have been helpless."
> —Victor Berge and Henry W. Lanier

What would you do to the arms of an octopus if you slashed them three or four times with a razor-sharp knife with a full sweep of your arms? You would *cut them off*, of course. *Severed* means "cut off."

And what would happen to your own arms if they were lassoed and gripped by the arms of an octopus? Obviously, they would be *bound fast*, so that you would not be able to use them. *Pinioned* means "bound fast."

The term *"commonsense" context,* as used in this book, means a context that yields the meaning of an unfamiliar word through clues other than a synonym or antonym. Such contexts, as we have seen, involve a bit of reasoning on your part.

Pretest 3

Try to discover the meaning of the italicized word in each of the following "commonsense" contexts:

1. A child wandering through a department store with its mother is *admonished* over and over again not to touch things.—Paul Gallico
2. My simple *repast* consisted of a sandwich and an apple.
3. Restrictions on the use of water will end as soon as our reservoirs are *replenished*.
4. A sufferer from *insomnia*, she lies awake most of the night.
5. The judge listened to the arguments of both attorneys before *rendering* her decision.
6. And take from seventy springs a *score*,
   It only leaves me fifty more.—A. E. Housman
7. In another year my father will have completed his first *decade* in business; he opened his shop nine years ago.
8. The blade slipped and cut my hand. Two *sutures* were needed to close the wound.
9. When the bald-headed fellow pretended he was the rightful King of France, Huck and Jim believed him. They were quite *gullible*.
10. While *confined* here in the Birmingham city jail, I came across your recent statement calling my present activities "unwise and untimely."—Martin Luther King, Jr.
11. A *probe* into the suspect's financial dealings disclosed evidence of large-scale fraud.
12. The dealer asked $190 for the radio, and I gave him his price; we did not *haggle*.
13. I know you asked for coleslaw, but I forgot to order it. I am sorry for the *lapse*.
14. We moved into first place, but our glory was *ephemeral*. The next day we lost a doubleheader and dropped to third.
15. It was not that he felt any emotion akin to love for Irene Adler. All emotions, and that one particularly, were *abhorrent* to his cold, precise but admirably balanced mind.—Arthur Conan Doyle
16. Jean greeted everyone, but when I said, "Hello," she walked past me as if I did not exist. The *snub* bothered me the rest of the day.
17. As I was leaving the meeting, I realized that I had *unwittingly* taken someone else's coat. Embarrassed, I ran back and apologized.

18. If the bomb had *detonated*, the consequences would have been frightful.
19. I *immersed* my hands in warm soapy water to loosen the dirt.
20. Perhaps in heaven, but certainly not until then, shall I ever taste anything so *ambrosial* as that fried chicken and coffee ice cream!—Dorothy Canfield Fisher

Study Your New Words, *Group 3*

You have just attempted to learn the meanings of twenty words from "commonsense" clues in their contexts. Now, for a firmer grasp of these words, study the following:

WORD	MEANING AND TYPICAL USE
abhorrent (*adj.*) ab-'hȯr-ənt	(followed by *to*) in conflict; utterly opposed; loathsome; repugnant (*ant.* **admirable**) Please do not ask me to tell an untruth; lying is *abhorrent* to me.
abhor (*v.*) əb-'hȯr	utterly detest; loathe; hate
admonish (*v.*) ad-'män-ish	reprove gently but seriously; warn of a fault; caution (*ant.* **commend**) The teacher *commended* me on my improvement in writing, but *admonished* me for my lateness to class.
admonition (*n.*) ,ad-mə-'nish-ən	gentle warning; friendly reproof
ambrosial (*adj.*) am-'brō-zhəl	extremely pleasing to taste or smell; delicious; like *ambrosia* (the food of the gods) Taste this ripe pineapple; it has an *ambrosial* flavor.
confine (*v.*) kən-'fīn	shut up; imprison; keep in narrow, cramped quarters (*ant.* **free**) On July 14, 1789, a Paris mob freed the prisoners *confined* in the Bastille.
confinement (*n.*) kən-'fīn-mənt	imprisonment
decade (*n.*) 'dek-,ād	period of ten years In the United States, the 1930's were the *decade* of the Great Depression.

detonate (*v.*) 'det-ə-ˌnāt	explode with suddenness and violence; cause (something) to explode Fallout showed that a nuclear device had probably been *detonated*.
detonation (*n.*) ˌdet-ᵊn-'ā-shən	explosion
ephemeral (*adj.*) i-'fem-ə-rəl	lasting one day only; fleeting; transitory; short-lived (*ant.* **permanent**) Day-lily blossoms are *ephemeral*; they last only for a day.
gullible (*adj.*) 'gəl-ə-bəl	easily deceived or cheated; credulous (*ant.* **astute**) A few investors were *gullible* enough to buy the worthless stock, but most were too *astute* to be deceived.
gull (*v.*) 'gəl	deceive; cheat
haggle (*v.*) 'hag-əl	dispute or argue over a price in a petty way; bargain; wrangle Have they agreed on a price yet, or are they still *haggling*?
immerse (*v.*) im-'ərs	1. plunge or place into a liquid; dip; duck I filled a basin with lukewarm water and *immersed* my foot in it. 2. engross; absorb She is *immersed* in her book.
immersion (*n.*) im-'ər-zhən	state of being deeply engrossed; absorption
insomnia (*n.*) in-'säm-nē-ə	inability to sleep; abnormal wakefulness; sleeplessness The former hostages now get a normal amount of sleep; during their imprisonment they suffered from *insomnia*.
insomniac (*n.*) in-'säm-nē-ˌak	person suffering from insomnia
lapse (*n.*) 'laps	1. slip; error; accidental mistake; trivial fault I wrote your name with one *t*, instead of two. Please forgive the *lapse*.

2. interval
He returned after a *lapse* of ten years.

lapse (*v.*)   cease being in force; become invalid
'laps

probe (*n.*)   critical inquiry into suspected illegal activity; inves-
'prōb   tigation
                          A *probe* is being conducted to learn what hap-
                          pened to the missing funds.

prober (*n.*)   investigator
'prōb-ər

render (*v.*)   hand down officially; deliver (as a verdict); give
'ren-dər   Tension was high in the courtroom as the jury filed
                          in to *render* its verdict.

rendering (*n.*)   presentation; interpretation
'ren-dər-iŋ

repast (*n.*)   food for one occasion of eating; meal
ri-'past   She eats little; her lunch would hardly make a *re-*
                          past for a sparrow.

replenish (*v.*)   bring back to condition of being full; refill
ri-'plen-ish   Every 200 miles we stopped at a service station to
                          replenish the gas tank.

score (*n.*)   group or set of twenty; twenty
'skȯ(ə)r   We have nineteen signatures already, and if we
                          get one more, we'll have an even *score*.

snub (*n.*)   act or instance of *snubbing* (treating with contempt);
'snəb   rebuff; slight; insult
                          Why did Sharon invite everyone but me? Was it
                          just an oversight, or a deliberate *snub*?

snub (*v.*)   treat with disdain or contempt; slight
'snəb

suture (*n.*)   strand or fiber used to sew parts of the living body;
'sü-chər   also, stitch made with such material
                          A few days after the cut finger was sewn together,
                          the patient returned for the removal of the *sutures*.

unwittingly (*adv.*) unintentionally; by accident; inadvertently (*ant.* **in-**
ən-'wit-iŋ-lē   **tentionally**)
                          I *unwittingly* opened a letter addressed to you.
                          Please forgive me.

Apply What You Have Learned

EXERCISE 2.13: SENTENCE COMPLETION

Which choice, A or B, makes the sentence correct? Enter the *letter* of your choice on your answer page.

1. When you __?__ , your body is totally immersed.
   (A) take a shower   (B) swim underwater

2. A probe of the corporation is under way; several of its top officers have been __?__ .
   (A) questioned   (B) promoted

3. Dawson entered the House in __?__ and served for a score of years until his defeat in 1991.
   (A) 1971   (B) 1961

4. The guests __?__ about the ambrosial food.
   (A) raved   (B) complained

5. Shoppers will find the selection __?__ because the shelves have been replenished.
   (A) poor   (B) excellent

6. If you regularly watch TV at 3 __?__ , you may be an insomniac.
   (A) A.M.   (B) P.M.

7. I offered my hand, and __?__ . I cannot forgive the snub.
   (A) we walked off the field together   (B) he didn't take it

8. Did you __?__ by yourself, or did someone join you in your repast?
   (A) study   (B) dine

9. For the first decade of her life, she lived on a farm. When she was __?__ , her family moved to the city.
   (A) ten   (B) eleven

10. They haggled. Joan wanted ten dollars for the used book, and Audrey thought that was __?__ .
    (A) too high   (B) a fair price

EXERCISE 2.14: CONCISE WRITING

Express the thought of each sentence below in no more than four words.

1. The fame that they achieved lasted only for a very short time.
2. She stays awake most of the night because she has a great deal of trouble falling asleep.
3. Some shoppers enjoy arguing over a price in a petty way.
4. Were the stitches that were used to sew up the wound removed?
5. No one who is serving a prison term likes being kept in narrow, confined quarters.
6. It is hard to believe how easy it is for others to cheat him.
7. Without realizing what I was doing, I treated you with contempt.
8. We utterly detest the way they have been behaving themselves.
9. Has the policy that you own ceased to be in force?
10. The people who had committed the offenses were reproved in a gentle but firm manner.

EXERCISE 2.15: SYNONYMS AND ANTONYMS

A. Find a SYNONYM on pages 26–28 for the italicized word.

1. We *bargained* for more than ten minutes.
2. She took it as an *insult*.
3. Has your glass been *refilled*?
4. What causes *sleeplessness*?
5. A mental *slip* prevented me from recalling your name.

B. Find an ANTONYM on pages 26–28 for the italicized word.

6. It was a *permanent* friendship.
7. Your opponent was quite *astute*.
8. Did she step on your foot *intentionally*?
9. The chief *commended* us.
10. On what grounds can the suspect be *freed*?

EXERCISE 2.16: CLOSE READING

Carefully read the statements below and answer the questions.

STATEMENTS

As a child, Roy believed that there were lions, tigers, and fire-breathing dragons in the woods near his home, as well as buried pirate treasure.

Andy consumed a seven-course dinner, but Margie had only a thin slice of cantaloupe.

Louise did not reach her cousin in her first try because she dialed 384-8439, instead of 384-8349.

The florist did exceptionally well on opening day, but after that there were so few customers that he had to go out of business.

Rivers favored an investigation, but Thompson said it would be a waste of time and money.

When Gail was gently reminded that it was getting late and that the bus would soon arrive, she said, ''Mom, I'll be right down.''

Olga had to invent an excuse for her friend, though it was something that she loathed doing.

The payroll clerk was given an office that was scarcely larger than a closet.

While Chuck and Jim were hesitating, wondering about the water temperature, Estelle dived in and swam two laps.

Evan sold forty-two tickets, Stella twenty-nine, and Terry nineteen.

QUESTIONS

1. Who enjoyed ephemeral success?
2. Who must have felt confined?
3. Who admonished someone?
4. Who had an abhorrent experience?
5. Who was gullible?
6. Who opposed a probe?
7. Who had a meager repast?
8. Who was short of a score?
9. Who was immersed?
10. Who committed a lapse?

EXERCISE 2.17: COMPOSITION

Answer in a sentence or two.

1. Should employees be required to reach the age of threescore and ten before becoming eligible to retire? Why, or why not?
2. Which could you more readily forgive, a snub or a lapse? Why?
3. Why is a gullible customer not likely to haggle?
4. Should someone who detonates firecrackers on the Fourth of July be admonished? Explain.
5. Describe one of the most ambrosial repasts you ever had.

EXERCISE 2.18: BRAINTEASERS

As clues to the complete word, you are given some of the letters and the number of missing letters. On your answer paper, write the complete word.

1. We respected them, but they treated us with (3)**tempt**.
2. If yellow is (1)**oath**(4) to you, choose another color.
3. Many windows were shattered by the (2)**ton**(5).
4. Liz read the poem beautifully, but your (1)**end**(5) was even better.
5. Gregg was so (2)**gross**(2) in his book that he didn't see us enter.
6. A team of experienced (1)**rob**(3) is investigating the crash.
7. If you are king or queen for a day, your glory will be (2)**hem**(4).
8. Most authors are soon forgotten, but a few achieve (3)**man**(3) fame.
9. The rebellious inmate was put into solitary (3)**fin**(5).
10. It was his first warning. Never before had he been (6)**shed**.

Part 4.
Mixed Contexts

This is a review section. It contains contexts of all the types we have met up to now—those with a contrasting word, or a similar word, or a commonsense clue. By this time, you should be able to deal with any of these contexts.

Pretest 4

Try to discover the meaning of the italicized word, in each of the following mixed contexts.

1. . . . then we examined the house itself. We divided its entire surface into compartments, which we numbered, so that none might be missed; then we *scrutinized* each individual square inch throughout the premises, including the two houses immediately adjoining, with the microscope, as before.
   —Edgar Allan Poe

2. "The two houses adjoining!" I exclaimed. "You must have had a great deal of trouble."
   "We had; but the reward offered is *prodigious*."
   —Edgar Allan Poe

3. They meant to be of help, but they *hampered* us by getting in our way.

4. The vacation *rejuvenated* her. She returned looking years younger.

5. If *acquitted*, the accused will walk out of the courtroom a free person.

6. . . . I have known since childhood that faced with a certain kind of simple problem I have sometimes made it so *complex* that there is no way out.—Lillian Hellman

7. Most of the merchandise was sold early in the season at regular prices. The *residue* is being marked down 50% for clearance.

8. Each of us carried a small cylinder of oxygen in his pack, but we used it only in emergencies and found that, while its immediate effect was *salutary*, it left us later even worse off than before.
   —James Ramsey Ullman

9. In the twentieth century the automobile *superseded* the horse-drawn vehicle as a means of transportation.

10. I would never have had the *effrontery* to do what they did. What nerve they had!

11. When he *withdrew* his hands from his gloves, the cold wind seemed to leap forward and grasp his unprotected fingers in an iron grip. —Edward A. Herron

12. There is great hardship in times of inflation and unemployment; they are *nettlesome* problems.

13. I was about to leave for the beach, *oblivious* of my appointment with the dentist, when Mother reminded me.

14. They do some *zany* things. For example, in one scene, having lost their employer's shopping money, they try to steal a chunk of meat from the cage of a hungry lion at the zoo.

15. When the neighbor mainland would be *sweltering*, day and night alike, under a breathless heat, out here on the island there was always a cool wind blowing.—Sir Charles G. D. Roberts

16. It was an *excruciating* headache. I had to stay in bed.

17. The package was so *unwieldy* that it was hard to get a grip on it, and I dreaded taking it on the bus.

18. We have not complained up to now; but our *forbearance* is coming to an end.

19. I thought you would be nervous when you were unexpectedly asked to give the first talk, but you were *unruffled*.

20. It was even whispered that Whymper and the Taugwalders had deliberately cut the rope, *consigning* their companions to death to save their own skins.—James Ramsey Ullman

Study Your New Words, *Group 4*

WORD	MEANING AND TYPICAL USE
acquit (*v.*) ə-'kwit	relieve from an accusation; pronounce not guilty; discharge; exculpate (*ant.* **convict**) Two of the defendants were *convicted* of first-degree murder; the third was *acquitted*.
acquittal (*n.*) ə-'kwit-ᵊl	exculpation; discharge (*ant.* **conviction**)
complex (*adj.*) käm-'pleks	having varied interrelated parts, and therefore hard to understand; complicated; intricate (*ant.* **simple**) I would never try to repair a mechanism so *complex* as a wristwatch, but I can easily replace a watchband.

complexity (*n.*)
ˌkəm-'plek-sət-ē

difficulty; intricacy (*ant.* **simplicity**)

consign (*v.*)
kən-'sīn

give, transfer, or deliver, as if by signing over; hand over; commit
After they were sentenced, the two convicts were *consigned* to prison.

consignee (*n.*)
ˌkän-sə-'nē

person to whom something is shipped

effrontery (*n.*)
i-'frənt-ə-rē

shameless boldness; insolence; gall; temerity
Her cousin had the *effrontery* to come to the party even though he had not been invited.

excruciating (*adj.*)
ik-'skrü-shē-ˌāt-iŋ

causing great pain or anguish; agonizing; unbearably painful
I had feared that the drilling of the tooth would be *excruciating*, but I barely felt any pain.

forbearance (*n.*)
fȯr-'ber-əns

act of forbearing (refraining); abstaining; leniency; patience (*ant.* **anger**)
If you stepped on my foot by accident, I would show *forbearance*. But if you tripped me on purpose, I would not be able to repress my *anger*.

hamper (*v.*)
'ham-pər

interfere with; hinder; impede (*ant.* **aid**)
We tried to leave the stadium quickly, but the dense crowd *hampered* our progress.

nettlesome (*adj.*)
'net-ᵊl-səm

literally, full of *nettles* (plants with stinging hairs); irritating; causing annoyance or vexation
How can we safely dispose of nuclear wastes? So far, no satisfactory answer has been found to this *nettlesome* question.

oblivious (*adj.*)
ə-'bli-vē-əs

(followed by *of*) forgetful; unmindful; not aware
She had promised to wait, but she walked off without me, *oblivious* of her promise.

oblivion (*n.*)
ə-'bliv-ē-ən

condition of being forgotten or unknown

prodigious (*adj.*)
prə-'dij-əs

extraordinary in amount or size; enormous; gigantic (*ant.* **tiny**)
In one year, there was a *prodigious* increase in the cost of oil; prices nearly tripled.

prodigy (*n.*)
'präd-ə-jē

person of extraordinary talent or ability; wonder

rejuvenate (*v.*)
ri-'jü-və-ˌnāt

make young or youthful again; give new vigor to; reinvigorate; refresh

A good night's sleep will *rejuvenate* you, and you will wake up feeling refreshed.

residue (*n.*)
'rez-ə-ˌd(y)ü

whatever is left after a part is taken, disposed of, or gone; remainder; rest

The floodwater receded, leaving a *residue* of mud in the streets.

residual (*adj.*)
ri-'zij-ə-wəl

remaining after a part is used or taken

salutary (*adj.*)
'sal-yə-ˌter-ē

favorable to health; healthful; curative; beneficial (*ant.* **deleterious**)

A winter in the South had a *salutary* effect on Manny; his cough disappeared. The icy Northern climate would have been *deleterious* to his health.

scrutinize (*v.*)
'skrüt-ᵊn-ˌīz

examine very closely; inspect

After *scrutinizing* my driver's license to see if there were any prior violations, the officer returned it to me.

scrutiny (*n.*)
'scrüt-ᵊn-ē

examination; inspection; review

supersede (*v.*)
ˌsü-pər-'sēd

force out of use; displace; supplant; replace

In many businesses, paper wrapping has been *superseded* by plastic.

sweltering (*adj.*)
'swel-tə-riŋ

oppressively hot; torrid (*ant.* **frigid**)

It was a *sweltering* day; everyone was perspiring.

swelter (*v.*)
'swel-tər

suffer from oppressive heat

unruffled (*adj.*)
ən-'rəf-əld

not upset or agitated; calm; cool; unflustered (*ant.* **discomposed**)

Most of us were *discomposed* by the new developments, but Elinor remained *unruffled*.

unwieldy (*adj.*)
ən-'wēl-dē

hard to *wield* (handle) because of size or weight; unmanageable; bulky; cumbersome

Will you please help me dispose of the empty refrigerator carton? It is too *unwieldy* for one person to carry out.

unwieldiness
ˌən-'wēl-dē-nəs

bulkiness

withdraw (*v.*)	1. take back; remove (*ant.* **deposit**)
wi<u>th</u>-'drȯ	I *deposited* a check for $87.50 and *withdrew* $50 in cash.
	2. draw back; go away; retreat; leave (*ant.* **advance**)
	As the officers *advanced* toward the scene, the mob *withdrew.*
withdrawal (*n.*)	departure (*ant.* **approach**)
wi<u>th</u>- 'drȯ-əl	
zany (*adj.*)	having the characteristics of a clown; mildly insane; crazy; clownish
'zā-nē	Warren would squirt you with a water pistol for a laugh; he has a *zany* sense of humor.
zany (*n.*)	clown; buffoon
'zā-nē	

Apply What You Have Learned

EXERCISE 2.19: SENTENCE COMPLETION

Which choice, A or B, makes the sentence correct? Enter the *letter* of your choice on your answer paper.

1. Your zany brother came to the meeting __?__ .
   (A) with a list of complaints   (B) in a gorilla costume
2. The treatments were salutary; the patient's condition __?__ .
   (A) improved   (B) worsened
3. Someone in the sweltering auditorium suggested that we turn off the __?__ .
   (A) air conditioning   (B) heat
4. After saying the pie you baked was not so delicious, Marge had the effrontery to __?__ .
   (A) apologize for her remark   (B) ask for a second helping
5. They thought that when they found __?__ , they would become rejuvenated.
   (A) Captain Kidd's treasure   (B) the Fountain of Youth
6. A superseded regulation __?__ .
   (A) is still in effect   (B) should be disregarded

7. In the imaginary country of Lilliput, where people were no more than six __?__ tall, an ordinary human like Gulliver must have seemed prodigious.
   (A) inches   (B) feet
8. After his acquittal, the suspect __?__ .
   (A) requested a new trial   (B) thanked the jury
9. When your sister is criticized, she shows forbearance; she __?__ .
   (A) becomes enraged   (B) listens patiently
10. Oblivious of the sudden drop in temperature, I left the house __?__ .
   (A) without taking a sweater   (B) thinking it would snow

EXERCISE 2.20: CONCISE WRITING

Express the thought of each sentence below in no more than four words.

1. The instructions that you have drawn up are not easy to understand.
2. Who is the person to whom the goods are to be shipped?
3. What are the reasons for their being found not guilty?
4. She examined very closely the application that you sent in.
5. Some packages are hard to handle because they are too big or too heavy.
6. The pain that he had was so agonizing that he could not bear it.
7. The forces that have invaded the country must draw back.
8. She has problems that are causing her a great deal of vexation.
9. The part that is left is not of much importance.
10. Everyone looks with contempt on the shamelessly bold manner in which they behave themselves.

EXERCISE 2.21: SYNONYMS

Find a SYNONYM on pages 34–37 for the italicized word.

1. They remained *cool* throughout the crisis.
2. She chose wallpaper with an *intricate* pattern.
3. The situation is rapidly becoming *unmanageable*.
4. Would you have had the *temerity* to open someone else's mail?
5. He ordered the most expensive dinner, *unmindful* of the cost.

EXERCISE 2.22: CLOSE READING

Carefully read the statements below and answer the questions.

STATEMENTS

When Martin asked permission to look through the files for the missing information, Muriel said, ''Not now. Come back next week.''

My aunt is more relaxed now that she has given up smoking, and her health has improved.

The recreation supervisor was able to find a way to stop the almost daily bitter fights we were having over the use of the tennis courts.

Though Simpson is still on the payroll, someone else has been put in charge.

Paul had been on the committee for a year, and we wanted him to stay, but he left.

When Jason's father died, Medea, an enchantress, brought him back to life and made him young again.

Humming the ''Blue Danube Waltz,'' Tony danced around the room with a mopstick for a partner.

When the carpenter had finished, his helper swept up the sawdust and tossed it into the fireplace.

Valerie has not paid back the money she borrowed from Eva last month, but so far Eva has said nothing.

In his poem about the outlaw Jesse James, William Rose Benét wrote, ''He was ten foot tall when he stood in his boots.''

QUESTIONS

1. Who was superseded?
2. Who withdrew?
3. Who disposed of a residue?
4. Who was alleged to be of prodigious stature?
5. Who hampered someone?
6. Who resolved a nettlesome problem?
7. Who was rejuvenated?
8. Who acted like a zany?
9. Who showed forbearance?
10. Who made a salutary move?

EXERCISE 2.23: COMPOSITION

Answer in a sentence or two.

1. How much forbearance should we have with a zany driver? Explain.
2. May we conclude that a person who seems unruffled has no nettlesome problems? Explain.
3. Is it salutary to sunbathe for hours under a sweltering sun? Why, or why not?
4. Should an official who hampers an investigation be superseded? Explain.
5. Would you be joking or serious if you said that a friend who is oblivious of faces, names, and appointments has a prodigious memory? Why?

EXERCISE 2.24: BRAINTEASERS

As clues to the complete word, you are given some of the letters and the number of missing letters. On your answer paper, write the complete word.

1. Greasy foods leave a(n) (4)**dual** film on dishes and silverware.
2. While we are sweltering here, people are shivering in (1)**rig**(2) temperatures up north.
3. There is still plenty of life left in the old car. It is much too early to (3)**sign** it to the scrap heap.
4. We cannot get Olly to stop clowning. He enjoys making a **buff**(3) of himself.
5. Our national debt has reached (3)**dig**(4) proportions, and it is still soaring.
6. Since the jury found no evidence against the defendants, it voted to (5)**pat**(1) them of all charges.
7. After spurning our offers of assistance, the members of the committee had the (2)**merit**(1) to say that we had never offered to help them.
8. Some of the concepts in advanced physics may be hard to understand at first because of their (5)**exit**(1).
9. One way to find a lost needle in a pile rug is to (2)**rut**(5) the area where it was dropped.
10. Her brother was **disco**(6). Obviously, something had upset him.

CHAPTER 3

Building Vocabulary Through Central Ideas

One way to expand your vocabulary is to study words related to a central idea. For example, you can learn **bliss, delectable, ecstasy, elation,** and **jubilation** as "joy" words, and **chagrin, compunction, dejected, disconsolate,** and **lamentable** as "sorrow" words. Grouping lesson words in this way may make vocabulary study easier and more interesting.

Here are a few suggestions for getting the most out of this chapter.

1. Pay careful attention to each illustrative sentence. Then construct, at least in your mind, a similar sentence of your own.

2. Do the drill exercises thoughtfully, not mechanically. Review the words you miss.

3. Deliberately *use* your new vocabulary as soon as possible in appropriate situations—in chats with friends, class discussions, letters, and compositions. Only by *exercising* new words will you succeed in making them part of your active vocabulary.

1. Joy, Pleasure

WORD	MEANING AND TYPICAL USE
bliss (*n.*) 'blis	perfect happiness The young movie star could conceive of no greater *bliss* than winning an "Oscar."

blissful (*adj.*)
'blis-fəl

very happy
The soldiers' reunion with their families was a *blissful* occasion.

blithe (*adj.*)
'blīth

1. merry; joyous
2. heedless
He was so enraptured with the scenery that he drove right through the intersection in *blithe* disregard of the "Full Stop" sign.

buoy (*v.*)
'bü-ē

keep afloat; raise the spirits of; encourage
Your encouragement *buoyed* us and gave us hope.

buoyant (*adj.*)
'bȯi-ənt

1. cheerful
We need your *buoyant* companionship to lift us from boredom.

2. able to float
The raft is sinking; it is not *buoyant*.

complacency (*n.*)
kəm-'plās-ᵊn-sē

self-satisfaction; smugness
Don't be too pleased with yourself; *complacency* is dangerous.

complacent (*adj.*)
kəm-'plās-ᵊnt

too pleased with oneself—often without awareness of possible dangers or defects; self-satisfied; smug
We should not be *complacent* about our security; we must be alert to potential threats.

convivial (*adj.*)
kən-'viv-ē-əl

1. fond of eating and drinking with friends
2. sociable
Our *convivial* host hates to dine alone.

conviviality (*n.*)
ˌkən-ˌviv-'ē-al-ə-tē

sociability
We enjoy the *conviviality* of holiday get-togethers.

delectable (*adj.*)
di-'lek-tə-bəl

very pleasing; delightful
The food was *delectable*; we enjoyed every morsel.

ecstasy (*n.*)
'ek-stə-sē

state of overwhelming joy; rapture
If we win tomorrow, there will be *ecstasy*; if we lose, gloom.

ecstatic (*adj.*)
ek-'stat-ik

in ecstasy; enraptured
The victors were *ecstatic*.

elated (*adj.*) i-'lāt-əd	in high spirits; joyful Except for my sister, who misses the old neighborhood, the family is *elated* with our new living quarters.
elation (*n.*) i-'lā-shən	state of being elated; euphoria Unfortunately, our *elation* was short-lived.
frolic (*v.*) 'fräl-ik	play and run about happily; have fun; romp Very young children need a safe place to *frolic*.
frolicsome (*adj.*) 'fräl-ik-səm	full of merriment; playful The clown's *frolicsome* antics amused the children.
gala (*adj.*) 'gā-lə	characterized by festivity The annual Mardi Gras in New Orleans is a *gala* carnival of parades and merriment.
jocund (*adj.*) 'jäk-ənd	merry; cheerful Our neighbor is a *jocund* fellow who tells amusing anecdotes.
jubilant (*adj.*) 'jü-bə-lənt	showing great joy; rejoicing; exultant The defendant's friends are *jubilant* over her acquittal.
jubilation (*n.*) ˌjü-bə-'lā-shən	rejoicing; exultation On election night there usually is *jubilation* at the campaign headquarters of the victorious party.

2. Sadness

ascetic (*adj.*) ə-'set-ik	shunning pleasures; self-denying The *ascetic* Puritans rigidly suppressed many forms of recreation.
ascetic (*n.*) ə-'set-ik	person who shuns pleasures and lives simply Carl never goes to the movies, plays, or parties. He must be an *ascetic*.
chagrin (*n.*) shə-'grin	embarrassment; mortification; disappointment Imagine my *chagrin* when I learned that I had not been invited to the party!
chagrined (*adj.*) shə-'grind	ashamed; mortified When my blunder was pointed out to me, I was deeply *chagrined*.

compunction (*n.*)   regret; remorse; misgiving; qualm
kəm-'pəŋ(k)-shən   We had no *compunction* about turning in the old car because it had become undependable.

contrite (*adj.*)   showing deep regret and sorrow for wrongdoing;
kən-'trīt   deeply penitent; repentant
    Believing the young offender to be *contrite*, the dean decided to give him another chance.

contrition (*n.*)   repentance
kən-'trish-ən   The ringleader showed no *contrition*, but his accomplices have expressed sorrow for their misdeeds.

dejected (*adj.*)   sad; in low spirits; depressed
di-'jek-təd   We are elated when our team wins, but *dejected* when it loses.

dejection (*n.*)   lowness of spirits; sadness; depression
di-'jek-shən   Cheer up. There is no reason for *dejection*.

disconsolate (*adj.*)   cheerless; inconsolable
dis-'kän-sə-lət   The mother could not stop her *disconsolate* son from sobbing over the loss of his dog.

disgruntled (*adj.*)   in bad humor; displeased; discontented
dis-'grənt-ᵊld   From her *disgruntled* expression I could tell she was not satisfied with my explanation.

doleful (*adj.*)   causing grief or sadness; mournful; dolorous
'dōl-fəl   The refugee told a *doleful* tale of hunger and persecution.

glum (*adj.*)   moody; gloomy; dour
'gləm   As they emerged from the conference, both the Mayor and the Governor were *glum* and refused to talk to reporters.

lament (*v.*)   mourn; deplore
lə-'ment   We *lament* the loss of life, and we sympathize with the victims' families.

lamentable (*adj.*)   pitiable; rueful
'lam-ən-tə-bəl   He described the *lamentable* hardships of the three miners trapped in the underground chamber.

maudlin (*adj.*)   weakly sentimental and tearful
'mȯd-lən   After singing a couple of *maudlin* numbers, the quartet was asked for something more cheerful.

nostalgia (*n.*)
nə-'stal-jə

1. homesickness
Toward the end of a vacation away from home, we usually experience a feeling of *nostalgia*.

2. yearning for the past
In moments of *nostalgia*, I long for the good old days.

nostalgic (*adj.*)
nä-'stal-jik

homesick
When away from home for too long, we tend to become *nostalgic*.

pathetic (*adj.*)
pə-'thet-ik

arousing pity
Despite his *pathetic* condition, the released hostage had a ready smile.

pathos (*n.*)
'pā-thäs

quality in events or in art (literature, music, etc.) that arouses our pity
The young seamstress who precedes Sydney Carton to the guillotine adds to the *pathos* of A TALE OF TWO CITIES.

pensive (*adj.*)
'pen-siv

thoughtful in a sad way; melancholy
Unlike her cheerful, outgoing sister, Elizabeth was *pensive* and shy.

plight (*n.*)
'plīt

unfortunate state; predicament
Numerous offers of assistance were received after the *plight* of the distressed family was publicized.

poignant (*adj.*)
'pói-nyənt

painfully touching; piercing
One of the most *poignant* scenes in MACBETH occurs when Macduff learns that his wife and children have been slaughtered.

sullen (*adj.*)
'səl-ən

resentfully silent; glum; morose; gloomy
The *sullen* suspect refused to give his name and address.

throes (*n. pl.*)
'thrōz

anguish; pangs
Fortunate are those who have never experienced the *throes* of separation from a loved one.

tribulation (*n.*)
ˌtrib-yə-'lā-shən

suffering; distress
The 1845 potato famine was a time of great *tribulation* in Ireland.

3. Stoutness

burly (*adj.*)
'bər-lē

strongly and heavily built; husky (*ant.* **lank**)
    Extra-large football uniforms were ordered to outfit our *burly* linemen.

buxom (*adj.*)
'bək-səm

plump and attractive
    By the side of her skinny city cousin, the farm girl looked radiant and *buxom.*

cherubic (*adj.*)
chə-'rü-bik

chubby and innocent-looking; like a *cherub* (angel in the form of a child)
    Your well-nourished nephew, despite his *cherubic* face, can be quite mischievous.

obese (*adj.*)
ō-'bēs

extremely overweight; corpulent; portly (*ant.* **skinny**)
    For a long, healthy life, one should give up smoking and avoid becoming *obese.*

obesity (*n.*)
o-'bē-sət-ē

excessive body weight; corpulence
    Dieting under professional guidance may help reduce *obesity.*

pudgy (*adj.*)
'pəj-ē

short and plump; chubby
    This ring is too small for a *pudgy* finger.

4. Thinness

attenuate (*v.*)
ə-'ten-yə-ˌwāt

make thin; weaken
    Photographs of President Lincoln reveal how rapidly the cares of leadership aged and *attenuated* him.

emaciated (*adj.*)
i-'mā-shē-ˌāt-əd

made unnaturally thin; abnormally lean because of starvation or illness (*ant.* **fleshy**)
    Emaciated by his illness, the patient found, on his recovery, that his clothes were too big.

haggard (*adj.*)
'hag-ərd

careworn; gaunt
    Haggard from their long ordeal, the rescued miners were rushed to the hospital for treatment and rest.

lank (*adj.*) 'laŋk	lean; ungracefully tall; lanky (*ant.* **burly**) Every basketball team longs for a *lank*, agile center who can control the boards.
svelte (*adj.*) 'svelt	slender; lithe Ballet dancers observe a strict diet to maintain their *svelte* figures.

5. Flattery

adulation (*n.*) ‚ad-yə-'lā-shən	excessive praise; flattery True leaders can distinguish sincere praise from blind *adulation*.
blandishment (*n.*) 'blan-dish-mənt	word or deed of mild flattery; allurement; enticement Suitors often use terms of endearment, flowers, and similar *blandishments*.
cajole (*v.*) kə-'jōl	persuade by pleasant words; wheedle; coax My sister *cajoled* Dad into raising her allowance.
cajolery (*n.*) kə-'jōl-ə-rē	persuasion by flattery; wheedling; coaxing The sly fox used *cajolery* to gain his ends.
curry (*v.*) **favor** (*n.*) 'kər-ē 'fā-və(r)	seek to gain favor by flattery The candidate tried to *curry favor* with the voters by praising their intelligence and patriotism.
fulsome (*adj.*) 'fúl-səm	offensive because of insincerity; repulsive; disgusting How can you endure the *fulsome* praises of your subordinate who lauds your every decision, right or wrong?
ingratiate (*v.*) in-'grā-shē-‚āt	work (oneself) into favor By trying to respond to every question, the new pupil tried to *ingratiate* herself with the teacher.
lackey (*n.*) 'lak-ē	follower who carries out another's wishes like a servant; toady The queen could never get a frank opinion from the *lackeys* surrounding her, for they would always agree with her.

obsequious (*adj.*)
əb-'sē-kwē-əs

showing excessive willingness to serve; subservient; fawning
> The *obsequious* subordinates vied with one another in politeness and obedience, each hoping to win the director's favor.

sycophant (*n.*)
'sik-ə-fənt

parasitic flatterer; truckler
> *Sycophants* live at the expense of vain persons who enjoy flattery.

truckle (*v.*)
'trək-əl

submit in a subservient manner to a superior; fawn; make a doormat of oneself
> Some employees, unfortunately, gain promotion by *truckling* to their supervisors.

Apply What You Have Learned

EXERCISE 3.1: SYNONYMS

For each word or expression in column I, write the *letter* of its correct synonym from column II.

COLUMN I	COLUMN II
1. delightful	(A) predicament
2. arousing pity	(B) attenuated
3. plight	(C) nostalgia
4. mild flattery	(D) haggard
5. careworn	(E) delectable
6. self-denying	(F) bliss
7. perfect happiness	(G) lackey
8. weakened	(H) blandishment
9. subservient follower	(I) pathetic
10. homesickness	(J) ascetic

EXERCISE 3.2: UNRELATED WORDS

On your answer page, enter the *letter* of the word unrelated in meaning to the other words on the line.

1. (A) ecstatic   (B) jubilant   (C) rapturous   (D) pensive
2. (A) svelte   (B) slender   (C) slippery   (D) lithe

3. (A) comedian   (B) lackey   (C) flatterer   (D) sycophant
4. (A) tribulation   (B) insincerity   (C) suffering   (D) pangs
5. (A) cajolery   (B) gloominess   (C) dejection   (D) melancholy
6. (A) elation   (B) frolicsomeness   (C) euphoria   (D) adulation
7. (A) wheedle   (B) attenuate   (C) ingratiate   (D) fawn
8. (A) pathos   (B) pity   (C) complacency   (D) compassion
9. (A) portly   (B) burly   (C) buxom   (D) contrite
10. (A) jovial   (B) jocund   (C) blithe   (D) disconsolate

EXERCISE 3.3: CONCISE WRITING

Express the thought of each sentence below in no more than four words. The first sentence has been rewritten as a sample.

1. What is the reason for your being in bad humor?
   Why are you disgruntled?
2. I was deeply regretful and full of sorrow for what I had done.
3. We look down on praise that is offered without sincerity.
4. Mom excels in the art of using pleasant words to persuade others.
5. They are altogether too willing to serve and obey their superiors.
6. The one who does the carpentry work is strongly and sturdily built.
7. Those who survived were little more than skin and bones.
8. The encouragement that we received from you brought our spirits up high.
9. A large number refused to take notice of the unfortunate situation that they saw we were in.
10. It is dangerous to be in a state of mind in which one is too satisfied with oneself.

EXERCISE 3.4: BRAINTEASERS

As clues to the complete word, you are given some of the letters and the number of missing letters. On your answer paper, write the complete word.

1. The workers are (6)**tent**(2) because they did not get a raise.
2. No one smiled. It was a(n) (6)**holy** occasion.
3. Whenever they try to (3)**rat**(4) themselves with us, we suspect they are looking for a favor.

4. I was (3)**grin**(2), when I went to pay for my lunch, to find that I had left my money at home.

5. We have no (3)**pun**(5) about not waiting for Sally because she has never waited for us.

6. The stolen car was in such **lame**(6) condition when it was recovered that its owner was moved to tears.

7. Anyone who enjoys adulation is an easy prey for (6)**ants**.

8. Don't expect them to cater to your wishes like servants. They are not your (3)**keys**.

9. This shop specializes in clothes for the tall and the (1)**or**(3).

10. It is unwise to adopt a(n) (4)**tic** lifestyle of "all work and no play."

EXERCISE 3.5: SENTENCE COMPLETION

On your answer paper write the most appropriate word from the vocabulary list below that will correctly complete the sentence.

VOCABULARY LIST

poignant	cajole	tribulation
buxom	burly	emaciated
throes	pathos	gala
fulsome	jubilation	elated
obesity	remorse	glum

1. The ___?___ movers lifted the piano with surprising ease.

2. After the game, there was wild ___?___ as supporters rushed onto the field to congratulate their heroes.

3. The President looked ___?___ as he announced the disappointing news.

4. To a young child, a birthday is certainly a(n) ___?___ occasion.

5. Newspapers reported the ___?___ details of the futile rescue attempt.

6. The new supervisor was repelled by the ___?___ compliments of some of her subordinates.

7. When Mr. Norwood was stopped for a traffic violation, he tried to ___?___ the officer into not writing a ticket.

8. The ___?___ appearance of the liberated prisoners shocked the world.

9. At the trial one of the suspects wept repeatedly, but the other showed no ___?___.

10. Many people watch their diets and exercise regularly to avoid ___?___.

EXERCISE 3.6: COMPOSITION

Answer in a sentence or two.

1. Who is more likely to do well in a marathon, a lank runner or a burly one? Why?
2. Give an example of something that can be done to buoy the spirits of a dejected friend.
3. Name two delectable foods that may have to be given up for a svelte waistline, and suggest substitutes for those foods.
4. If you accidentally hurt someone, would you be complacent or contrite? Explain.
5. Would you enjoy working for a company where some of the employees are obsequious and truckle to the boss? Explain.

EXERCISE 3.7: ANALOGIES

Write the *letter* of the pair of words related to each other in the same way as the capitalized pair.

Sample

ECSTASY : JOY

a. thrift : wealth   *d.* terror : fear
b. certainty : doubt   *e.* frigid : cold
c. fondness : adoration

Solution

The first step is to find the relationship in the capitalized pair. Obviously ECSTASY is a state of overwhelming JOY. If we designate ECSTASY by the letter X, and JOY by the letter Y, we can express the ECSTASY : JOY relationship by saying, "X is a state of overwhelming Y."

a. Thrift : Wealth

> *Thrift* is a means by which one may acquire *wealth*. *Thrift* is NOT a state of overwhelming *wealth*.

b. Certainty : Doubt

> *Certainty* is the opposite of *doubt*. It is definitely NOT a state of overwhelming *doubt*.

c. Fondness : Adoration

> *Fondness* is a much milder expression of liking than *adoration*. Note that the trouble with this pair is the order. If it were reversed (ADORATION : FONDNESS), this pair would be a correct answer because *adoration* is a state of overwhelming *fondness*.

d. Terror : Fear

> *Terror* is a state of overwhelming *fear*. This choice looks very good, but let us also check the final pair.

e. Frigid : Cold

> *Frigid* is overwhelmingly *cold*. The relationship is correct. However, *frigid* and *cold* are adjectives, whereas the capitalized pair, ECSTASY : JOY, are nouns. If choice *e* were changed to FRIGIDITY : COLD (*nouns*), it would be acceptable.

Note that *terror* and *fear* in choice *d* are both nouns. This, plus the fact that *terror* is a state of overwhelming *fear*, makes *d* the correct choice.

1. NOSTALGIA : PAST
- *a.* regret : deed
- *b.* yearning : eternity
- *c.* anticipation : future
- *d.* absence : presence
- *e.* memory : forgetfulness

2. SYCOPHANT : SINCERITY
- *a.* thief : cleverness
- *b.* deceiver : truth
- *c.* coward : fear
- *d.* friend : loyalty
- *e.* hero : courage

3. ASCETIC : PLEASURE
- *a.* politician : votes
- *b.* plant : light
- *c.* scientist : truth
- *d.* root : water
- *e.* hermit : society

4. FOOD : OBESITY
- *a.* slip : fall
- *b.* spark : explosion
- *c.* fatigue : work
- *d.* rainfall : flood
- *e.* landslide : earthquake

5. DISCONSOLATE : CHEER
- *a.* intrepid : fear
- *b.* compassionate : sympathy
- *c.* repentant : regret
- *d.* frolicsome : merriment
- *e.* plaintive : sorrow

Going Over the Answers

Since this is our first exercise in analogies, check your answers with the following, paying careful attention to the reasoning involved.

QUESTION	RELATIONSHIP OF X AND Y	ANSWER AND EXPLANATION
1.	*Nostalgia* is a yearning for the *past*.	c. *Anticipation* is a yearning for the *future*.
2.	A *sycophant* makes a pretense of *sincerity*.	b. A *deceiver* makes a pretense of *truth*.
3.	An *ascetic* shuns *pleasure*.	e. A *hermit* shuns *society*.
4.	Excessive *food* intake may cause *obesity*.	d. Excessive *rainfall* may cause a *flood*.
5.	A *disconsolate* person is without *cheer*.	a. An *intrepid* person is without *fear*.

---

6. Animal

WORD	MEANING AND TYPICAL USE
apiary (*n.*) 'ā-pē-,er-ē	place where bees are kept A beekeeper maintains an *apiary*.
aviary (*n.*) 'ā-vē-,er-ē	place where birds are kept Some interesting birds of prey are confined in an *aviary* on the zoo grounds.
badger (*v.*) 'baj-ə(r)	tease; annoy; nag (originally to harass a trapped badger) *Badgered* by the children's persistent pleas, their parents finally relented and allowed them to go to the movies.
halcyon (*adj.*) 'hal-sē-ən	calm; peaceful (from *halcyon*, a bird thought to calm the waves) Most adults nostalgically recall the *halcyon* days of their youth.
lionize (*v.*) 'lī-ə-,nīz	treat as highly important With the first publication of his poems, Robert Burns gained immediate fame and was *lionized* by Edinburgh society.

menagerie (*n.*)
mə-'naj-ə-rē

place where animals are kept and trained; collection of wild animals
    P. T. Barnum called his traveling circus, museum, and *menagerie* ''the greatest show on earth.''

molt (*v.*)
'mōlt

shed feathers, skin, hair, etc.
    Birds, mammals, and snakes *molt* periodically.

ornithology (*n.*)
‚ȯr-nə-'thäl-ə-jē

study of birds
    Ellen developed an interest in *ornithology* after reading John Burroughs' writings on birds.

parasite (*n.*)
'par-ə-‚sīt

animal, plant, or person living on others
    Instead of seeking employment, he preferred to live as a *parasite* on his brother.

parasitic (*adj.*)
‚par-ə-'sit-ik

living at the expense of another; sponging
    Fleas are *parasitic* insects.

parrot (*v.*)
'par-ət

repeat mechanically, like a *parrot* (tropical bird that imitates human speech)
    Does he really understand what he is saying, or is he merely *parroting* his teacher?

scavenger (*n.*)
'skav-ən-jə(r)

animal or person removing refuse, decay, etc.
    Sea gulls are useful harbor *scavengers*, since they feed on garbage.

7. Health, Medicine

antidote (*n.*)
'ant-i-‚dōt

remedy for a poison or evil
    A bottle containing poison must have the *antidote* specified on the label.

astringent (*n.*)
ə-'strin-jənt

substance that shrinks tissues and checks flow of blood
    According to its label, this after-shave lotion acts as an *astringent* by helping to check the bleeding of nicks and scrapes.

astringent (*adj.*)
ə-'strin-jənt

1. severe; stern
    Instead of mild criticism, I got an *astringent* rebuke.
2. causing contraction

benign (*adj.*)
bi-'nīn

1. not dangerous (*ant.* **malignant**)
The patient was relieved to learn that his tumor was *benign*, not *malignant*.

2. gentle; kindly
The doorman is a kind, elderly man with a *benign* smile.

convalesce (*v.*)
ˌkän-və-'les

recover health after illness; recuperate
After the appendectomy you will have to *convalesce* for about a week before returning to school.

convalescent (*n.*)
ˌkän-və-'les-ᵊnt

person recovering from sickness
A *convalescent* should not be taxed with chores.

fester (*v.*)
'fes-tə(r)

form pus; rankle; rot; putrefy
When a wound *festers*, it becomes inflamed, swollen, and painful.

hypochondriac (*n.*)
ˌhī-pə-'kän-drē-ˌak

one who is morbidly anxious about personal health, or suffering from imagined illness
The *hypochondriac* often interprets a normal condition as a symptom of serious illness.

immunity (*n.*)
im-'yü-nət-ē

1. resistance (to a disease)
Most people acquire life-long *immunity* to German measles once they have had that disease.

2. freedom (from an obligation)
Federal and state properties within the city limits enjoy *immunity* from taxation.

immunize (*v.*)
'im-yə-ˌnīz

make *immune* (resistant to a disease)
Infants receive a series of injections to *immunize* them against serious childhood diseases.

lesion (*n.*)
'lē-zhən

injury; hurt
The slightest *lesion* on a tree's bark, if left untended, may kill the tree.

malignant (*adj.*)
mə-'lig-nənt

1. threatening to cause death (*ant.* **benign**)
An emergency operation was scheduled to remove the *malignant* tissues.

2. very evil
The brothers came under the *malignant* influence of a criminal who taught them to steal.

morbid (*adj.*)
'mȯr-bəd

1. gruesome
In describing his illness, he discreetly omitted the *morbid* details.

2. having to do with disease
   One sign of Lady Macbeth's *morbid* condition is that she was troubled by hallucinations and fantasies.

pestilential (*adj.*)
,pes-tə-'len-shəl

1. morally harmful
   Parents, teachers, and spiritual leaders have attacked certain TV programs as *pestilential*.

2. pertaining to a *pestilence* (plague)
   The flu is a *pestilential* disease.

regimen (*n.*)
'rej-ə-mən

set of rules, esp. to improve health
   After the operation I had to follow a *regimen* of diet and exercise prescribed by my physician.

salubrious (*adj.*)
sə-'lü-brē-əs

healthful
   Southern Florida's *salubrious* climate attracts many convalescents.

sebaceous (*adj.*)
si-'bā-shəs

greasy; secreting *sebum* (fatty matter secreted by the glands of the skin)
   The *sebaceous* glands in the skin secrete an oily substance essential for skin health.

therapeutic (*adj.*)
,ther-ə-'pyüt-ik

curative
   The "get-well" cards have had a *therapeutic* effect on the hospitalized patient.

toxic (*adj.*)
'täk-sik

poisonous
   Operating a gasoline engine in a closed garage may cause death, as the exhaust fumes are dangerously *toxic*.

unguent (*n.*)
'əŋ-gwənt

salve; ointment
   Flora's skin irritation was relieved after she applied the *unguent* prescribed by her physician.

virulent (*adj.*)
'vir-(y)ə-lənt

1. extremely poisonous; deadly; venomous
   Some insecticides and weed killers contain arsenic, a *virulent* substance.

2. very bitter
   The rebels show a *virulent* antagonism to the present ruler.

viral (*adj.*)
'vī-rəl

caused by a *virus*
   The flu is a *viral* disease.

virus (*n.*)
'vī-rəs

1. disease-causing substance too small to be seen through a microscope
   Diseases like AIDS, rabies, smallpox, and polio are caused by a *virus*.
2. corruptive force
   What further measures are needed to combat the *virus* of prejudice?

---

8. Praise

---

acclaim (*v.*)
ə-'klām

welcome with approval; applaud loudly
   I did not enjoy that novel although it was *acclaimed* by several leading reviewers.

encomium (*n.*)
en-'kō-mē-əm

speech or writing of high praise; tribute; eulogy
   Lincoln's "Gettysburg Address" is, in part, an *encomium* of those who fought at the Battle of Gettysburg.

eulogize (*v.*)
'yü-lə-ˌjīz

praise; extol; laud; glorify (*ant.* **vilify**)
   The late composer was *eulogized* for his contributions to American music.

laudable (*adj.*)
'lȯd-ə-bəl

praiseworthy; commendable
   The bus driver's *laudable* safety record evoked high praise from her superiors.

laudatory (*adj.*)
'lȯd-ə-ˌtȯr-ē

expressing praise; eulogistic
   Most of the critics wrote *laudatory* reviews of the new film; only one found fault with it.

plaudit (*n.*)
'plȯd-ət

(used mainly in the plural) applause; enthusiastic praise
   Responding to the *plaudits* of their admirers, the singers reappeared for an encore.

---

9. Defamation

---

calumnious (*adj.*)
kə-'ləm-nē-əs

falsely and maliciously accusing; defamatory; slanderous
   Witnesses who heard the *calumnious* attack offered to testify in behalf of the slandered person.

derogatory (*adj.*)
di-'räg-ə-,tȯr-ē

expressing low esteem; belittling; disparaging (*ant.* **complimentary**)
  Despite *derogatory* comments by some reviewers, the film is a box-office success.

imputation (*n.*)
,im-pyə-'tā-shən

charge, esp. an unjust or false charge; insinuation; accusation
  My rival has tried to besmirch my character with the cowardly *imputation* that I am untrustworthy.

libel (*n.*)
'lī-bəl

false and defamatory printed (or written) statement
  We shall certainly sue the newspaper that printed this *libel* against our company.

libelous (*adj.*)
'lī-bə-ləs

injurious to reputation; defamatory; calumnious

malign (*v.*)
mə-'līn

speak evil of; vilify; traduce
  I cannot bear to hear you *malign* so good a man.

slander (*n.*)
'slan-də(r)

false and defamatory spoken statement; calumny
  The rumor that she was discharged is a vicious *slander*; the fact is that she resigned.

stigma (*n.*)
'stig-mə

mark of disgrace
  With the *stigma* of a prison record, the ex-convict had difficulty in finding employment.

stigmatize (*v.*)
'stig-mə-,tīz

brand with a mark of disgrace
  Surely no one would enjoy being *stigmatized* by a nickname like ''Dopey.''

---

10. Jest

---

banter (*n.*)
'bant-ə(r)

playful teasing; joking; raillery
  The retiring employees were subjected to gentle *banter* about their coming life of ease.

caricature (*n.*)
'kar-i-kə-,chu̇(ə)r

drawing, imitation, or description that ridiculously exaggerates peculiarities or defects
  The Class Night skit that drew the loudest plaudits was a *caricature* of the first day in high school.

droll (*adj.*)
'drōl

odd and laughter-provoking
  ''On Eating Crackers in Bed'' is surely a *droll* title for an essay.

facetious (*adj.*)
fə-'sē-shəs

1. in the habit of joking
   Our *facetious* club president has a way of turning almost every comment into a joke.

2. said in jest without serious intent
   When you are carrying a heavily loaded lunch tray, some joker may try to upset you with a *facetious* remark, like "Hey, do you have a pen?"

flippant (*adj.*)
'flip-ənt

treating serious matters lightly
   One should not be so *flippant* about the need for studying; it is a serious matter that may affect your graduation.

harlequin (*n.*)
'här-li-k(w)ən

buffoon; clown
   The *harlequin's* clowning endeared him to all.

hilarious (*adj.*)
hil-'ar-ē-əs

boisterously merry; very funny
   The comedian was *hilarious.*

hilarity (*n.*)
hil-'ar-ət-ē

noisy gaiety; mirth; jollity; glee
   The laughter and shouting made passersby curious to learn what all the *hilarity* was about.

ironic or
ironical (*adj.*)
'ī-'rän-ik
'ī-'rän-i-kəl

containing or expressing irony
   It is *ironic* that a joyous event, like leaving for a vacation, should result in the tragic loss of life.

irony (*n.*)
'ī-rə-nē

1. species of humor whose intended meaning is the opposite of the words used
   In *irony*, the basketball players nicknamed their 6'6" center "Shorty."

2. state of affairs contrary to what would normally be expected
   The breakdown occurred just after the car was inspected and found to be in perfect condition. What *irony*!

jocose (*adj.*)
jō-'kōs

given to jesting; playfully humorous; jocular
   Some columnists write in a *jocose* vein; others are inclined to be serious.

levity (*n.*)
'lev-ət-ē

lack of proper seriousness; trifling gaiety; frivolity
Some of us felt that George's giggling during the ceremony was an unforgivable *levity*.

ludicrous (*adj.*)
'lüd-ə-krəs

exciting laughter; ridiculous; farcical; absurd
Pie-throwing, falling down stairs, and similar *ludicrous* antics were common in early film comedies.

parody (*n.*)
'par-əd-ē

humorous imitation
The Washington press corps entertained the Chief Executive with a *parody* of a Presidential message to Congress.

sarcasm (*n.*)
'sär-ˌkaz-əm

sneering language intended to hurt a person's feelings
Instead of helping, he offered such *sarcasm* as "You have made your bed; now lie in it."

sarcastic (*adj.*)
sär-'kas-tik

given to or expressing sarcasm
Sarcastic language can deeply hurt a person.

sardonic (*adj.*)
sär-'dän-ik

bitterly sarcastic; mocking; sneering
Villains are often portrayed with a *sardonic* grin that suggests contempt for others.

satire (*n.*)
'sa-ˌtī(ə)r

language or writing that exposes follies or abuses by holding them up to ridicule
Jonathan Swift's GULLIVER'S TRAVELS is a brilliant *satire* on human follies.

satiric or
satirical (*adj.*)
sə-'tir-ik
sə-'tir-i-kəl

given to or expressing satire
In *Catch-22*, a *satirical* novel, Joseph Heller ridicules the inflexibility of military bureaucrats.

travesty (*n.*)
'trav-ə-stē

imitation that makes a serious thing seem ridiculous; mockery
It is a *travesty* of justice that a notorious criminal should escape trial because of a technicality.

Apply What You Have Learned

EXERCISE 3.8: ANTONYMS

For each word or expression in column I there is an ANTONYM (opposite) in column II. Write the *letter* of the correct ANTONYM on your answer paper.

COLUMN I	COLUMN II
1. mark of honor	(A) complimentary
2. susceptible	(B) poisonous
3. nontoxic	(C) halcyon
4. treat (someone) as unimportant	(D) doleful
5. hilarious	(E) levity
6. derogatory	(F) stigma
7. turbulent	(G) encomium
8. seriousness	(H) lionize
9. denunciation	(I) vilify
10. extol	(J) immune

EXERCISE 3.9: DEFINITIONS

Write the *letter* of the word or expression that best defines the italicized word.

1. *Astringent* rebuke (A) mild (C) undeserved (B) friendly (D) stern

2. Effective *antidote* (A) harlequin (C) remedy (B) punishment (D) precaution

3. *Derogatory* comment (A) unfair (C) congratulatory (B) belittling (D) false

4. *Benign* ruler (A) healthful (C) kindly (B) aging (D) tyrannical

5. *Ironical* development (A) contrary to expectation (C) discouraging (B) very sudden (D) unfortunate

6. *Festering* slums (A) decaying (C) poverty-stricken (B) crime-ridden (D) spreading

7. Utterly *farcical*   (A) hopeless   (C) irresponsible
                           (B) incompetent   (D) absurd
8. Prescribed *regimen*   (A) rules   (C) dose
                           (B) medicine   (D) enforcement
9. *Venomous* fangs   (A) vigorous   (C) dangerous
                           (B) virulent   (D) pointed
10. *Halcyon* atmosphere   (A) cloudy   (C) calm
                           (B) noisy   (D) clear

EXERCISE 3.10: CONCISE WRITING

Express the thought of each sentence below in no more than four words. The first sentence has been rewritten as a sample.

1. We look down with contempt on those who live on others.
   We despise parasites.
2. Who is the person who wrote that false and defamatory statement?
3. He deliberately uses sneering language that can hurt people's feelings.
4. Those who suffer from imaginary illnesses are in urgent need of help.
5. They visited a place where animals are kept and trained.
6. At the present time, she is recovering from an illness.
7. He makes remarks that are meant as jokes and are not intended to be taken seriously.
8. The outcome was the opposite of what one would normally have expected.
9. Some tumors do not threaten the life of the patient.
10. At no time in the past did she speak evil of anyone.

EXERCISE 3.11: SENTENCE COMPLETION

Write the *letter* of the word (or set of words) that best completes the sentence.

1. Newspapers generally withhold the names of criminal offenders under sixteen so as not to __?__ them.
   (A) popularize   (C) stigmatize   (E) traduce
   (B) libel   (D) slander

2. DON QUIXOTE, a __?__ novel by Cervantes, ridicules exaggerated notions of chivalry.
   (A) satirical   (C) historical   (E) eulogistic
   (B) sentimental   (D) realistic

3. The __?__ currently being exhibited in the __?__ have attracted numerous students of ornithology.
   (A) apes . . aviary   (D) monkeys . . apiary
   (B) parrots . . apiary   (E) vultures . . aviary
   (C) bees . . menagerie

4. The Olympic medal winner was __?__ by the citizens of her hometown.
   (A) badgered   (C) maligned   (E) caricatured
   (B) parodied   (D) lionized

5. Winston Churchill __?__ the heroes of the Battle of Britain in this memorable __?__ : "Never was so much owed by so many to so few."
   (A) congratulated . . travesty   (D) acclaimed . . tribute
   (B) defended . . encomium   (E) extolled . . oration
   (C) vilified . . plaudit

EXERCISE 3.12: BRAINTEASERS

As clues to the complete word, you are given some of the letters and the number of missing letters. On your answer paper, write the complete word.

1. At the dedication ceremony, the mayor will **e (1) l o g (3)** the scientist for whom the school is being named.

2. Fearing that failure to win a promotion might **(4) m a t (3)** her, Margaret did her best to succeed on the job.

3. It is **i r o n (4)** that the severely paralyzed lad should have the name Hale, which means "healthy."

4. Swimming is believed to have **(4) a p e (4)** benefits for people who suffer from arthritis.

5. **F a c e (5)** remarks on solemn occasions are entirely inappropriate.

6. The person who accidentally swallowed the poison was given a(n) **(4) d o t (1)** and rushed to the hospital.

7. Several newspaper editors commended the governor for his **(3) d a b (2)** efforts to prevent the strike.

8. Beneath the outer layer of the skin are the **(3) a c e (3)** glands, which secrete oil to lubricate the skin and the hair.

9. Many a life has been saved by the timely surgical removal of a(n) **(6) a n t** growth.

10. Though responsible for the fatal collision, the envoy could not be arrested because of diplomatic **(3) u n i t (1)**.

EXERCISE 3.13: COMPOSITION

Answer in a sentence or two.

1. Is badgering a convalescent forgivable? Explain.
2. Would you feel maligned if someone called you a hypochondriac when you were not feeling well? Why, or why not?
3. Is it a travesty for suspects who testify against fellow suspects to receive immunity from prosecution? Explain.
4. Why is it derogatory to be called a "parasite"?
5. Why would it be ironical for an ordinary high school tennis player to win a match from an acclaimed world champion?

EXERCISE 3.14: ANALOGIES

Write the *letter* of the word that best completes the analogy.

Sample

Aviary is to *birds* as *apiary* is to ___e___ .
    a. flowers *b.* apes *c.* worms *d.* reptiles *e.* bees

Explanation

The first step is to find the relationship of *aviary* and *birds*. As you have learned, an *aviary* is a "place where birds are kept." Then say to yourself, an *apiary* is a "place in which what is kept?" The answer, of course, is *e,* bees.

1. *Invalid* is to *hypochondriac* as *real* is to __?__ .
    a. sickly *b.* genuine *c.* healthful *d.* imagined *e.* impossible
2. *Birds* are to *ornithologist* as *poisons* are to __?__ .
    a. bacteriologist   *b.* pharmacist   *c.* toxicologist   *d.* physician
    e. coroner
3. *Waste* is to *scavenger* as *dirt* is to __?__ .
    a. oil *b.* parasite *c.* cleanser *d.* ant *e.* weed
4. *Photograph* is to *caricature* as *fact* is to __?__ .
    a. drawing *b.* exaggeration *c.* sketch *d.* truth *e.* description
5. *Ludicrous* is to *laugh* as *dolorous* is to __?__ .
    a. weep *b.* laud *c.* exult *d.* condemn *e.* smile

11. Willingness—Unwillingness

WORD	MEANING AND TYPICAL USE
alacrity (*n.*) ə-'lak-rət-ē	cheerful willingness; readiness; liveliness Dr. Burke's class is one which pupils attend with *alacrity* and leave with reluctance.
aversion (*n.*) ə-'vər-zhən	strong dislike; repugnance; antipathy Philip's *aversion* to work led to his dismissal.
involuntary (*adj.*) in-'väl-ən-ˌter-ē	not done of one's own free will; automatic; unintentional; spontaneous (*ant.* **voluntary**) Sneezing is *involuntary*.
loath (*adj.*) 'lōth	unwilling; averse; disinclined; reluctant We were *loath* to leave our friends, but my father's transfer to California left us no choice.
loathe (*v.*) 'lō<u>th</u>	have an intense aversion to; detest We *loathe* liars.
volition (*n.*) vō-'lish-ən	will Were you discharged or did you leave of your own *volition*?

12. Height

WORD	MEANING AND TYPICAL USE
acclivity (*n.*) ə-'kliv-ət-ē	upward slope (*ant.* **declivity**) The sharp *acclivity* compelled us to drive in low gear.
acme (*n.*) 'ak-mē	highest point; pinnacle; summit Many believe that Shakespeare reached his *acme* as a playwright when he wrote *Hamlet*.
apogee (*n.*) 'ap-ə-jē	1. farthest point from the earth in the orbit of a heavenly body (*ant.* **perigee**) At its *apogee*, the satellite was 560 miles (903 kilometers) from the earth, and at its perigee 150 miles (242 kilometers). 2. highest point; culmination The use of solar energy, though increasing, is still exceedingly far from its *apogee*.

climactic (*adj.*)
klī-'mak-tik

arranged in order of increasing force and interest (*ant.* **anticlimactic**)
    Notice the *climactic* order of ideas in this sentence: "Swelled by heavy rains, brooks became creeks, creeks rivers, and rivers torrents."

consummate (*adj.*)
kən-'səm-ət

perfect, superb; carried to the highest degree
    The pilot guided the plane onto the runway with *consummate* skill.

eminence (*n.*)
'em-ə-nəns

high rank
    Raised suddenly to an *eminence* for which he was ill qualified, the executive could not get along with his new subordinates.

eminent (*adj.*)
'em-ə-nənt

standing out; notable; famous
    Emily Dickinson was an *eminent* poet.

ethereal (*adj.*)
i-'thir-ē-əl

of the heavens; celestial; airy; delicate; intangible
    Charles was told by his employer, "Get rid of your *ethereal* notions and come down to earth."

exalt (*v.*)
ig-'zȯlt

1. lift up with joy, pride, etc.; elate (*ant.* **humiliate**)
    My parents were *exalted* to learn that I had won a scholarship.
2. raise in rank, dignity, etc.; extol; glorify
    Some films have *exalted* criminals to the level of heroes.

precipice (*n.*)
'pres-ə-pəs

very steep, overhanging place; cliff
    The climbers had to make a lengthy detour around an insurmountable *precipice*.

precipitous (*adj.*)
pri-'sip-ət-əs

1. steep as a precipice
    She descended from the summit in low gear, using her brakes all the way, since the road was so *precipitous*.
2. hasty; rash
    Don't rush into a *precipitous* action that you may later regret. Take your time.

preeminent (*adj.*)
prē-'em-ə-nənt

standing out above others; superior
    As a violinmaker, Stradivarius remains *preeminent*.

sublimate (*v.*)
'səb-lə-,māt

1. redirect the energy of a person's bad impulses into socially and morally higher channels
    With the aid of dedicated social workers, energies that had once found release in gang fights were *sublimated* into wholesome club activities and sports.

2. purify; refine
The alchemists failed in their efforts to *sublimate* baser metals, such as lead and copper, into gold.

sublime (*adj.*)
sə-'blīm

elevated; noble; exalted; uplifting
Visitors to the Grand Canyon are uplifted and refreshed by its *sublime* scenery.

vertex (*n.*)
'vər-ˌteks

farthest point opposite the base, as in a triangle or pyramid; apex
The *vertex* of the largest Egyptian pyramid was originally 482 feet (147 meters) from the base.

zenith (*n.*)
'zē-nəth

1. highest point; culmination (*ant.* **nadir**)
Her election to the Senate marked the *zenith* of her long career in politics.
2. point in the heavens directly overhead
At noon, the sun reaches the *zenith*.

---

13. Lowness, Depth

---

abject (*adj.*)
'ab-ˌjekt

deserving contempt; sunk to a low condition; wretched
For your *abject* submission to your tyrannical associate, we have the utmost contempt.

abysmal (*adj.*)
ə-'biz-məl

deep; profound; immeasurably great
I was ashamed of my *abysmal* ignorance.

abyss (*n.*)
ə-'bis

bottomless, immeasurably deep space
The sudden death of his closest friend threw Tennyson into an *abyss* of despair.

anticlimax (*n.*)
ˌant-i-'klī-maks

abrupt decline from the dignified or important to the trivial or ludicrous; comedown; bathos (*ant.* **climax**)
Sally used *anticlimax* when she said that my friend has a boundless appetite for classical music, Renaissance painting, and roasted peanuts.

chasm (*n.*)
'kaz-əm

deep breach; wide gap or rift
Prospects for a settlement became remote, as the *chasm* between the rival parties deepened.

declivity (*n.*)
di-'kliv-ət-ē

downward slope (*ant.* **acclivity**)
The hill was ideal for beginning skiers because of its gentle *declivity*.

dregs (*n. pl.*)
'dregz

most worthless part; sediment at the bottom of a liquid
  Thieves and hoodlums are among the *dregs* of society.

earthy (*adj.*)
'ər-thē

coarse; low
  The contractor's helpers were excellent, though we did not exactly enjoy their *earthy* humor.

humble (*adj.*)
'həm-bəl

1. of low position or condition
  Despite his *humble* origin, Lincoln rose to the highest office in the land.
2. not proud; unpretentious; modest; courteously respectful
  Though Stella has done far more than anyone else, she has never boasted of her achievement; she is *humble*.

humiliate (*v.*)
hyü-'mil-ē-,āt

lower the pride, position, or dignity of; abase; degrade; mortify (*ant.* **exalt**)
  Ted feels that I *humiliated* him at the meeting when I said that his motion was unnecessary.

humility (*n.*)
hyü-'mil-ət-ē

freedom from pride; humbleness; lowliness; modesty
  Boasters and braggarts need a lesson in *humility*.

menial (*adj.*)
'mē-nē-əl

low; mean; subservient; servile
  Some might consider mowing lawns *menial* work, but Harvey loves it.

nadir (*n.*)
'nā-də(r)

lowest point (*ant.* **zenith**)
  Hopes of the American Revolutionary forces were at their *nadir* in the bitter winter of 1777–78 at Valley Forge.

plumb (*v.*)
'pləm

get to the bottom of; ascertain the depth of; fathom
  Sherlock Holmes amazes readers by his ability to *plumb* the deepest mysteries.

profound (*adj.*)
prə-'faúnd

very deep; deeply felt; intellectually deep
  Einstein's theories are understood by relatively few because they are so *profound*.

ravine (*n.*)
rə-'vēn

deep, narrow gorge worn by running water
  Survivors of the plane that crashed in the mountain *ravine* were rescued by helicopter.

14. Relatives

filial (*adj.*)
'fil-ē-əl

of or like a son or daughter
Cordelia was the only one of King Lear's daughters that showed him *filial* affection.

fraternal (*adj.*)
frə-'tərn-əl

of or like a brother
There was much *fraternal* affection between the brothers; they were devoted to one another.

genealogy (*n.*)
ˌjē-nē-'äl-ə-jē

a person's or family's descent; lineage; pedigree
Most people can trace their *genealogy* back to a grandparent, or a great-grandparent, but they know almost nothing about their earlier ancestors.

gentility (*n.*)
jen-'til-ət-ē

1. good manners
George Bernard Shaw's PYGMALION shows how a cockney flower girl quickly acquires the *gentility* necessary to pass as a duchess.
2. gentry; upper class
The duke scandalized some members of the *gentility* by marrying a commoner.

kith and kin (*n. pl.*)
'kith; 'kin

friends and relatives; kindred
Because he married in a distant state, the soldier had few of his *kith and kin* at the wedding.

maternal (*adj.*)
mə-'tərn-əl

of or like a mother
The kindergarten teacher has a kindly, *maternal* concern for each pupil.

nepotism (*n.*)
'nep-ə-ˌtiz-əm

favoritism to relatives by those in power
Whenever a President appoints a relative to a government position, the cry of *nepotism* is raised by the opposition party.

paternal (*adj.*)
pə-'tərn-əl

of or like a father
The molding of a child's character is an important maternal and *paternal* obligation.

progenitor (*n.*)
prō-'jen-ət-ə(r)

forefather
Adam is the Biblical *progenitor* of the human race.

progeny (*n.*)
'präj-ə-nē

offspring; children; descendants
Josiah Franklin's *progeny* numbered seventeen, the fifteenth being his son Benjamin.

sibling (*n.*)   one of two or more children of a family
'sib-liŋ   Eileen has three *siblings*—two younger brothers and an older sister.

---

15. Smell

---

aroma (*n.*)   pleasant odor; bouquet
ə-'rō-mə   What a smoker may describe as a rich tobacco *aroma*, a nonsmoker may consider a disgusting stench.

aromatic (*adj.*)   sweet-scented; fragrant
ˌar-ə-'mat-ik   Honeysuckle is *aromatic*.

fragrant (*adj.*)   having a pleasant odor; pleasantly odorous or odor-
'frā-grənt   iferous
    A florist's shop is a *fragrant* place.

fusty (*adj.*)   1. stale-smelling; musty; moldy
'fəs-tē   To rid the unused room of its *fusty* smell, we opened the windows and let the fresh air in.

    2. old-fashioned
    The *fusty* tenant refused to allow any modern appliance to be installed in the apartment.

incense (*n.*)   substance yielding a pleasant odor when burned
'in-ˌsens   Ancient Greek and Roman worshipers often burned *incense* to please their gods.

malodorous (*adj.*)   ill-smelling; stinking; fetid; unpleasantly odorous
mal-'ōd-ə-rəs   The air was *malodorous*; someone nearby must have been burning garbage illegally.

noisome (*adj.*)   1. offensive to smell; disgusting
'nȯi-səm   The bus discharged *noisome* exhaust fumes that offended our nostrils.

    2. harmful; noxious
    People were advised to remain indoors until the *noisome* fog was dispersed.

olfactory (*adj.*)   pertaining to the sense of smell
äl-'fak-t(ə-)rē   Because of their superior *olfactory* sense, bloodhounds can pick up the trails of fleeing criminals.

pungent (*adj.*)
'pən-jənt

sharp in smell or taste; acrid; biting; stimulating
When you slice onions, the *pungent* fumes may cause your eyes to tear.

putrid (*adj.*)
'pyü-trəd

1. stinking from decay
An occasional rinse with a soapy solution will keep garbage cans free of *putrid* odors.

2. extremely bad; corrupt
Any system that requires applicants for promotion to pay bribes is *putrid*.

rancid (*adj.*)
'ran-səd

unpleasant to smell or taste from being spoiled or stale
Butter or fish that has a *rancid* odor is unfit to eat.

rank (*adj.*)
'raŋk

1. having a strong, bad odor or taste; offensively gross or coarse
When threatened, a skunk protects itself effectively by emitting a *rank* odor.

2. extreme
Many felt that the murderer's acquittal on the grounds of insanity was a *rank* injustice.

reek (*v.*)
'rēk

emit a strong, disagreeable smell; be permeated with
Even after the fire was extinguished and the tenants were allowed to return, the building *reeked* of smoke.

scent (*n.*)
'sent

smell; perfume
The room was fragrant with the *scent* of freshly cut lilacs.

scent (*v.*)

get a suspicion of
When I saw my two rivals putting their heads together in a whispered conference, I *scented* a plot.

unsavory (*adj.*)
'ən-'sāv(-ə)-rē

1. unpleasant to taste or smell
The *unsavory* odor was traced to a decaying onion in the vegetable bin.

2. morally offensive
Opponents of the nominee alleged that he was an *unsavory* character with connections to the underworld.

Apply What You Have Learned

EXERCISE 3.15: SYNONYMS

Match each word or expression in column I, with its synonym in II.

COLUMN I	COLUMN II
1. spicy	(A) abyss
2. most worthless part	(B) eminence
3. chasm	(C) humility
4. consummate	(D) precipitous
5. disinclined	(E) dregs
6. humiliated	(F) loath
7. descent	(G) pungent
8. high rank	(H) lineage
9. hasty	(I) humbled
10. freedom from pride	(J) perfect

EXERCISE 3.16: UNRELATED WORDS

Write the letter of the word NOT related in meaning to the other words on the line.

1. (A) contemptible (B) abject (C) reluctant (D) wretched (E) low
2. (A) putrid   (B) unsavory   (C) involuntary   (D) fusty (E) malodorous
3. (A) children   (B) offspring   (C) scent   (D) progeny (E) descendants
4. (A) vertex (B) apex (C) climax (D) acme (E) base
5. (A) rank (B) position (C) gross (D) offensive (E) coarse
6. (A) abyss (B) precipice (C) elevation (D) peak (E) cliff
7. (A) modesty (B) humility (C) unpretentiousness (D) pride (E) humbleness
8. (A) unwillingness (B) repugnance (C) antipathy (D) aversion (E) alacrity
9. (A) rift (B) acclivity (C) breach (D) ravine (E) gorge
10. (A) servile (B) paternal (C) obsequious (D) submissive (E) subservient

EXERCISE 3.17: SENTENCE COMPLETION

Which word, selected from the vocabulary list, will correctly complete the sentence?

VOCABULARY LIST

maternal	progeny	exalted
rancid	bathos	kith and kin
attraction	aversion	chasm
gentility	delectable	humiliated
filial	climax	declivity

1. Janet's __?__ to the water made her dread our swimming class.
2. It is only natural that we should be __?__ by our successes.
3. Mother's Day gives children an opportunity to express their __?__ love.
4. The gripping suspense at the __?__ of the play held the audience breathless.
5. As we came down the steep __?__, the speed of our car increased sharply.
6. The meal was wholesome and delicious except for the butter, which was __?__ .
7. The youngsters received kinder treatment from total strangers than from their own __?__ .
8. Coming as it did after three excellent skits, the rather dull final number produced an effect of __?__ .
9. Your companion's earthy manner of speaking suggests that he has no __?__ .
10. I felt __?__ when I was notified that I had not passed the driving test.

EXERCISE 3.18: CONCISE WRITING

Express the thought of each sentence below in no more than four words. The first sentence has been rewritten as a sample.

1. Does the soap that you use have a pleasant odor?
   Is your soap fragrant?
2. This downward slope is as steep as a precipice.
3. The American people look down on favoritism to relatives by those in power.
4. Hell is an immeasurably deep place that has no bottom.
5. We saw no sediment at the bottom of the liquid.

6. Look at the point in the heavens directly over your head.
7. Their freedom from pride is something that is worthy of praise.
8. The record that she has compiled stands out above that of others.
9. This cheese is stale, and it has an unpleasant odor.
10. The yawning that I did was beyond the control of my will.

EXERCISE 3.19: BRAINTEASERS

As clues to the complete word, you are given some of the letters and the number of missing letters. On your answer paper, write the complete word.

1. One whiff of that **(3)some** air made us hold our noses.
2. The eminent guitarist displayed her usual **(3)sum(4)** control of her instrument.
3. After an occasional short trip to earth, the king of the gods would return to his **(2)here(2)** palace.
4. By comparison to a mansion, a log cabin is a **hum(3)** dwelling.
5. We want no part of that deal! It is corrupt! It is **(3)rid**!
6. Destructive energy can be **(5)mat(2)** towards constructive ends.
7. In a world torn by war and dissension, wouldn't you agree that peace and harmony would be **(3)lime**?
8. No one forced us to do it. We did it of our own **(2)lit(3)**.
9. The **(2)as(1)** between the opposing sides is widening.
10. For a scientist, the award of a Nobel Prize is the **(2)me** of fame.

EXERCISE 3.20: COMPOSITION

Answer in two or three sentences.

1. Describe a noisome situation to which you had a strong aversion.
2. Give an example of a necessary menial task that you were not loath to do.
3. Tell how a parent succeeded or failed to bridge a chasm between siblings.
4. Would you feel humiliated if someone said you were a student of consummate intelligence? Explain.
5. Is it humiliating to be called a consummate zany? Why, or why not?

EXERCISE 3.21: ANALOGIES

Write the *letter* of the pair of words that most nearly approaches the relationship between the capitalized words.

1. INFINITE : END
   a. wealthy : money
   b. blithe : happiness
   c. abysmal : bottom
   d. contrite : repentance
   e. delectable : delight

2. AUDITORY : HEARING
   a. keen : observing
   b. gustatory : touching
   c. tactile : tasting
   d. olfactory : smelling
   e. irritable : feeling

3. VERTEX : TRIANGLE
   a. peak : mountain
   b. summit : foot
   c. slope : base
   d. hill : ravine
   e. index : preface

4. PROGENY : PROGENITOR
   a. root : branch
   b. river : source
   c. genius : protector
   d. bricks : house
   e. orchestra : conductor

5. FETID : FRAGRANT
   a. imperfect : consummate
   b. humble : pretentious
   c. shallow : profound
   d. fresh : stale
   e. reeking : aromatic

---

16. Age

WORD	MEANING AND TYPICAL USE
adolescent (*adj.*) ˌad-ᵊl-ˈes-ᵊnt	growing from childhood to adulthood; roughly, of the teenage period Boys and girls undergo many changes in their *adolescent* years.
adolescent (*n.*)	teenager As *adolescents* develop into adults, they tend to become more self-confident.
antediluvian (*adj.*) ˌant-i-də-ˈlü-vē-ən	antiquated; belonging to the time before the Biblical Flood (when all except Noah and his family perished)

Compared with today's supersonic jets, the plane the Wright brothers flew in 1903 seems *antediluvian*.

archaic (*adj.*)
är-'kā-ik

no longer used, except in a special context; old-fashioned
An *archaic* meaning of the word "quick" is "living," as in the Biblical phrase "the quick and the dead."

callow (*adj.*)
'kal-ō

young and inexperienced; unfledged
A prudent executive cannot be expected to entrust the management of a company to a *callow* youth just out of college.

contemporary (*adj.*)
kən-'tem-pə-,rer-ē

of the same period or duration
The English Renaissance was not *contemporary* with the Italian Renaissance; it came two centuries later.

contemporary (*n.*)

person who lives at the same time as another
Benjamin Franklin was Thomas Jefferson's *contemporary*.

crone (*n.*)
'krōn

withered old woman
The use of the word *crone* is unfair to women because there is no corresponding word for a "withered old man."

decrepit (*adj.*)
di-'krep-ət

weakened by old age
Several *decrepit* inmates had to be carried to safety when the nursing home was evacuated during the fire.

defunct (*adj.*)
di-'fəŋ(k)t

dead; deceased; extinct
The Acme Lumber Company is still in business, but the Equity Appliance Corporation has long been *defunct*.

forebear (*n.*)
'fȯr-,be(ə)r

forefather, ancestor
The world of our *forebears* centuries ago was much less polluted.

hoary (*adj.*)
'hȯr-ē

1. white or gray with age
Santa Claus is usually portrayed as an elderly, stout man with a *hoary* beard.
2. ancient
The plot of the novel is based on one of the *hoary* legends of Ancient Greece.

infantile (*adj.*)
'in-fən-ˌtīl

of or like an infant or infancy; childish
A child may revert to the *infantile* act of thumb-sucking when insecure.

inveterate (*adj.*)
in-'vet-ə-rət

1. firmly established by age; deep-rooted
From their ancestors, Americans have inherited an *inveterate* dislike of tyranny.
2. habitual
My cousin would like to give up cigarettes, but it will not be easy; she is an *inveterate* smoker.

juvenile (*adj.*)
'jü-və-ˌnīl

1. of or for youth; youthful
Books for grade-school children are usually located in the *juvenile* section of the library.
2. immature
Jody suggested we play hide-and-seek, but we told her not to be *juvenile*.

longevity (*n.*)
län-'jev-ət-ē

1. long life
Methuselah is renowned for his *longevity*; according to the Bible, he lived for 969 years.
2. length of life
Medical advances are prolonging the average person's *longevity*.

matriarch (*n.*)
'mā-trē-ˌärk

1. mother and ruler of a family
Mama, in *A Raisin in the Sun*, is the *matriarch* of the Younger family.
2. highly respected elderly lady

mature (*adj.*)
mə-'t(y)ù(ə)r

1. full-grown; ripe
Rita, 23, was not appointed manager because the employer wanted a more *mature* person in that position.
2. carefully thought out
These are *mature* plans; they were not devised hastily.

nonage (*n.*)
'nän-ij

legal minority; period before maturity
On his twenty-first birthday, the heir assumed control of his estate from the trustees who had administered it during his *nonage*.

nonagenarian (*n.*)
ˌnō-nə-jə-'ner-ē-ən

person in his or her 90's
(Note also **octogenarian,** person in the 80's, and **septuagenarian,** person in the 70's.)
George Bernard Shaw, among his many other distinctions, was a *nonagenarian*, for he lived to be 94.

obsolescent (*adj.*)
ˌäb-sə-'les-ᵊnt

going out of use; becoming obsolete
The company will soon have to replace its *obsolescent* machinery if it is to compete successfully with rivals who have state-of-the-art equipment.

obsolete (*adj.*)
ˌäb-sə-'lēt

no longer in use; out-of-date
The calculator has made the slide rule *obsolete*.

patriarch (*n.*)
'pā-trē-ˌärk

1. venerable old man
Practically all of the *patriarch's* children, grandchildren, and great-grandchildren attended his eightieth birthday.
2. father and ruler of a family or tribe; founder
According to the Bible, the human family is descended from the *patriarch* Adam and his wife Eve.

posthumous (*adj.*)
'päs-chə-məs

1. published after the author's death
Only two of Emily Dickinson's poems were published before her death; the rest are *posthumous*.
2. occurring after death
Posthumous fame is of no use to an artist who struggles for a lifetime and dies unknown.

primeval (*adj.*)
prī-'mē-vəl

pertaining to the world's first ages; primitive
From the exposed rock strata in the Grand Canyon, scientists have learned much about *primeval* life on this planet.

primordial (*adj.*)
prī-'mȯrd-ē-əl

1. existing at the very beginning
Humanity's *primordial* conflict with the environment has continued to the present day.
2. elementary; primary; first in order
One of the *primordial* concepts of science is that light travels at the rate of 186,000 miles per second.

pristine (*adj.*)
'pris-ˌtēn

in original, long-ago state; uncorrupted
A diamond in its *pristine* state as it comes from the mine looks altogether different from the diamond in a ring.

puberty (*n.*)
'pyü-bərt-ē

physical beginning of manhood (at about age 14) or womanhood (at about age 12)
Among the changes in boys at *puberty* are a deepening of the voice and the growth of hair on the face.

puerile (*adj.*)
'pyü(-ə)r-əl

foolish for a grown person to say or do; childish
    Some thought it was fun to throw snowballs at passing cars; others considered it *puerile*.

senile (*adj.*)
'sēn-ˌīl

showing the weakness of age
    Grandfather no longer has the energy he used to have. He often forgets things. He is becoming *senile*.

superannuated (*adj.*)
ˌsü-pər-'an-yə-wāt-əd

retired on a pension; extremely old
    Some *superannuated* citizens can be more productive than many still in the work force.

venerable (*adj.*)
'ven-ər-ə-bəl

worthy of respect because of advanced age, achievement, virtue, or historical importance
    At family reunions, our *venerable* grandmother, now past 80, sits at the head of the table.

veteran (*n.*)
'vet-ə-rən

1. person experienced in some occupation, art, or profession
    In her bid for reelection, the mayor—a *veteran* of twenty years in public service—cited her opponent's lack of experience.

2. ex-member of the armed forces
    Many *veterans* of the Vietnam War found it hard to readjust to civilian life.

yore (*n.*)
'yȯ(ə)r

(always preceded by *of*) long ago
    In days of *yore* there was trial by combat; today, we have trial by jury.

17. Sobriety—Intoxication

abstemious (*adj.*)
ab-'stē-mē-əs

sparing in eating and drinking; temperate; abstinent
    Employers usually do not hire known alcoholics, preferring personnel who are *abstemious* in their habits.

carousal (*n.*)
kə-'raù-zəl

jovial feast; drinking party
    While the enemy was celebrating Christmas Eve in a merry *carousal*, Washington and his troops—quite sober—crossed the Delaware and took them by surprise.

dipsomania (*n.*)
,dip-sə-'mā-nē-ə

abnormal, uncontrollable craving for alcohol; alcoholism
   An organization that has helped many persons to overcome *dipsomania* is Alcoholics Anonymous.

inebriated (*adj.*)
in-'ē-brē-,āt-əd

drunk; intoxicated
   Captain Billy Bones, *inebriated* from too much rum, terrorized the other patrons of the Admiral Benbow Inn.

sober (*adj.*)
'sō-bə(r)

1. not drunk; temperate (*ant.* **drunk; intoxicated**)
   The motorist's obligation to be *sober* must be emphasized in driver-training programs.
2. serious; free from excitement or exaggeration
   My immediate thought was to leave but, after *sober* consideration, I decided not to.

sobriety (*n.*)
sə-'brī-ət-ē

temperance; abstinence
   Sobriety is a virtue.

sot (*n.*)
'sät

person made foolish by excessive drinking; drunkard
   Don't ask a *sot* for directions; consult someone whose mind is clear.

teetotaler (*n.*)
'tē-'tōt-ᵊl-ə(r)

person who totally abstains from intoxicating beverages (*ant.* **dipsomaniac**)
   Former dipsomaniacs who are now *teetotalers* deserve admiration for their courage and willpower.

18. Sea

bow (*n.*)
'baủ

forward part of a ship; prow (*ant.* **stern**)
   A search from *bow* to *stern* before sailing disclosed that no stowaways were on board.

brine (*n.*)
'brīn

1. salty water
   Brine can be converted to drinking water, but at high cost.
2. ocean; sea; the deep
   Anything on deck that was not firmly secured would have been blown into the *brine*.

doldrums (*n. pl.*)
'dōl-drəmz

1. calm, windless part of the ocean near the equator
   Becalmed in the *doldrums*, the sailing vessel was ''As idle as a painted ship/Upon a painted ocean.''

2. listlessness

The rise in sales and employment showed that America was emerging from the economic *doldrums*.

flotsam (*n.*)
'flät-səm

wreckage of a ship or its cargo found floating on the sea; driftage

Flotsam from the sunken freighter littered the sea for miles around.

jetsam (*n.*)
'jet-səm

goods cast overboard to lighten a ship in distress

Jetsam washed ashore indicated that frantic efforts had been made to lighten the ship's cargo.

jettison (*v.*)
'jet-ə-sən

throw (goods) overboard to lighten a ship or plane; discard

The pilot of the distressed plane *jettisoned* surplus fuel before attempting an emergency landing.

leeward (*adj.*)
'lē-wərd

in the direction away from the wind (*ant.* **windward**)

To avoid the wind, we chose deck chairs on the *leeward* side of the ship.

marine (*adj.*)
mə-'rēn

of the sea or shipping; nautical; maritime

If you are fascinated by undersea plants and animals, you may want to study *marine* biology.

mariner (*n.*)
'mar-ə-nər

sailor; seaman

Her uncle is an experienced *mariner*.

starboard (*adj.*)
'stär-bərd

pertaining to the right-hand side of a ship when you face the bow (forward) (*ant.* **port**)

When a ship follows a southerly course, sunrise is on the *port* side and sunset on the *starboard* side.

19. Cleanliness—Uncleanliness

carrion (*n.*)
'kar-ē-ən

decaying flesh of a carcass

Vultures fed for several days on the air-polluting *carrion* left by hunters.

contaminate (*v.*)
kən-'tam-ə-ˌnāt

make impure by mixture; pollute (*ant.* **decontaminate**)

Many of our rivers have been *contaminated* by sewage.

dross (*n.*)
'dräs

waste; refuse
When you revise your composition, eliminate all meaningless expressions, repetitions, and similar *dross*.

expurgate (*v.*)
'ek-spər-ˌgāt

remove objectionable material from a book; bowdlerize; purify
In his FAMILY SHAKESPEARE (published 1818), Bowdler *expurgated* Shakespeare's works, removing words and expressions that he considered improper for reading aloud in a family.

immaculate (*adj.*)
im-'ak-yə-lət

spotless; absolutely clean; pure; faultless
With some water, a cloth, and a little energy, a dirty windshield can be made *immaculate*.

offal (*n.*)
'ä-fəl

waste parts of a butchered animal; refuse; garbage
Sea gulls hovered about the wharf where fish was being sold, waiting to scoop up any *offal* cast into the water.

purge (*v.*)
'pərj

cleanse; purify; rid of undesired element or person
If elected, the candidate vowed he would *purge* the county administration of corruption and inefficiency.

slatternly (*adj.*)
'slat-ərn-lē

untidy; dirty from habitual neglect; slovenly
There were cobwebs on the walls, dust on the shelves, and dirty dishes in the sink; it was a *slatternly* kitchen.

sloven (*n.*)
'sləv-ən

person habitually untidy, dirty, or careless in dress, habits, etc.
It is difficult for an immaculate person to share a room with a *sloven*.

sordid (*adj.*)
'sȯrd-əd

filthy; vile
As soon as the athlete received the bribe offer, he informed his coach of the *sordid* affair.

squalid (*adj.*)
'skwäl-əd

filthy from neglect; dirty; degraded
If we had entered without removing our muddy boots, we would have made the house *squalid*.

squalor (*n.*)
'skwäl-ər

filth; degradation; sordidness
People do a great deal of washing, vacuuming, and mopping because they do not want to live in *squalor*.

sully (*v.*)
'səl-ē

tarnish; besmirch; defile
The celebrity felt that her name had been *sullied* by the publicity given her son's arrest for speeding.

20. Nearness

adjacent (*adj.*)
ə-'jās-ᵊnt

lying near or next to; bordering; adjoining
Alaska is *adjacent* to northwestern Canada.

approximate (*adj.*)
ə-'präk-sə-mət

nearly correct (*ant.* **exact; precise**)
The *approximate* length of a year is 365 days; its *exact* length is 365 days, 5 hours, 48 minutes, and 46 seconds.

contiguous (*adj.*)
kən-'tig-yə-wəs

touching; adjoining
England and France are not *contiguous*; they are separated by the English Channel.

environs (*n. pl.*)
in-'vī-rənz

districts surrounding a place; suburbs
Many of the city's former residents now live in its immediate *environs*.

juxtapose (*v.*)
'jək-stə-ˌpōz

put side by side; put close together
If you *juxtapose* the two cabinets, you will see that one is slightly taller than the other.

juxtaposition (*n.*)
ˌjək-stə-pə-'zish-ən

close or side-by-side position
Soap should not be placed in *juxtaposition* with foods because it may impart its scent to them.

propinquity (*n.*)
prō-'piŋ-kwət-ē

1. kinship
   Disregarding *propinquity*, the executive gave the post to a highly recommended stranger rather than to his own nephew.
2. nearness of place; proximity
   There were large shrubs too close to the house, and their *propinquity* added to the dampness indoors.

Apply What You Have Learned

EXERCISE 3.22: ANTONYMS

Each word in column I has an *antonym* in column II. Write the *letter* of that antonym.

COLUMN I	COLUMN II
1. full-fledged	(A) teetotaler
2. sturdy	(B) abstinent
3. dipsomaniac	(C) filthy
4. right	(D) callow
5. intemperate	(E) bow
6. windward	(F) approximate
7. exact	(G) intoxication
8. immaculate	(H) leeward
9. stern	(I) decrepit
10. sobriety	(J) port

EXERCISE 3.23: SYNONYMS

Select the *synonym* of the italicized word.

1. *Unexpurgated* edition
   (A) abbreviated (C) purified
   (B) unpurified (D) bowdlerized

2. Jefferson's *forebears*
   (A) contemporaries (C) ancestors
   (B) rivals (D) followers

3. *Defunct* princess
   (A) dead (C) intemperate
   (B) infantile (D) slatternly

4. *Inveterate* latecomer
   (A) strange (C) juvenile
   (B) extinct (D) habitual

5. *Sober* estimates
   (A) approximate (C) exaggerated
   (B) calm (D) inaccurate

6. Venerable *patriarch*
   (A) founder (C) monument
   (B) martyr (D) philosopher

7. *Jettisoned* cargo
   (A) surplus (C) discarded
   (B) wrecked (D) loaded

8. *Primordial rights*
   (A) inherited (C) elementary
   (B) secondary (D) royal

9. Surface *dross*

    (A) waste   (C) dregs
    (B) flotsam (D) polish

10. *Contiguous* properties

    (A) sordid   (C) noxious
    (B) contagious (D) touching

EXERCISE 3.24: SENTENCE COMPLETION

Which word, selected from the vocabulary list will correctly complete the sentence?

VOCABULARY LIST

juxtaposition	puberty	primeval
obsolescent	abstemious	dross
squalid	puerile	obsolete
senility	immaculate	nonage
longevity	jetsam	carrion

1. Aunt Matilda thinks it childish for grown-ups to yell and boo at ball games. She cannot understand their _?_ behavior.
2. When individuals distinguished for their advanced age are interviewed by the press, they are usually asked for the secret of their _?_.
3. As a means of transportation, the horse-drawn carriage has long been _?_.
4. In the hospital, every room was spotless. The corridors, too, were _?_.
5. During his legal minority, the young monarch had heeded his advisers, but, once past his _?_, he took absolute personal control.
6. Most eighth-graders have reached the stage of development known as _?_.
7. The two troublemakers sat side by side. This _?_ gave them ample opportunity to create disturbances.
8. Jackals feed on the decaying flesh of a carcass. Kites, hawks, and buzzards also subsist on _?_.
9. By studying fossils, scientists have learned a great deal about _?_ plants and animals.
10. When pedestrians track in mud from dirty streets, the custodial staff has to mop the halls and stairways frequently to keep them from becoming _?_.

EXERCISE 3.25: CONCISE WRITING

Express the thought of each sentence below in no more than four words. The first sentence has been rewritten as a sample.

1. Some former members of the armed forces are between eighty and eighty-nine years of age.
   Some veterans are octogenarians.
2. Our uniforms are so clean that there is not a spot on them.
3. Was Shakespeare living at the time that Elizabeth was alive?
4. Most of the men and women in their seventies no longer go to work.
5. We know several men and women who totally abstain from alcohol.
6. The computer that we own is going out of use.
7. Was this play published after the death of its author?
8. Move those two tables so that one is right alongside the other.
9. She had a craving for intoxicating beverages that she could not control.
10. Wreckage from the ship and its cargo is drifting ashore.

EXERCISE 3.26: BRAINTEASERS

As clues to the complete word, you are given some of the letters and the number of missing letters. On your answer paper, write the complete word.

1. The office staff consists of three newcomers and one (4)ran.
2. The guests helped themselves generously, except for a few dieters who were noticeably (2)stem(4).
3. What Mama says goes in this house. She is the (5)arch of the family.
4. The city is congested, but its (3)iron(1) are sparsely populated.
5. Merchants are complaining that business has been in the (1)old(4).
6. Thanks to the cleanup sponsored by the Block Association, the vacant lot is now (6)late.
7. The edifice is still called the Price Corporation Building, even though that company has long been (2)fun(2).
8. This must be the room of a(n) (2)oven; it is so untidy!
9. She can play tennis almost every day because of the (2)ox(5) of her house to the courts.
10. The (5)tale(1) next to us didn't even taste his champagne.

EXERCISE 3.27: COMPOSITION

Answer in two or three sentences.

1. What can apartment house dwellers do to prevent an adjacent vacant lot from becoming squalid?
2. Is it puerile for a mature person to play chess? Explain.
3. If you were an employer, would you hire a former dipsomaniac? Why, or why not?
4. Suggest one thing you can do to ease the plight of a grandparent who is becoming senile?
5. How does the jettisoning of sludge by oil tankers affect marine plant and animal life?

EXERCISE 3.28: ANALOGIES

Write the *letter* of the word that best completes the analogy.

1. *Drought* is to *rain* as *doldrums* is to __?__ .
   a. sea *b.* calm *c.* sails *d.* sunshine *e.* wind
2. *Refrigerator* is to *chill* as *brine* is to __?__ .
   a. moisten *b.* preserve *c.* spoil *d.* fill *e.* spill
3. *Employed* is to *salary* as *superannuated* is to __?__ .
   a. bonus *b.* wages *c.* pension *d.* royalties *e.* commission
4. *Banana* is to *peel* as *carcass* is to __?__ .
   a. offal *b.* meat *c.* game *d.* hunter *e.* carrion
5. *Front* is to *rear* as *bow* is to __?__ .
   a. leeward *b.* prow *c.* port *d.* stern *e.* starboard

---

21. Reasoning

WORD	MEANING AND TYPICAL USE
analogy (*n.*) ə-'nal-ə-jē	likeness in some respects between things otherwise different; similarity; comparison An *analogy* is frequently made between life and a candle, since each lasts a relatively short time, and each is capable of being snuffed out.

arbitrary (*adj.*)
'är-bə-ˌtrer-ē

autocratic; despotic; tyrannical; proceeding from a whim or fancy (*ant.* **legitimate**)
   A promotion should depend on an employee's record rather than on some official's *arbitrary* decision.

arbitrate (*v.*)
'är-bə-ˌtrāt

1. decide a dispute, acting as an *arbiter* or *arbitrator* (judge)
   When the opposing claimants asked me to *arbitrate*, it was understood they would abide by my decision.

2. submit a dispute to arbitration
   Neither side has shown any eagerness to *arbitrate*.

axiom (*n.*)
'ak-sē-əm

self-evident truth; maxim
   It is an *axiom* that practice makes perfect.

axiomatic (*adj.*)
ˌak-sē-ə-'mat-ik

self-evident; universally accepted as true
   It is *axiomatic* that expenditures should not exceed income.

bias (*n.*)
'bī-əs

opinion formed before there are grounds for it; prejudice; predilection; partiality
   Prospective jurors with a *bias* for or against the defendant were not picked for the jury.

bigoted (*adj.*)
'big-ət-əd

intolerant; narrow-minded
   It is futile to argue with *bigoted* persons; they hold stubbornly to their prejudices.

bigotry (*n.*)
'big-ə-trē

views or behavior of a *bigot* (one intolerantly devoted to one's own beliefs and prejudices); narrow-mindedness; intolerance
   On hearing the verdict, the defendant accused the judge and the jury of *bigotry*.

cogitate (*v.*)
'käj-ə-ˌtāt

think over; consider with care; ponder
   Since the matter is important, I must have time to *cogitate* before announcing my decision.

criterion (*n.*)
krī-'tir-ē-ən

standard; rule or test for judging (*pl.* **criteria**)
   Two of the *criteria* that experts consider in judging an automobile are fuel consumption and frequency of repair.

crux (*n.*)
'krəks

most important point; essential part
   Skip over the minor points and get to the *crux* of the matter.

deduce (*v.*)
di-'d(y)üs

derive by reasoning; infer

From the fact that the victim's wallet and jewelry were not taken, we *deduced* that robbery had not been a motive for the murder.

dilemma (*n.*)
də-'lem-ə

situation requiring a choice between two equally bad alternatives; predicament

Trapped by the flames, the guests on the upper stories faced the *dilemma* of leaping or waiting for an uncertain rescue.

dogmatic (*adj.*)
dȯg-'mat-ik

asserting opinions as if they were facts; opinionated; asserted without proof

Without offering any proof at all, you keep insisting that the plan will not work; you are being *dogmatic*.

eclectic (*adj.*)
e-'klek-tik

choosing (ideas, methods, etc.) from various sources

In some matters I follow the progressives and in others the conservatives; you may consider me *eclectic*.

fallacious (*adj.*)
fə-'lā-shəs

based on a *fallacy* (erroneous idea); misleading; deceptive (*ant.* **sound; valid**)

For centuries people held the *fallacious* view that the sun revolves around the earth.

fallible (*adj.*)
'fal-ə-bəl

liable to be mistaken (*ant.* **infallible**)

Umpires occasionally make mistakes; like other human beings, they too are *fallible*.

heterodox (*adj.*)
'het-ə-rə-‚däks

rejecting regularly accepted beliefs or doctrines; heretical; nonconformist (*ant.* **orthodox**)

Political dissenters in dictatorships are often persecuted for their *heterodox* beliefs.

hypothetical (*adj.*)
‚hī-pə-'thet-i-kəl

supposed; having the characteristics of a *hypothesis*, a supposition made as a basis for reasoning or research. (If supported by considerable evidence, a hypothesis becomes a *theory*, and eventually, if no exceptions are found, a *law*.)

The detective investigated each employee because of a *hypothetical* notion that the robber had received ''inside'' information.

illusion (*n.*)
il-'ü-zhən

misleading appearance; false impression; misconception

Barbara had thought that no college student could be dishonest, but the theft of her textbooks shattered that *illusion*.

indubitable (*adj.*)
in-'d(y)ü-bət-ə-bəl

certain; incontrovertible; indisputable (*ant.* **questionable; doubtful**)

The defendant's confession, added to the witnesses' testimony, makes his guilt *indubitable*.

orthodox (*adj.*)
'òr-thə-ˌdäks

generally accepted, especially in religion; conventional; approved (*ant.* **heterodox; unorthodox**)

At the dinner table, it is *orthodox* to use a knife and fork instead of your fingers.

paradoxical (*adj.*)
ˌpar-ə-'däk-si-kəl

having the characteristics of a *paradox* (a self-contradictory statement which may nevertheless be true)

It is *paradoxical* but true that teachers may be taught by their pupils.

plausible (*adj.*)
'plò-zə-bəl

superficially true or reasonable; apparently trustworthy

In the Middle Ages, the view that the earth is flat seemed *plausible*.

preposterous (*adj.*)
pri-'päs-t(ə-)rəs

senseless; absurd; irrational

The choice of Stella for the leading role is *preposterous*; she can't act.

rational (*adj.*)
'rash-ə-nəl

1. able to think clearly; intelligent; sensible (*ant.* **absurd; irrational**)

Humans are *rational*; animals have little power of reason.

2. based on reason

Mobs, as a rule, do not make *rational* decisions.

rationalize (*v.*)
'rash-ə-nəl-ˌīz

invent excuses for one's actions, desires, failures, etc.

The fox in the fable *rationalized* his failure to get at the grapes by claiming that they were sour.

sophistry (*n.*)
'säf-ə-strē

clever but deceptive reasoning

Imagine the *sophistry* of that child! He denied having a water pistol because, as he later explained, he had two.

specious (*adj.*)
'spē-shəs

apparently reasonable, but not really so

The contractor's claim that her employees have an average experience of five years is *specious*; one has had twenty years of experience, but the other three are beginners.

speculate (*v.*)
'spek-yə-ˌlāt

1. reflect; meditate; conjecture
Space exploration may solve a problem on which we have long *speculated*—whether or not human life exists elsewhere in the universe.

2. buy or sell with the hope of profiting by price fluctuations
Aunt Susan never invests in risky stocks; she does not *speculate*.

tenable (*adj.*)
'ten-ə-bəl

capable of being maintained or defended (*ant.* **untenable**)
An argument supported by facts is more *tenable* than one based on hearsay.

---

22. Shape

---

amorphous (*adj.*)
ə-'mȯr-fəs

shapeless; having no definite form; unorganized
At first my ideas for a term paper were *amorphous*, but now they are beginning to assume a definite shape.

concave (*adj.*)
kän-'kāv

curved inward, creating a hollow space (*ant.* **convex**)
In its first and last quarters, the moon is crescent-shaped; its inner edge is *concave* and its outer *convex*.

contour (*n.*)
'kän-ˌtu̇(ə)r

outline of a figure
The *contour* of our Atlantic coast is much more irregular than that of our Pacific coast.

distort (*v.*)
dis-'tȯrt

1. twist out of shape
My uncle suffered a minor stroke that temporarily *distorted* his face.
2. change from the true meaning
A company that speaks of the "average experience" of its technicians may be *distorting* the truth, as some of them may have had no experience.

malleable (*adj.*)
'mal-yə-bəl

1. capable of being shaped by hammering, as a metal
Copper is easily shaped into thin sheets because it is very *malleable*.
2. adaptable
Had they asked me, I would not have reduced the price, but they bargained with my partner, who is more *malleable*.

rotund (*adj.*)
rō-'tənd

1. rounded out; plump
   Santa Claus has a white beard and a *rotund* figure.

2. full-toned
   The announcer introduced each of the players in a clear, *rotund* voice.

sinuous (*adj.*)
'sin-yə-wəs

bending in and out; winding; serpentine
   Signs that forewarn motorists of a *sinuous* stretch of road often indicate a safe speed for negotiating the curves.

symmetrical (*adj.*)
sə-'me-tri-kəl

balanced in arrangement; capable of division by a central line into similar halves (*ant.* **asymmetrical**)
   This badly misshapen bumper was perfectly *symmetrical* before the accident.

symmetry (*n.*)
'sim-ə-trē

balance; harmony
   It is amazing how a flock of wild geese can maintain perfect *symmetry* in flight.

23. Importance—Unimportance

grave (*adj.*)
'grāv

deserving serious attention; weighty; momentous
   The President summoned the cabinet into emergency session on receipt of the *grave* news.

nugatory (*adj.*)
'n(y)ü-gə-ˌtȯr-ē

of little or no value; trifling; worthless; useless
   My last-minute cramming was *nugatory*; at the examination, I didn't remember a thing.

paltry (*adj.*)
'pȯl-trē

practically worthless; trashy; piddling; petty
   I complain not because of the *paltry* few pennies I was overcharged but because of the principle involved.

paramount (*adj.*)
'par-ə-ˌmaunt

chief; above others; supreme
   A *paramount* concern of the parents is the welfare of their children.

relevant (*adj.*)
'rel-ə-vənt

bearing upon the matter in hand; pertinent (*ant.* **irrelevant; extraneous**)
   The prosecutor objected that the witness' testimony had nothing to do with the case, but the judge ruled that it was *relevant*.

24. Modesty

coy (*adj.*)
'kȯi

pretending to be shy
Annabelle's shyness was just a pretense; she was being *coy*.

demure (*adj.*)
di-'myu̇(ə)r

1. falsely modest or serious; coy
The children giggled behind the teacher's back, but as soon as he turned around they looked *demure*.

2. grave; prim
Who would have guessed that so *demure* a person as Mr. Lee was addicted to betting on horse races?

diffident (*adj.*)
'dif-əd-ənt

lacking self-confidence; unduly timid; shy (*ant.* **confident**)
Though Carlo's teachers were confident that he would succeed, he himself was *diffident*.

modest (*adj.*)
'mäd-əst

not thinking too highly of one's merits; unpretentious; humble (*ant.* **ambitious**)
Joe is the real hero, but he is too *modest* to talk about it.

modesty (*n.*)
'mäd-əs-tē

freedom from conceit or vanity; unpretentiousness; humility
Modesty prevents Donna from wearing any of the medals she has won.

staid (*adj.*)
'stād

of settled, quiet disposition; sedate
Shocking pink is much too loud; beige is more *staid*.

25. Vanity

brazen (*adj.*)
'brāz-ᵊn

1. shameless; impudent
Two persons in the audience were smoking in *brazen* defiance of the "No Smoking" sign.

2. made of brass or bronze
We have a pair of *brazen* candlesticks.

egoism (*n.*)
'ē-gə-ˌwiz-əm

excessive concern for oneself; selfishness; conceit (*ant.* **altruism**)

By assuming full credit for our committee's hard work, the chairperson has disclosed her *egoism*.

ostentatious (*adj.*)
ˌäs-tən-'tā-shəs

done to impress others; showy; pretentious

Parked next to our staid family car was an *ostentatious* red convertible.

overweening (*adj.*)
ˌō-və(r)-'wē-niŋ

thinking too highly of oneself; arrogant; presumptuous

After his initial victories, the *overweening* pugilist boasted that he was invincible.

pert (*adj.*)
'pərt

too free in speech or action; bold; saucy; impertinent

Most of us addressed the speaker as ''Dr. Bell,'' but one sophomore began a question with a *pert* ''Doc.''

vain (*adj.*)
'vān

1. conceited; excessively proud or concerned about one's personal appearance or achievements

Oscar boasts about his awards to everyone, even strangers. I have never seen such a *vain* person.

2. empty; worthless

We have had enough of your *vain* promises; you never keep your word.

3. futile

Anna made a valiant but *vain* effort to get her sister to stop smoking.

vainglorious (*adj.*)
vān-'glōr-ē-əs

excessively proud or boastful; elated by vanity

Vainglorious Ozymandias had these words inscribed on the pedestal of his statue, now shattered: ''Look on my works, ye Mighty, and despair!''

vanity (*n.*)
'van-ə-tē

condition of being too vain about one's appearance or achievements; conceit (*ant.* **humility**)

If you are free of *vanity*, you will not be fooled by flatterers.

Apply What You Have Learned

EXERCISE 3.29: ANTONYMS

Each italicized word in column I has an *antonym* in column II. Write the *letter* of that antonym.

COLUMN I	COLUMN II
1. *confident* outlook	(A) altruism
2. *legitimate* ruling	(B) fallacious
3. shows *vanity*	(C) diffident
4. *questionable* evidence	(D) arbitrary
5. example of *egoism*	(E) rational
6. *sound* reasoning	(F) indubitable
7. *ambitious* expectations	(G) concave
8. *absurd* conclusion	(H) humility
9. *relevant* details	(I) modest
10. *convex* surface	(J) extraneous

EXERCISE 3.30: UNRELATED WORDS

Write the letter of the word unrelated in meaning to the other words on the line.

1. (A) deceptive (B) infallible (C) erroneous (D) fallacious
2. (A) bold (B) immodest (C) pertinent (D) impudent
3. (A) intolerance (B) prejudice (C) impartiality (D) bias
4. (A) concave (B) buxom (C) rotund (D) corpulent
5. (A) unrelated (B) impertinent (C) rude (D) irrelevant
6. (A) petty (B) piddling (C) paltry (D) prim
7. (A) heretical (B) paradox (C) heterodox (D) unorthodox
8. (A) preposterous (B) vain (C) proud (D) conceited
9. (A) shy (B) diffident (C) arrogant (D) coy
10. (A) indisputable   (B) axiomatic   (C) incontrovertible   (D) hypothetical

EXERCISE 3.31: SENTENCE COMPLETION

Complete the sentence with the most appropriate word from the vocabulary list below.

VOCABULARY LIST

axiomatic	analogy	saucy
dilemma	staid	hypothesis
theory	paradox	dogmatic
paramount	illusion	speculating
sophistry	relevant	ostentatious

1. Scientific research usually begins with a(n) __?__ .
2. Grandmother and Grandfather look dignified and __?__ in their wedding picture.
3. Jack never wears any of his medals because he doesn't want to appear __?__ .
4. On a sinking ship, saving the lives of the passengers is the __?__ consideration.
5. When exasperated with my little brother, I call him a "snake," but my parents do not like the __?__ .
6. It is __?__ that the shortest distance between any two points on a plane surface is a straight line.
7. As we were discussing tomorrow's picnic, Dinah interrupted with a(n) __?__ question about the weather forecast.
8. The company faces the __?__ of going into bankruptcy or seeing its debts mount further.
9. __?__ always involves risk, as prices fluctuate.
10. What I had been reasonably certain was a ship approaching on the horizon turned out to be a mere __?__ .

EXERCISE 3.32: CONCISE WRITING

Express the thought of each sentence below in no more than four words. The first sentence has been rewritten as a sample.

1. His weakness is that he is excessively concerned about his personal appearance.
   His weakness is vanity.
2. People dislike commands that proceed from someone's whim or fancy.
3. We're in a situation in which we must make a choice between two equally bad alternatives.

4. The reasons that he gave seemed reasonable, but they really were not.
5. She sometimes expresses opinions without offering proof to support them.
6. The questions you are asking have no bearing on the matter in hand.
7. What is the supposition on which she is basing her research?
8. Traders like to buy or sell with the expectation of making profits from price fluctuations.
9. The thoughts that I had in my brain had no definite shape or form.
10. What is the reason for your lack of confidence in yourself?

EXERCISE 3.33: BRAINTEASERS

As clues to the complete word, you are given some of the letters and the number of missing letters. On your answer paper, write the complete word.

1. The (4)**our** of the distant peak grew more distinct in the sky.
2. Why must you insist that you are always right? Don't you know that everyone is (1)**all**(4)?
3. These (2)**tent**(6) furnishings were meant to impress guests.
4. A deer's antlers are perfectly (3)**met**(5).
5. It is (4)**mat**(2) that opposites attract.
6. The older settlers found it hard to adapt to the new circumstances; the younger ones were much more (1)**all**(5).
7. It is a maxim that a person with (4)**wee**(4) ambitions is almost surely headed for a downfall.
8. The path was so **sin**(4) that we soon lost our sense of direction.
9. Most investors were dissatisfied with their (3)**at**(3) gains.
10. Are you so wrapped up in your own (1)**go**(3) that you give no thought to others?

EXERCISE 3.34: COMPOSITION

Answer in two or three sentences.

1. Why is it difficult for vain individuals to admit that they are fallible?
2. Who is more likely to be popular—a modest champion, or an overweening one? Why?

3. What would be your most important criterion in arbitrating a dispute between two members of your family? Explain.
4. Would you regard it as nugatory if your opponent in an election distorted one of your statements? Why, or why not?
5. Why is it preposterous for a person with a bias against consumers to be nominated to head a consumer protection agency?

EXERCISE 3.35: ANALOGIES

Write the *letter* of the best choice.

1. CONTOUR : STATUE
   a. shadow : body
   b. coastline : island
   c. peak : mountain
   d. area : surface
   e. original : imitation
2. CRUX : ARGUMENT
   a. title : book
   b. bridge : river
   c. kernel : nut
   d. door : house
   e. costume : actor
3. CONCAVE : CONVEX
   a. bowl : platter
   b. bulge : dent
   c. cup : saucer
   d. cavity : swelling
   e. building : dome
4. HYPOTHESIS : TRUTH
   a. supposition : fact
   b. proof : conclusion
   c. deceit : honesty
   d. folly : wisdom
   e. guess : blunder
5. RATIONALIZING : SELF-DECEPTION
   a. speculating : thrift
   b. egoism : shyness
   c. cogitating : brain
   d. brazenness : courtesy
   e. boasting : vanity

CHAPTER 4

Words Derived From Greek

A great revival of interest in ancient Greek and Latin civilizations took place in England during the years 1500–1650, a period known as the Renaissance. At that time numerous ancient Greek and Latin words and their derivatives were incorporated into our language. This pattern of language growth has continued to the present day. When modern scientists need to name a new idea, process, or object, they tend to avoid existing English words because these already may have several other meanings. Instead they prefer to construct a new English word out of one or more ancient Greek or Latin words. Ancient Greek has been especially preferred as a source of new words in the scientific and technical fields.

Here are twenty-five ancient Greek prefixes and roots that have enriched our language. Each one, as you can see, has produced a group of useful English words.

1. PHOBIA: "fear," "dislike," "aversion"

WORD	MEANING
acrophobia (*n.*) ˌak-rə-ˈfō-bē-ə	fear of being at a great height
agoraphobia (*n.*) ˌag-ə-rə-ˈfō-bē-ə	fear of open spaces

Anglophobia (*n.*) ˌaŋ-glə-'fō-bē-ə	dislike of England or the English (*ant.* **Anglophilia**)
claustrophobia (*n.*) ˌklȯ-strə-'fō-bē-ə	fear of enclosed or narrow spaces
Germanophobia (*n.*) jer-ˌman-ə-'fō-bē-ə	dislike of Germany or the Germans (*ant.* **Germanophilia**)
hydrophobia (*n.*) ˌhī-drə-'fō-bē-ə	1. morbid (abnormal) fear of water 2. rabies
monophobia (*n.*) ˌmä-nō-'fō-bē-ə	fear of being alone
phobia (*n.*) 'fō-bē-ə	fear; dread; aversion
photophobia (*n.*) ˌfōt-ə-'fō-bē-ə	morbid aversion to light
xenophobia (*n.*) ˌzen-ə-'fō-bē-ə	aversion to foreigners

The form *phobe* at the end of a word means "one who fears or dislikes."
For example:

Russophobe (*n.*) 'rə-sə-ˌfōb	one who dislikes Russia or the Russians (*ant.* **Russophile**)

Also: **Francophobe, Anglophobe, Germanophobe,** etc.

EXERCISE 4.1

On your answer paper, write the most appropriate word from group 1,
phobia.

1. You would not expect a professional mountain climber to have __?__ .
2. As we grow up, we overcome our childhood __?__ of the dark.
3. Passage of the Chinese Exclusion Act of 1882 proves that some degree of __?__ existed in our nation at that time.
4. Youngsters who suffer from __?__ do not make a habit of hiding in closets.
5. After many decades of __?__ , the French joined the West Germans in close economic ties following World War II.

2. PHIL (PHILO): "loving," "fond of"

philanthropist (*n.*)
fə-'lan-thrə-pəst

lover of humanity; person active in promoting human welfare
(*ant.* **misanthrope**)

philanthropy (*n.*)
fə-'lan-thrə-pē

love of humanity, especially as shown in donations to charitable and socially useful causes
(*ant.* **misanthropy**)

philatelist (*n.*)
fə-'lat-ᵊl-əst

stamp collector

philately (*n.*)
fə-'lat-ᵊl-ē

collection and study of stamps

philharmonic (*adj.*)
ˌfil-ər-'män-ik

pertaining to a musical organization, such as a symphony orchestra (originally, "loving music")

philhellenism (*n.*)
fil-'hel-ə-ˌniz-əm

support of Greece or the Greeks

philogyny (*n.*)
fə-'läj-ə-nē

love of women
(*ant.* **misogyny**)

philology (*n.*)
fə-'läl-ə-jē

study (love) of language and literature

philosopher (*n.*)
fə-'läs-ə-fə(r)

lover of, or searcher for, wisdom or knowledge; person who regulates his or her life by the light of reason

The form *phile* at the end of a word means "one who loves or supports." For example:

Anglophile (*n.*)
'aŋ-glə-ˌfīl

supporter of England or the English
(*ant.* **Anglophobe**)

audiophile (*n.*)
'òd-ē-ō-ˌfīl

one who is enthusiastic about high-fidelity sound reproduction on records and tapes

bibliophile (*n.*)
'bib-lē-ə-ˌfīl

lover of books
(*ant.* **bibliophobe**)

Francophile (*n.*)
'fraŋ-kə-ˌfīl

supporter of France or the French
(*ant.* **Francophobe**)

EXERCISE 4.2

Write the most appropriate word from group 2, *phil* (*philo*).

1. Socrates, the great Athenian __?__, devoted his life to seeking truth and exposing error.

2. The __?__ was proud of his fine collection of beautifully bound volumes.

3. Do you collect stamps? I, too, was once interested in __?__ .

4. The __?__s among the American colonists were opposed to the war with England.

5. In her will, the __?__ bequeathed more than a million dollars to charity.

6. __?__s are especially eager to listen to newly released recordings by outstanding artists.

---

3. MIS: "hate" (MIS means the opposite of PHIL.)

---

misandry (*n.*) 'mi-ˌsan-drē	hatred of males
misanthrope (*n.*) 'mis-ᵊn-ˌthrōp	hater of humanity (*ant.* **philanthropist**)
misanthropy (*n.*) mis-'an-thrə-pē	hatred of humanity (*ant.* **philanthropy**)
misogamy (*n.*) mə-'säg-ə-mē	hatred of marriage
misogyny (*n.*) mə-'säj-ə-nē	hatred of women (*ant.* **philogyny**)
misology (*n.*) mə-'säl-ə-jē	hatred of argument, reasoning, or discussion
misoneism (*n.*) ˌmis-ə-'nē-ˌiz-əm	hatred of anything new

EXERCISE 4.3

Write the most appropriate word from group 3, *mis.*

1. Hamlet's __?__ resulted from his mistaken conclusion that he had been betrayed by a woman—Ophelia.
2. When Gulliver returned from his travels, he could not endure the sight of fellow humans; he had become a __?__ .
3. Surprisingly, the first of the fraternity members to marry was the one who had been the loudest advocate of __?__ .
4. Isabel enjoys discussion and debate; she cannot be accused of __?__ .
5. Some oppose innovation out of sheer __?__ ; they dislike change.

---

4. DYS: "bad," "ill," "difficult"

---

dysentery (*n.*)
dis-ᵊn-ˌter-ē
inflammation of the large intestine

dysfunction (*n.*)
dis-'fəŋk-shən
abnormal functioning, as of an organ of the body

dyslexia (*n.*)
də-'slek-sē-ə
impairment of the ability to read

dyslogistic (*adj.*)
ˌdis-lə-'jis-tik
expressing disapproval or censure; uncomplimentary (*ant.* **eulogistic**)

dyspepsia (*n.*)
dis-'pep-shə
difficult digestion; indigestion
(*ant.* **eupepsia**)

dysphagia (*n.*)
dis-'fā-jə
difficulty in swallowing

dysphasia (*n.*)
dis-'fā-zhə
speech difficulty resulting from brain injury

dysphoria (*n.*)
dis-'fōr-ē-ə
sense of great unhappiness or dissatisfaction
(*ant.* **euphoria**)

dystopia (*n.*)
dis-'tō-pē-ə
imaginary place where living conditions are dreadful
(*ant.* **utopia**)

dystrophy (*n.*)
'dis-trə-fē
faulty nutrition

EXERCISE 4.4

Write the most appropriate word from group 4, *dys.*

1. To aid digestion, eat slowly; rapid eating may cause __?__ .
2. Those who ate the contaminated food became ill with __?__ .
3. Injury to the brain may result in __?__ , a complicated speech disorder.
4. Muscular __?__ is a disease in which the muscles waste away.
5. When your throat is badly inflamed, you may experience some __?__ at mealtime.
6. George Orwell's *Nineteen Eighty-Four* is about a totalitarian __?__ where life is incredibly horrible.

5. EU: "good," "well," "advantageous" (EU means the opposite of DYS.)

eugenics (*n.*) yù-'jen-iks	science dealing with improving the hereditary qualities of the human race
eulogize (*v.*) 'yü-lə-ˌjīz	write or speak in praise of someone (*ant.* **vilify**)
eupepsia (*n.*) yù-'pep-shə	good digestion (*ant.* **dyspepsia**)
euphemism (*n.*) 'yü-fə-ˌmiz-əm	substitution of a "good" expression for an unpleasant one. Example: *sanitation* for *garbage collection.*
euphonious (*adj.*) yù-'fō-nē-əs	pleasing in sound (*ant.* **cacophonous**)
euphoria (*n.*) yù-'fòr-ē-ə	sense of great happiness or well-being (*ant.* **dysphoria**)
euthanasia (*n.*) ˌyü-thə-'nā-zhə	controversial practice of mercifully putting to death a person suffering from an incurable, painfully distressing disease (literally "advantageous death")
euthenics (*n.*) yù-'then-iks	science dealing with improving living conditions

EXERCISE 4.5

Write the most appropriate word from group 5, *eu.*

1. The audience liked the organist's __?__ melodies.
2. Before conferring the award, the presiding officer will probably __?__ the recipient.
3. The employee formerly called a ''janitor'' is now known by a __?__ such as ''superintendent'' or ''custodian.''
4. Many believe that anyone who commits __?__, regardless of the circumstances, is a murderer.
5. The __?__ I felt when my teacher complimented my work this morning stayed with me for the rest of the day.

---

6. MACRO: ''large,'' ''long''
7. MICRO: ''small,'' ''minute''

---

macrocosm (*n.*)
'mak-rə-ˌkaz-əm

great world; universe
(*ant.* **microcosm**)

macron (*n.*)
'māk-ˌrän

horizontal mark indicating that the vowel over which it is placed is long

macroscopic (*adj.*)
ˌmak-rə-'skäp-ik

large enough to be visible to the naked eye
(*ant.* **microscopic**)

microbe (*n.*)
'mī-ˌkrōb

microscopic living animal or plant; microorganism

microbicide (*n.*)
mī-'krō-bə-ˌsīd

agent that destroys microbes

microdont (*adj.*)
'mī-krə-ˌdänt

having small teeth

microfilm (*n.*)
'mī-krə-ˌfilm

film of very small size

microgram (*n.*)
'mī-krə-ˌgram

millionth of a gram

micrometer (*n.*)
'mi-krō-ˌmēt-ər

millionth of a meter

microorganism (*n.*)
‚mī-krō-'ȯr-gə-‚niz-əm

microscopic living animal or plant

microsecond (*n.*)
'mī-krə-‚sek-ənd

millionth of a second

microsurgery (*n.*)
‚mī-krō-'serj-ə-rē

surgery with the aid of microscopes and minute instruments or laser beams

microvolt (*n.*)
'mī-krə-‚vōlt

millionth of a volt

microwatt (*n.*)
'mī-krə-‚wät

millionth of a watt

microwave (*n.*)
'mī-krə-wāv

1. very short electromagnetic wave
2. microwave oven (oven that cooks quickly by using microwaves)

EXERCISE 4.6

Write the most appropriate word from groups 6 and 7, *macro* and *micro*.

1. Documents can be recorded in a minimum of space if photographed on __?__ .
2. Space exploration has made us more aware of the vastness of the __?__ .
3. A __?__ enables us to measure very minute distances that cannot be measured accurately with a ruler.
4. An ant is visible to the naked eye, but an ameba is __?__ .
5. The dictionary uses a __?__ to tell us that the *e* in *ēra* is a long vowel.
6. Thanks to the miracle of __?__ , the patient's detached retina was successfully reattached.

8. A (AN): "not," "without"

amoral (*adj.*)
ā-'mȯr-əl

not moral; without a sense of moral responsibility

amorphous (*adj.*)
ə-'mȯr-fəs

without (having no) definite form or shape

anarchy (*n.*)
'an-ər-kē

total absence of rule or government; confusion; disorder

anemia (*n.*)
ə-'nē-mē-ə

lack of a normal number of red blood cells

anesthesia (*n.*)
ˌan-əs-'thē-zhə

loss of feeling or sensation resulting from ether, chloroform, novocaine, etc.

anesthetic (*n.*)
ˌan-əs-'thet-ik

drug that produces anesthesia

anhydrous (*adj.*)
an-'hī-drəs

destitute of (without) water

anomalous (*adj.*)
ə-'näm-ə-ləs

not normal; abnormal

anomaly (*n.*)
ə-'näm-ə-lē

deviation from the common rule

anonymous (*adj.*)
ə-'nän-ə-məs

nameless; of unknown or unnamed origin

anoxia (*n.*)
a-'näk-sē-ə

deprivation of (state of being without) oxygen

apnea (*n.*)
'ap-nē-ə

temporary cessation of breathing

aseptic (*adj.*)
ā-'sep-tik

free from disease-causing microorganisms

asymptomatic (*adj.*)
ˌā-ˌsim-tə-'mat-ik

showing no symptoms of disease

atheism (*n.*)
'ā-thē-ˌiz-əm

godlessness; denial of the existence of a Supreme Being

atrophy (*n.*)
'a-trə-fē

lack of growth from disuse or want of nourishment
(*ant.* **hypertrophy**, hī-'pər-trə-fē, enlargement of a body part, as from excessive use)

atypical (*adj.*)
ā-'tip-i-kəl

unlike the typical

EXERCISE 4.7

Write the most appropriate word from group 8, *a(an)*.

1. The gift is __?__. We have no idea who sent it.
2. In the tropics a snowstorm would be a(n) __?__.
3. The administration of a(n) __?__ prevents the patient from feeling pain during and immediately after an operation.
4. Wendy is __?__ in one respect: she doesn't care for ice cream.
5. In __?__ surgery, rigid precautions are taken to exclude disease-causing microorganisms.
6. Dan is cured. Medical tests show that he is __?__.

---

9. MONO (MON): "one," "single," "alone"
10. POLY: "many"

---

monarchy (*n.*) 'män-ər-kē	rule by a single person (*ant.* **polyarchy**)
monochromatic (*adj.*) ‚män-ə-krō-'mat-ik	of one color (*ant.* **polychromatic**)
monocle (*n.*) 'män-i-kəl	eyeglass for one eye
monogamy (*n.*) mə-'näg-ə-mē	marriage with one mate at a time (*ant.* **polygamy**)
monogram (*n.*) 'män-ə-‚gram	two or more letters interwoven to represent a name
monograph (*n.*) 'män-ə-‚graf	written account of a single thing or class of things
monolith (*n.*) 'män-ᵊl-‚ith	single stone of large size
monolog(ue) (*n.*) 'män-ᵊl-‚og	long speech by one person in a group
monomania (*n.*) ‚män-ə-'mā-nē-ə	excessive concentration on one idea or subject

monomorphic (*adj.*)
ˌmän-ō-'mȯr-fik

having a single form
(*ant.* **polymorphic**)

monosyllabic (*adj.*)
ˌmän-ə-sə-'lab-ik

having one syllable
(*ant.* **polysyllabic**)

monotheism (*n.*)
'män-ə-thē-ˌiz-əm

belief that there is one God
(*ant.* **polytheism**)

monotonous (*adj.*)
mə-'nät-ᵊn-əs

continuing in an unchanging tone; wearying

polyarchy (*n.*)
'pä-lē-ˌär-kē

rule by many
(*ant.* **monarchy**)

polychromatic (*adj.*)
ˌpäl-i-krō-'mat-ik

having a variety of colors; multicolored
(*ant.* **monochromatic**)

polygamy (*n.*)
pə-'lig-ə-mē

marriage to several mates at the same time
(*ant.* **monogamy**)

polyglot (*adj.*)
'päl-i-ˌglät

speaking several languages

polyglot (*n.*)

person who speaks several languages

polygon (*n.*)
'päl-i-ˌgän

closed plane figure having, literally, "many angles"—and therefore many sides

polymorphic (*adj.*)
ˌpäl-i-'mȯr-fik

having various forms
(*ant.* **monomorphic**)

polyphonic (*adj.*)
ˌpäl-i-'fän-ik

having many sounds or voices
(*ant.* **homophonic**, having the same sound)

polysyllabic (*adj.*)
ˌpäl-i-sə-'lab-ik

having more than three syllables
(*ant.* **monosyllabic**)

polytechnic (*adj.*)
ˌpäl-i-'tek-nik

dealing with many technical arts or sciences

polytheism (*n.*)
'päl-i-thē-ˌiz-əm

belief that there is a plurality of gods
(*ant.* **monotheism**)

EXERCISE 4.8

Write the most appropriate word from groups 9 and 10, *mono* and *poly*.

1. The idea of getting revenge on Moby Dick was never absent from Ahab's mind—it was his __?__ .
2. Books for beginning readers contain relatively few __?__ words.
3. The Romans obviously practiced __?__ , for they worshiped many gods.
4. A relative gave me a jacket embroidered with my own __?__ .
5. A discussion in which you take part is practically a __?__ ; you hardly give anyone else a chance to speak.
6. Our __?__ neighbor speaks French, German, Russian, and English.
7. Professor Shaw's __?__ on garden insecticides is being widely read.
8. A __?__ institute offers instruction in many applied sciences and technical arts.
9. Repetitive work soon becomes __?__ .
10. A huge __?__ , the 555-foot Washington Monument dominates the skyline of our nation's capital.

Review Exercises

REVIEW 1: GREEK PREFIXES AND ROOTS

Match each Greek prefix or root in column I with its correct meaning in column II.

COLUMN I	COLUMN II
1. PHOBIA	*a.* bad; ill; difficult
2. MACRO	*b.* small; minute
3. PHIL (PHILO)	*c.* not; without
4. MONO (MON)	*d.* one; single; alone
5. A (AN)	*e.* fear; dislike; aversion
6. DYS	*f.* one who loves or supports
7. POLY	*g.* many
8. PHOBE	*h.* loving; fond of
9. MIS	*i.* large; long
10. MICRO	*j.* good; well; advantageous
11. EU	*k.* hate
12. PHILE	*l.* one who fears or dislikes

REVIEW 2: OPPOSITES

Write the word that means the OPPOSITE of the word defined. (For your guidance, your first answer should be *atheism*.)

DEFINITION	WORD
1. belief in God	theism
2. supporter of Russia	Russophile
3. conforming to a type	typical
4. good digestion	eupepsia
5. one who dislikes books	bibliophobe
6. lover of humanity	philanthropist
7. believing there is but one God	monotheistic
8. harsh in sound	cacophonous
9. showing a variety of colors	polychromatic

10. infected	septic
11. without a sense of moral responsibility	amoral
12. married to several mates at the same time	polygamous
13. invisible to the naked eye	microscopic
14. enlargement, as from excessive use	hypertrophy
15. rule by many	polyarchy
16. sense of great happiness	euphoria
17. expressing censure or disapproval	dyslogistic
18. having but one syllable	monosyllabic
19. the great world; universe	macrocosm
20. having various forms	polymorphic

REVIEW 3: SENTENCE COMPLETION

Write the most appropriate word from the vocabulary list below.

VOCABULARY LIST

euphemistic	euphoria	dysentery
monogram	dysphagia	acrophobia
euthanasia	anesthesia	dystrophy
misanthropy	anomalous	philatelist
anonymous	monograph	xenophobia

1. There is a conflict in the minds of many between the commandment "Thou shalt not kill" and the practice of __?__ .

2. A two-headed horse would be a(n) __?__ sight.

3. The new regime dislikes foreigners; it exhibits a profound __?__ .

4. Though the letter was __?__ , I was able to discover who had written it.

5. The term "mortician" is a(n) __?__ term for "undertaker."

6. The drinking of contaminated water can cause __?__ , an inflammation of the large intestine.

7. A(n) __?__ collects stamps.

8. I had no dread of heights, but my companion's __?__ became more severe as we approached the summit.

9. So effective was the local __?__ that the patient experienced practically no pain during the surgery.

10. The biology professor is the author of a(n) __?__ on earthworms.

REVIEW 4: CONCISE WRITING

Express the thought of each sentence below in no more than four words. The first sentence has been rewritten as a sample.

1. Scrooge has nothing but hate and contempt for other human beings.
    Scrooge is a misanthrope.
2. That patient does not have the normal number of red blood cells.
3. It is impossible to see viruses with the naked eye.
4. Beret suffered from a fear of being in the midst of open spaces.
5. It is against the law for people to be married to several mates at the same time.
6. Clouds in the sky generally have no definite shape or form.
7. Carnegie used his millions to promote the welfare of his fellow human beings.
8. Many inhabitants had a disease characterized by an inflammation of the large intestine.
9. The fear of being at a great height is quite common.
10. Mama is an individual who lives her life by the light of reason.

REVIEW 5: BRAINTEASERS

As clues to the complete word, you are given some of the letters and the number of missing letters. On your answer paper, write the complete word.

1. Stop using (7)**lab**(2) words just to impress others.
2. Many (3)**late**(5) own stamps from almost every nation.
3. The dog owner used a(n) (3)**hem**(3) when he told us that his ailing poodle had been ''put to sleep'' by the veterinarian.
4. One would not expect a **bib**(8) to have a library card.
5. If we had no laws or government, there would be total (2)**arc**(2).
6. Is there really a(n) (1)**top**(2), where living conditions are ideal?
7. Under favorable conditions, an accident victim's detached limb can be reattached through (6)**urge**(2).
8. My (4)**hag**(2) has eased, but it is still hard for me to swallow.
9. The star was delighted when critics wrote (2)**log**(5) reviews about her new film.
10. In heated discussions, people may sometimes lose their heads, call each other names, and (3)**if**(1) each other.

REVIEW 6: COMPOSITION

Answer in two or three sentences.

1. If you were a discussion leader, what could you do to prevent an audience from having to listen to a monotonous monologue?
2. How would an invasion by hundreds of cacophonous birds affect the euphoria of people living in the neighborhood?
3. Would it be an anomaly for a well-known Francophobe to choose to live permanently in France? Why, or why not?
4. In your opinion, has the ready availability of anesthesia affected the phobias that people have about surgery? Explain.
5. Is it atypical for an immigrant to encounter no xenophobia whatsoever? Explain.

REVIEW 7: ANALOGIES

Write the *letter* of the word that best completes the analogy.

1. *Anemia* is to *red blood cells* as *anoxia* is to __?__ .
   a. corpuscles   *b.* disease   *c.* oxygen   *d.* tissue   *e.* surgery
2. *Euthenics* is to *environment* as *eugenics* is to __?__ .
   a. surroundings   *b.* heredity   *c.* nutrition   *d.* health   *e.* education
3. *Dysphagia* is to *swallowing* as *dysphasia* is to __?__ .
   a. digestion   *b.* hearing   *c.* sight   *d.* speech   *e.* tasting
4. *Misanthropy* is to *humanity* as *misogamy* is to __?__ .
   a. women   *b.* novelty   *c.* marriage   *d.* argument   *e.* foreigners
5. *Polychromatic* is to *colors* as *polytechnic* is to __?__ .
   a. arts   *b.* sounds   *c.* forms   *d.* syllables   *e.* angles

---

11. LOGY: "science," "study," "account"

WORD	MEANING
anthropology (*n.*) ˌan-thrə-ˈpäl-ə-jē	science dealing with the origin, races, customs, and beliefs of humankind
bacteriology (*n.*) bak-ˌtir-ē-ˈäl-ə-jē	science dealing with the study of bacteria

biology (*n.*)
bī-'äl-ə-jē

science dealing with the study of living organisms

cardiology (*n.*)
ˌkärd-ē-'äl-ə-jē

science dealing with the action and diseases of the heart

criminology (*n.*)
ˌkrim-ə-'näl-ə-jē

scientific study of crimes and criminals

dermatology (*n.*)
ˌdər-mə-'täl-ə-jē

science dealing with the skin and its diseases

ecology (*n.*)
i-'käl-ə-jē

science dealing with the relation of living things to their environment and to each other

ethnology (*n.*)
eth-'näl-ə-jē

branch of anthropology dealing with human races, their origin, distribution, culture, etc.

genealogy (*n.*)
ˌjē-nē-'äl-ə-jē

account of the descent of a person or family from an ancestor

geology (*n.*)
jē-'äl-ə-jē

science dealing with the earth's history as recorded in rocks

meteorology (*n.*)
ˌmēt-ē-ə-'räl-ə-jē

science dealing with the atmosphere and weather

morphology (*n.*)
mȯr-'fäl-ə-jē

1. scientific study of the forms and structures of plants and animals
2. form and structure of an organism or any of its parts

mythology (*n.*)
mith-'äl-ə-jē

account or study of myths

necrology (*n.*)
nə-'kräl-ə-jē

list of persons who have died recently

neurology (*n.*)
n(y) u̇-'räl-ə-jē

scientific study of the nervous system and its diseases

paleontology (*n.*)
ˌpā-lē-än-'täl-ə-jē

science dealing with life in the remote past as recorded in fossils

pathology (*n.*)
pə-'thäl-ə-jē

1. science dealing with the nature and causes of disease
2. something abnormal

petrology (*n.*)
pə-'träl-ə-jē

scientific study of rocks

physiology (*n.*)
ˌfiz-ē-'äl-ə-jē

science dealing with the functions of living things or their organs

psychology (*n.*)
sī-'käl-ə-jē

science of the mind

sociology (*n.*)
ˌsō-sē-'äl-ə-jē

study of the evolution, development, and functioning of human society

technology (*n.*)
tek-'näl-ə-jē

use of science to achieve a practical purpose; applied science

theology (*n.*)
thē-'äl-ə-jē

study of religion and religious ideas

EXERCISE 4.9

Write the most appropriate word from group 11, *logy.*

1. Both ethnology and __?__ deal with the origin and races of humankind.
2. The tale of Pyramus and Thisbe is one of the most appealing in Greek __?__ .
3. Advances in __?__ have enabled industries to manufacture products at lower costs.
4. Sherlock Holmes is a fictional character who excels in __?__ .
5. Sufferers from skin disorders are often referred to a specialist in __?__ .
6. The good news is that the patient's medical tests show no evidence of __?__ .

12. BIO: ''life''

abiogenesis (*n.*)
ˌā-ˌbī-ō-'jen-ə-səs

spontaneous generation (development of life from lifeless matter)
(*ant.* **biogenesis**)

amphibious (*adj.*)
am-'fib-ē-əs

able to live both on land and in water

antibiotic (*n.*)
ˌant-i-bī-'ät-ik

antibacterial substance produced by a living organism

autobiography (*n.*)
ˌȯt-ə-bī-'äg-rə-fē

story of a person's life written by that person

biochemistry (*n.*)
‚bī-ō-'kem-ə-strē

chemistry dealing with chemical compounds and processes in living plants and animals

biocidal (*adj.*)
‚bī-ə-'sīd-ᵊl

destructive to life or living things

biodegradable (*adj.*)
‚bī-ō-di-'grād-ə-bəl

capable of being readily decomposed into harmless substances by living microorganisms (*ant.* **nonbiodegradable**)

biogenesis (*n.*)
‚bī-ō-'jen-ə-səs

development of life from preexisting life (*ant.* **abiogenesis**)

biography (*n.*)
bī-'äg-rə-fē

story of a person's life written by another person

biology (*n.*)
bī-'äl-ə-jē

science dealing with the study of living organisms

biometry (*n.*)
bī-'äm-ə-trē

statistical calculation of the probable duration of human life

or **biometrics** (*n.*)
‚bī-ō-'me-triks

statistical analysis of biologic data

biopsy (*n.*)
'bī-‚äp-sē

diagnostic examination of a piece of tissue from the living body

biota (*n.*)
bī-'ōt-ə

the living plants (flora) and living animals (fauna) of a region

microbe (*n.*)
'mī-‚krōb

very minute living organism; microorganism; germ

symbiosis (*n.*)
‚sim-bi-'ō-səs

the living together in mutually helpful association of two dissimilar organisms

EXERCISE 4.10

Write the most appropriate word from group 12, *bio.*

1. Fish can live only in water, but frogs are __?__ .
2. One __?__ widely used to arrest the growth of harmful bacteria is penicillin.
3. In his __?__ AN AMERICAN DOCTOR'S ODYSSEY, Victor Heiser tells how he survived the Johnstown flood.

4. An example of __?__ is provided by the fungus that lives in a mutually beneficial partnership with the roots of an oak tree.

5. A(n) __?__ is a microscopic living organism.

6. The use of the pesticide DDT was discontinued when it was found to be too __?__ .

---

13. TOMY (TOM): "cutting," "operation of incision"

anatomy (*n.*) ə-'nat-ə-mē	1. dissection of plants, animals, or anything else for the purpose of studying their structure 2. structure of a plant or animal
appendectomy (*n.*) ˌap-ən-'dek-tə-mē	surgical removal of the appendix
atom (*n.*) 'at-əm	smallest particle of an element (literally, "not cut," "indivisible")
atomizer (*n.*) 'at-ə-ˌmī-zə(r)	device for converting a liquid to a fine spray
dichotomy (*n.*) dī-'kät-ə-mē	cutting or division into two; division
gastrectomy (*n.*) ga-'strek-tə-mē	surgical removal of part or all of the stomach
lobotomy (*n.*) lō-'bät-ə-mē	brain surgery for treatment of certain mental disorders
mastectomy (*n.*) ma-'stek-tə-mē	surgical removal of a breast
phlebotomy (*n.*) fli-'bät-ə-mē	opening of a vein to diminish the blood supply
tome (*n.*) 'tōm	one volume, or "cut," of a work of several volumes; scholarly book
tonsillectomy (*n.*) ˌtän-sə-'lek-tə-mē	surgical removal of the tonsils
tracheotomy (*n.*) ˌtrā-kē-'ät-ə-mē	surgical operation of cutting into the *trachea* (windpipe)

EXERCISE 4.11

Write the most appropriate word from group 13, *tomy* (*tom*).

1. The sharp __?__ between your promises and your deeds suggests that you are not reliable.
2. Even though I have had a number of colds and sore throats, my physician feels I do not need a(n) __?__ .
3. In former times __?__ (*bleeding*) was used indiscriminately as a treatment for practically all illnesses.
4. You will learn about the structure of the skeleton, the muscles, the heart, and other parts of the body when you study human __?__ .
5. Only in certain cases of extremely serious mental illness is a(n) __?__ to be considered.

---

14. POD: "foot"

---

antipodes (*n. pl.*)
an-'tip-ə-ˌdēz

parts of the globe (or their inhabitants) diametrically opposite (literally, "with the feet opposite")

arthropod (*n.*)
'är-thrə-ˌpäd

any invertebrate (animal having no backbone) with jointed legs. Example: insects.

chiropodist (*n.*)
kə-'räp-əd-əst

one who treats ailments of the human foot

dipody (*n.*)
'dip-əd-ē

verse (line of poetry) consisting of two feet; a dimeter

podiatrist (*n.*)
pə-'dī-ə-trəst

chiropodist

podium (*n.*)
'pōd-ē-əm

1. dais; raised platform
2. low wall serving as a foundation

pseudopod (*n.*)
'süd-ə-ˌpäd

(literally, "false foot") temporary extension of the protoplasm, as in the ameba, to enable the organism to move and take in food

  or **pseudopodium**
    ˌsüd-ə-'pōd-ē-əm

tripod (*n.*)
'trī-ˌpäd

utensil, stool, or caldron having three legs

unipod (*n.*)   one-legged support
'yü-nə-,päd

EXERCISE 4.12

Write the most appropriate word from group 14, *pod*.

1. One who treats ailments of the feet is known as a chiropodist or a(n)
   _?_ .
2. The English often call Australia and New Zealand the _?_ , since these countries are almost diametrically opposite England on the globe.
3. As the guest conductor stepped onto the _?_ , the audience burst into applause.
4. A crab is a(n) _?_ ; so, too, are lobsters, bees, flies, spiders, and other invertebrates with segmented legs.
5. Joined at the top, the three poles supporting a tent form a(n) _?_ .

---

15. HOMO: "one and the same," "like"
16. HETERO: "different"

---

homochromatic (*adj.*)   having the same color
,hō-mō-krə-'mat-ik

heterochromatic (*adj.*)   having different colors
,het-ə-rō-krə-'mat-ik

homogeneous (*adj.*)   of the same kind; similar; uniform
,hō-mə-'jē-nē-əs

heterogeneous (*adj.*)   differing in kind; dissimilar; varied
,het-ə-rə-'jē-nē-əs

homology (*n.*)   fundamental similarity of structure
hō-'mäl-ə-jē

heterology (*n.*)   lack of correspondence between parts
,het-ə-'räl-ə-jē

homomorphic (*adj.*)   exhibiting similarity of form
,hō-mə-'mȯr-fik

heteromorphic (*adj.*)   exhibiting diversity of form
ˌhet-ə-rō-'mȯr-fik

homonym (*n.*)   word that sounds like another but differs in
'häm-ə-ˌnim   meaning and spelling
   Examples: *principal* and *principle.*

heteronym (*n.*)   word spelled like another, but differing in
'het-ə-rə-ˌnim   sound and meaning
   Examples: *bass* (the tone, pronounced
   ''base'') and *bass* (the fish, rhyming with
   ''pass'').

homocentric (*adj.*)   having the same center; concentric
hō-mō-'sen-trik

homophonic (*adj.*)   having the same sound
ˌhäm-ə-'fän-ik   (*ant.* **polyphonic,** ˌpäl-i-'fän-ik, having many
   sounds or voices)

heteroclite (*adj.*)   deviating from the common rule; abnormal;
'het-ə-rə-ˌklīt   atypical

heteroclite (*n.*)   person or thing deviating from the common
   rule

heterodox (*adj.*)   opposed to accepted beliefs or established doc-
'het-ə-rə-ˌdäks   trines; unorthodox
   (*ant.* **orthodox,** 'ȯr-thə-ˌdäks, conforming to
   accepted doctrines, especially in religion)

EXERCISE 4.13

Write the most appropriate word from groups 15 and 16, *homo* and *het-ero.*

1. The butterfly is __?__ ; it goes through four stages in its life cycle, and in each of these it has a different form.
2. An archery target usually consists of several __?__ circles.
3. People of many races and religions can be found in the __?__ population of large American cities.
4. The words *write* and *right* are __?__ .

5. The foreleg of a horse and the wing of a bird exhibit __?__ ; they have a fundamental similarity of structure.

6. To escape persecution for his __?__ views, Roger Williams fled from Massachusetts Bay Colony and founded the colony of Rhode Island.

7. *Lead*, as in "lead the way," and *lead*, as in "lead pipe," are a pair of __?__ s.

8. Stained-glass windows are __?__ ; they are composed of glass sections of many colors.

9. The newly admitted students, though fairly __?__ in age, were quite heterogeneous in ability.

10. One would not expect heteroclite opinions from a(n) __?__ person.

---

17. HYPER: "over," "above," "beyond the ordinary"
18. HYPO: "under," "beneath," "less than the ordinary"

---

hyperacidity (*n.*)   excessive acidity
ˌhī-pər-ə-'sid-ət-ē

hypoacidity (*n.*)   weak acidity
ˌhī-pō-ə-'sid-ət-ē

hyperglycemia (*n.*)   excess of sugar in the blood
ˌhī-pər-glī-'sēm-ē-ə

hypoglycemia (*n.*)   abnormally low level of sugar in the blood
ˌhī-pə-glī-'sēm-ē-ə

hypertension (*n.*)   abnormally high blood pressure
ˌhī-pər-'ten-shən

hypotension (*n.*)   low blood pressure
ˌhī-pō-'ten-shən

hyperthermia (*n.*)   especially high fever; hyperpyrexia
ˌhī-pər-'thər-mē-ə

hypothermia (*n.*)   subnormal body temperature
ˌhī-pō-'thər-mē-ə

hyperthyroid (*adj.*) ˌhī-pər-'thī-ˌrȯid	marked by excessive activity of the thyroid gland
hypothyroid (*adj.*) ˌhī-pō-'thī-ˌrȯid	marked by deficient activity of the thyroid gland
hyperactive (*adj.*) ˌhī-pə-'rak-tiv	overactive
hyperbole (*n.*) hī-'pər-bə-lē	extravagant exaggeration of statement
hypercritical (*adj.*) ˌhī-pər-'krit-i-kəl	overcritical
hyperemia (*n.*) ˌhī-pə-'rē-mē-ə	superabundance of blood
hyperopia (*n.*) ˌhī-pə-'rō-pē-ə	farsightedness (*ant.* **myopia,** mī-'ō-pē-ə, nearsightedness)
hypersensitive (*adj.*) ˌhī-pər-'sen-sət-iv	excessively sensitive; supersensitive
hypertrophy (*n.*) ˌhī-'pər-trə-fē	enlargement of a body part or organ, as from excessive use (*ant.* **atrophy,** 'a-trə-fē, lack of growth from want of nourishment or from disease)
hypodermic (*adj.*) ˌhī-pə-'dər-mik	injected under the skin
hypothesis (*n.*) ˌhī-'päth-ə-səs	theory or supposition assumed as a basis for reasoning (something "placed under")
hypothetical (*adj.*) ˌhī-pə-'thet-i-kəl	assumed without proof for the purpose of reasoning; conjectural

EXERCISE 4.14

Write the most appropriate word from groups 17 and 18, *hyper* and *hypo.*

1. Try not to hurt Ann's feelings when you criticize her work, as she is
   __?__ .

2. In __?__ , the blood pressure is lower than normal.

3. The critic who judged the story was __?__; he exaggerated minor faults and gave no credit at all for the author's style and humor.
4. Nobody finished the lemonade because of its __?__. Evidently, too much lemon juice had been used.
5. The following statement is an example of __?__: "I've told you a *million* times to wear your boots when it rains."
6. A __?__ syringe and needle are used to administer injections under the skin.
7. Billy is a __?__ youngster; he won't sit still for a minute.
8. If your __?__ is disproved by facts, you should abandon it.
9. In __?__, the blood pressure is abnormally high.
10. Excessive activity of the thyroid gland is described as a __?__ condition.

19. ENDO: "within"
20. EXO: "out of," "outside"

endocrine (*adj.*)
'en-də-krən
secreting internally

exocrine (*adj.*)
'ek-sə-krən
secreting externally

endogamy (*n.*)
en-'däg-ə-mē
marriage within the tribe, caste, or social group

exogamy (*n.*)
ek-'säg-ə-mē
marriage outside the tribe, caste, or social group

endogenous (*adj.*)
en-'däj-ə-nəs
produced from within; due to internal causes

exogenous (*adj.*)
ek-'säj-ə-nəs
produced from without; due to external causes

endoskeleton (*n.*)
,en-dō-'skel-ət-ᵊn
internal skeleton or supporting framework in an animal

exoskeleton (*n.*)
,ek-sō-'skel-ət-ᵊn
hard protective structure developed outside the body, as the shell of a lobster

endosmosis (*n.*)
,en-,däs-'mō-səs
osmosis inward

exosmosis (*n.*)
ˌek-ˌsäs-'mō-səs

osmosis outward

endocarditis (*n.*)
ˌen-dō-kär-'dīt-əs

inflammation of the lining of the heart

endoderm (*n.*)
'en-də-ˌdərm

membranelike tissue lining the digestive tract

endoparasite (*n.*)
ˌen-dō-'par-ə-ˌsīt

parasite living in the internal organs of an animal (*ant.* **ectoparasite,** ˌek-tō-'par-ə-ˌsīt, parasite living on the exterior of an animal)

endophyte (*n.*)
'en-də-ˌfīt

plant growing within another plant

exoteric (*adj.*)
ˌek-sə-'ter-ik

external; exterior; readily understandable
(*ant.* **esoteric,** ˌes-ə-'ter-ik, inner; private; difficult to understand)

exotic (*adj.*)
eg-'zät-ik

1. introduced from a foreign country; not native
2. excitingly strange

EXERCISE 4.15

Write the most appropriate word from groups 19 and 20, *endo* and *exo*.

1. Algae that live within other plants are known as __?__s.
2. Foreign visitors can often be identified by their __?__ dress.
3. __?__ glands discharge their secretions externally through ducts or tubes.
4. __?__ glands, having no ducts or tubes, secrete internally.
5. Some primitive tribes observe __?__, forbidding marriage outside the tribe.
6. The body louse is a most annoying __?__, as it moves freely over the body of its host.
7. The lobster has a thick protective shell known as an __?__.
8. Unlike lobsters, humans have an inside skeleton called an __?__.
9. Refusing to admit that the rebellion was __?__, the dictator blamed "foreign agitators."
10. Once established in the intestines of its host, an __?__ leads a life of ease.

21. ARCHY: "rule"

anarchy (*n.*)
'an-ər-kē

total absence of rule or government; confusion; disorder

autarchy (*n.*)
'ȯ-ˌtär-kē

rule by an absolute sovereign

hierarchy (*n.*)
'hī-ə-ˌrär-kē

body of rulers or officials grouped in ranks, each being subordinate to the rank above it

matriarchy (*n.*)
'mā-trē-ˌär-kē

form of social organization in which the mother rules the family or tribe, descent being traced through the mother

monarchy (*n.*)
'män-ər-kē

state ruled over by a single person, as a king or queen

oligarchy (*n.*)
'äl-ə-ˌgär-kē

form of government in which a few people have the power

patriarchy (*n.*)
'pā-trē-ˌär-kē

form of social organization in which the father rules the family or tribe, descent being traced through the father

EXERCISE 4.16

Write the most appropriate word from group 21, *archy.*

1. In the naval __?__, a rear admiral ranks below a vice admiral.
2. Many a supposedly "democratic" organization is controlled by a(n) __?__ of three or four influential members.
3. In a constitutional __?__, the power of the king or queen is usually limited by a constitution and a legislature.
4. A family in which the mother alone makes all the final decisions could be called a(n) __?__ .
5. Those who declare that the best form of government is no government at all are advocating __?__ .

22. GEO: "earth," "ground"

geocentric (*adj.*)
ˌjē-ō-'sen-trik

measured from the earth's center; having the earth as a center

geodetic (*adj.*)
ˌjē-ə-'det-ik

pertaining to *geodesy* (mathematics dealing with the earth's shape and dimensions)

geography (*n.*)
jē-'äg-rə-fē

study of the earth's surface, climate, continents, people, products, etc.

geology (*n.*)
jē-'äl-ə-jē

science dealing with the earth's history as recorded in rocks

geometry (*n.*)
jē-'äm-ə-trē

mathematics dealing with lines, angles, surfaces, and solids (literally, "measurement of land")

geomorphic (*adj.*)
ˌjē-ə-'mȯr-fik

pertaining to the shape of the earth or the form of its surface

geophysics (*n.*)
ˌjē-ə-'fiz-iks

science treating of the forces that modify the earth

geopolitics (*n.*)
ˌjē-ō-'päl-ə-ˌtiks

study of government and its policies as affected by physical geography

geoponics (*n.*)
ˌjē-ə-'pän-iks

art or science of agriculture (literally, "working of the earth")

georgic (*adj.*)
'jȯr-jik

agricultural

georgic (*n.*)

poem on husbandry (farming)

geotropism (*n.*)
jē-'ä-trə-ˌpiz-əm

response to earth's gravity, as the growing of roots downward in the ground

The form *gee* is used at the end of a word. For example:

apogee (*n.*)
'ap-ə-jē

farthest point from the earth in the orbit of a satellite

perigee (*n.*)
'per-ə-jē

nearest point to the earth in the orbit of a satellite

EXERCISE 4.17

Write the most appropriate word from group 22, *geo*.

1. At its apogee the moon is nearly 252,000 miles from the earth; at its __?__ it is less than 226,000 miles away.
2. Heliotropism attracts leaves to sunlight; __?__ draws roots downward in the earth.
3. To make precise earth measurements, __?__ engineers use sensitive instruments.
4. Some earthquakes have little effect on the form of the earth's surface, but others result in noticeable __?__ changes.
5. The atmosphere, the sun, and other forces that modify the earth are dealt with in the science of __?__ .

---

23. PATH (PATHO, PATHY): (1) "feeling," "suffering,"; (2) "disease"

FEELING, SUFFERING

antipathy (*n.*) an-'tip-ə-thē	aversion ("feeling against"); dislike (*ant.* **sympathy**)
apathy (*n.*) 'ap-ə-thē	lack of feeling, emotion, interest, or excitement; indifference
empathy (*n.*) 'em-pə-thē	the complete understanding of another's feelings, motives, etc.
pathetic (*adj.*) pə-'thet-ik	arousing pity
pathos (*n.*) 'pā-thäs	quality in drama, speech, literature, music, or events that arouses a feeling of pity or sadness
sympathy (*n.*) 'sim-pə-thē	a sharing of ("feeling with") another's trouble; compassion (*ant.* **antipathy**)
telepathy (*n.*) tə-'lep-ə-thē	transference of the thoughts and feelings of one person to another by no apparent means of communication

DISEASE

homeopathy (*n.*) ˌhō-mē-'äp-ə-thē	system of medical practice that treats disease by administering minute doses of a remedy which, if given to healthy persons, would produce symptoms of the disease treated
osteopath (*n.*) 'äs-tē-ə-ˌpath	practitioner of *osteopathy* (treatment of diseases by manipulation of bones, muscles, nerves, etc.)
pathogenic (*adj.*) ˌpath-ə-'jen-ik	causing disease
pathological (*adj.*) ˌpath-ə-'läj-i-kəl	due to disease
psychopathic (*adj.*) ˌsī-kə-'path-ik	1. pertaining to mental disease 2. insane

EXERCISE 4.18

Write the most appropriate word from group 23, *path* (*patho, pathy*).

1. Among the diseases caused by __?__ bacteria are pneumonia and scarlet fever.
2. Sometimes, as if by __?__, one may know the thoughts of an absent friend or relative.
3. The __?__ expression on the youngster's face made everyone feel sorry for him.
4. Such intense __?__ resulted from their quarrel that the sisters haven't spoken to each other for years.
5. The reunion of the rescued miners with their families was full of __?__ .

---

24. MORPH: "form"

---

amorphous (*adj.*) ə-'mȯr-fəs	without definite form; shapeless
anthropomorphic (*adj.*) ˌan-thrə-pə-'mȯr-fik	attributing human form or characteristics to beings not human, especially gods

dimorphous (*adj.*)   occurring under two distinct forms
dī-'mȯr-fəs

endomorphic (*adj.*)   occurring within; internal
‚en-də-'mȯr-fik

heteromorphic (*adj.*)   exhibiting diversity of form
'het-ə-rō-'mȯr-fik

metamorphosis (*n.*)   change of form
‚met-ə-'mȯr-fə-səs

monomorphic (*adj.*)   having a single form
‚män-ō-'mȯr-fik

morphology (*n.*)   1. branch of biology dealing with the form
mȯr-'fäl-ə-jē   and structure of animals and plants
          2. form and structure of an organism or any
          of its parts

EXERCISE 4.19

Write the most appropriate word from group 24, *morph*.

1. As the fog slowly lifted, __?__ objects began to assume definite shapes.
2. When you study cell __?__, you will learn about the nucleus, the cell membrane, and other features of cell structure.
3. The drastic __?__ from forested area to attractive residential neighborhood was accomplished in less than three years.
4. Individual members of a(n) __?__ species are identical or similar in form.
5. The ancient Greeks had a(n) __?__ conception of deity; they gave their gods and goddesses the characteristics of men and women.

25. PERI: "around," "about," "near," "enclosing"

pericardium (*n.*)   membranous sac enclosing the heart
‚per-ə-'kärd-ē-əm

perigee (*n.*)   nearest point to the earth in the orbit of a sat-
'per-ə-jē   ellite (*ant.* **apogee**, 'ap-ə-jē, farthest point from
          the earth in the orbit of a satellite)

perihelion (*n.*)
ˌper-ə-'hēl-yən

nearest point to the sun in the orbit of a planet or comet
(*ant.* **aphelion,** a-'fēl-yən, farthest point from the sun in the orbit of a planet or comet)

perimeter (*n.*)
pə-'rim-ət-ə(r)

the whole outer boundary or measurement of a surface or figure

periodontics (*n.*)
ˌper-ē-ō'dänt-iks

branch of dentistry dealing with diseases of the bone and gum tissues supporting the teeth

peripheral (*adj.*)
pə-'rif-ə-rəl

1. on the *periphery* (outside boundary); outside or away from the central part, as in *peripheral* vision
2. only slightly connected with what is essential; merely incidental

periphrastic (*adj.*)
ˌper-ə-'fras-tik

expressed in a roundabout way

periscope (*n.*)
'per-ə-ˌskōp

instrument permitting those in a submarine a view ("look around") of the surface

peristalsis (*n.*)
ˌper-ə-'stȯl-səs

wavelike contraction of the walls of the intestines which propels contents onward

peristyle (*n.*)
'per-ə-ˌstīl

1. row of columns around a building or court
2. the space so enclosed

peritonitis (*n.*)
ˌper-ət-ᵊn-'īt-əs

inflammation of the *peritoneum* (membrane lining the abdominal cavity and covering the organs)

EXERCISE 4.20

Write the most appropriate word from group 25, *peri*.

1. The __?__ of a rectangle is twice its width plus twice its length.
2. At its aphelion, the earth is 152,516,120 kilometers (94,560,000 miles) from the sun; at its __?__, it is only 147,496,770 kilometers (91,448,000 miles) away.
3. We will not be able to reach a decision on the main issue if we waste too much time on __?__ matters.
4. By a series of wavelike contractions, known as __?__, food is moved through the intestines.
5. Before changing its position, the cautious turtle raised its head like a __?__ to survey surrounding conditions.

Review Exercises

REVIEW 8: GREEK PREFIXES AND ROOTS

For each Greek prefix or root in column I, write the *letter* of its correct meaning.

COLUMN I		COLUMN II
1. POD	*a.*	different
2. EXO	*b.*	life
3. HETERO	*c.*	under; beneath; less than ordinary
4. GEO	*d.*	one and the same; like
5. LOGY	*e.*	rule
6. HYPO	*f.*	around; about; near; enclosing
7. BIO	*g.*	cutting; operation of incision
8. MORPH	*h.*	feeling; suffering; disease
9. PATH (PATHO, PATHY)	*i.*	earth; ground
10. ARCHY	*j.*	within
11. PERI	*k.*	foot
12. TOMY (TOM)	*l.*	form
13. HYPER	*m.*	out of; outside
14. ENDO	*n.*	over; above; beyond the ordinary
15. HOMO	*o.*	science; study; account

REVIEW 9: SYNONYMS

Write the *letter* of the word that most nearly has the SAME MEANING as the italicized word or expression.

1. *hypercritical* reviewer:
   a. uncritical *b.* hypersensitive *c.* esoteric *d.* overcritical
2. complete *metamorphosis*:
   a. change *b.* course *c.* process *d.* misunderstanding
3. eminent *foot specialist*:
   a. criminologist *b.* world traveler *c.* podiatrist *d.* osteopath
4. trace one's *genealogy*:
   a. career *b.* descent *c.* downfall *d.* personality

5. *hypothetical* statement:
      a. conjectural   *b.* introductory   *c.* unbiased   *d.* incontrovertible
6. *anatomical* defect:
      a. minor   *b.* irremediable   *c.* structural   *d.* inherited
7. *homogeneous* in size:
      a. different   *b.* perfect   *c.* heteromorphic   *d.* similar
8. seems *psychopathic*:
      a. pathetic   *b.* indifferent   *c.* insane   *d.* unsympathetic
9. *exotic* customs:
      a. native   *b.* foreign   *c.* familiar   *d.* cultured
10. *amorphous* ideas:
      a. organized   *b.* original   *c.* exaggerated   *d.* shapeless

REVIEW 10: OPPOSITES

Write the word that means the OPPOSITE of the word defined. (For your guidance, your first answer should be *homogeneous*.)

DEFINITION	WORD
1. differing in kind	heterogeneous
2. conforming to an acknowledged standard	orthodox
3. lack of growth from want of nourishment	atrophy
4. a feeling of accord	sympathy
5. having many sounds	polyphonic
6. difficult to understand	esoteric
7. fundamental similarity in structure	homology
8. parasite living on the exterior of an animal	ectoparasite
9. low blood pressure	hypotension
10. nearsightedness	myopia
11. excessive acidity	hyperacidity
12. osmosis outward	exosmosis
13. secreting internally	endocrine
14. excess of sugar in the blood	hyperglycemia
15. nearest point to the earth in the orbit of a satellite	perigee
16. development of life from preexisting life	biogenesis
17. due to external causes	exogenous
18. nearest point to the sun in the orbit of a planet	perihelion
19. exhibiting diversity of form	heteromorphic
20. marriage outside the tribe, caste, or social group	exogamy

REVIEW 11: BRAINTEASERS

As clues to the complete word, you are given some of the letters and the number of missing letters. On your answer paper, write the complete word.

1. Many citizens do not bother to vote on Election Day. What is the reason for their **(1)path(1)**?
2. The **(2)rim(4)** of a 7-inch square is 28 inches.
3. TV weather programs teach us a great deal about **(7)log(1)**.
4. A country ruled by a(n) **(4)arch(1)** of three powerful officials is not a true democracy.
5. Continued progress in **(4)no(4)** is enabling factories to turn out more and more products with fewer and fewer employees.
6. The feelings of a(n) **(8)sit(3)** person are easily hurt.
7. If there were no laws, and we all could do as we pleased, our nation would be in a state of **an(5)**.
8. Some of the lecturer's remarks were so **(1)sot(4)** that nobody but advanced scholars could understand them.
9. When it is noon here, it is midnight in the **(2)tip(4)**.
10. Seals are **am(8)**; they spend a part of the year on land.

REVIEW 12: CONCISE WRITING

Express the thought of each sentence below in no more than four words.

1. Shock may cause a person's body temperature to drop to a subnormal level.
2. Some wastes cannot readily be decomposed into harmless substances by living microorganisms.
3. Galileo had ideas that were contrary to the accepted beliefs of his time.
4. The science that deals with the study of living things is fascinating.
5. Some chiefs forbid the marriage of any member of their tribe to an outsider.
6. Is the supposition that you are making as a basis for your reasoning logical?
7. The operation for the surgical removal of her appendix was a success.
8. These very minute living organisms are invisible to the naked eye.
9. We are studying the science that deals with the earth's history as told in rocks.
10. He goes to a physician who specializes in the treatment of foot problems.

REVIEW 13: COMPOSITION

Answer in two or three sentences.

1. Is our nation's population more homogeneous or more heterogeneous than it was a hundred years ago? Explain.
2. Why would most Americans have an antipathy to the establishment of a monarchy in their country?
3. Would it encourage or discourage apathy in a lesson on amphibious animals if a living frog were brought into the classroom? Why?
4. How would a hypersensitive individual react to criticism by a hyper-critical person?
5. Describe one metamorphosis in the way we live that was brought on by a technological discovery.

REVIEW 14: ANALOGIES

Write the *letter* of the word that best completes the analogy.

1. *Environment* is to *ecology* as *skin* is to __?__ .
   a. osteopathy
   b. dermatology
   c. peritonitis
   d. neurology
   e. endoderm
2. *Lobotomy* is to *brain* as *phlebotomy* is to __?__ .
   a. throat   b. nerve   c. foot   d. vein   e. muscle
3. *Government* is to *anarchy* as *sympathy* is to __?__ .
   a. pathos   b. compassion   c. apathy   d. empathy   e. telepathy
4. *Pathology* is to *disease* as *morphology* is to __?__ .
   a. structure   b. function   c. descent   d. health   e. race
5. *Animal* is to *tapeworm* as *plant* is to __?__ .
   a. earthworm   b. biota   c. microbe   d. ectoparasite   e. endophyte

CHAPTER 5

Words Derived From Latin

When the Latin-speaking Romans ruled Britain, approximately 75–410 A.D., there was no English language. The native Britons spoke Celtic, a language akin to Irish and Welsh. After the Romans withdrew, the Britons were overwhelmed by Germanic invaders, the Angles and Saxons. The English we speak today is a continuation of the language of the Angles and Saxons.

Before invading Britain, the Angles and Saxons had adopted some Latin words from contacts with the vast neighboring Roman Empire. In Britain, they undoubtedly acquired a few more Latin words from the Britons, who had lived so long under Roman domination. And after 597, when the Roman monk St. Augustine introduced Christianity and the Holy Scripture—in Latin—to Britain, the Anglo-Saxons absorbed more words from Latin. But Latin had no major impact on English until 1066, when the Normans conquered England.

The Normans spoke French, a *Romance* language, i.e., a language developed from the language of the *Romans*. French, which is 85 percent descended from Latin, was England's official language for two hundred years after the Norman Conquest. The language of the Normans gradually blended with the Anglo-Saxon spoken by the common people. In the process, a considerable number of Latin words were incorporated into English indirectly, by way of French.

Later, a substantial number of other words came into English directly from Latin itself. From the Renaissance, in the sixteenth century, to the present day, as English-speaking authors and scientists have needed new words to express new ideas, they have been able to form them from Latin—or Greek.

It is no wonder, then, that more than 50 percent of the vocabulary of English derives directly or indirectly from Latin.

To boost your word power, study the common Latin prefixes and roots presented in this chapter. Each of them, as the following pages will show, can help you learn a cluster of useful English words.

Latin Prefixes 1–15

PREFIX	MEANING	SAMPLE WORDS
1. **a, ab**	away, from	*a*vert (turn *away*), *ab*duct (lead *from*)
2. **ad**	to	*ad*mit (grant entrance *to*)
3. **ante**	before	*ante*room (a room *before* another)
4. **bi**	two	*bi*cycle (a vehicle having *two* wheels)
5. **circum**	around	*circum*navigate (sail *around*)
6. **con (col, com, cor)**	together, with	*con*spire (plot *together* or *with*), *col*loquy (a talking *together*; conference), *com*pose (put *together*), *cor*respond (agree *with*; communicate *with* by exchange of letters)
7. **contra**	against	*contra*dict (speak *against*; deny)
8. **de**	from, down	*de*duction (a conclusion drawn *from* reasoning), *de*mote (move *down* in rank)
9. **dis**	apart, away	*dis*rupt (break *apart*), *dis*miss (send *away*)
10. **e, ex**	out	*e*mit (send *out*; utter), *ex*pel (drive *out*)
11. **extra**	beyond	*extra*ordinary (*beyond* the ordinary)
12. **in (il, im, ir)**	not	*in*significant (*not* significant), *il*legal (*not* legal), *im*moral (*not* moral), *ir*regular (*not* regular)
13. **in (il, im, ir)**	in, into, on	*in*ject (throw or force *in*), *il*luminate (direct light *on*; light

up), *import* (bring *into* one
country from another), *ir*rigate
(pour water *on*)

14. **inter**   between   *inter*rupt (break *between*; stop)
15. **intra**   within   *intra*mural (*within* the walls; inside)

EXERCISE 5.1

On your answer paper, write (1) the prefix required in column I and (2)
the new word in column III. (In question 1, the prefix is *in*, and the new
word is *intangible*.)

COLUMN I	COLUMN II	COLUMN III
1. ___?___ *not*	+ tangible *able to be touched*	= ___?___ (*not able to be touched*)
2. ___?___ *against*	+ vene *come; go*	= ___?___ (*go against or contrary to*)
3. ___?___ *out*	+ hale *breathe*	= ___?___ (*breathe out*)
4. ___?___ *down*	+ mote *move*	= ___?___ (*reduce to lower rank*)
5. ___?___ *to*	+ here *stick*	= ___?___ (*stick to*)
6. ___?___ *together*	+ gregate *gather*	= ___?___ (*gather together; assemble*)
7. ___?___ *from*	+ normal	= ___?___ (*deviating from the normal*)
8. ___?___ *around*	+ scribe *write; draw*	= ___?___ (*write or draw a line around; encircle; limit*)
9. ___?___ *between*	+ cede *go*	= ___?___ (*go between arguing parties; mediate*)
10. ___?___ *two*	+ sect *cut*	= ___?___ (*cut into two parts*)
11. ___?___ *beyond*	+ mural *pertaining to a wall*	= ___?___ (*occurring beyond the walls*)
12. ___?___ *before*	+ diluvian *pertaining to a flood*	= ___?___ (*belonging to the period before the Biblical Flood; therefore, very old*)
13. ___?___ *within*	+ venous *pertaining to a vein*	= ___?___ (*within a vein*)

14. ___?___	+ pel	= ___?___ (*drive apart; scatter*)
apart	*drive*	
15. ___?___	+ fuse	= ___?___ (*pour in; fill; instill*)
in	*pour*	
16. ___?___	+ scend	= ___?___ (*climb down*)
down	*climb*	
17. ___?___	+ sensory	= ___?___ (*beyond the scope of the*
beyond	*pertaining to the*	*senses*)
	senses	
18. ___?___	+ sect	= ___?___ (*cut apart*)
apart	*cut*	
19. ___?___	+ solve	= ___?___ (*loose from; release from*)
from	*loose*	
20. ___?___	+ pute	= ___?___ (*think apart (differently*
apart	*think*	*from others); argue*)

EXERCISE 5.2

Match each Latin prefix in column I, with the *letter* of its correct meaning in column II.

COLUMN I	COLUMN II
1. contra	*a.* within
2. ante	*b.* between
3. de	*c.* in; into; on
4. extra	*d.* from; down
5. a, ab	*e.* out
6. in (il, im, ir)	*f.* against
7. bi	*g.* around
8. intra	*h.* beyond
9. dis	*i.* apart; away
10. e, ex	*j.* to
11. ad	*k.* together; with
12. inter	*l.* before
13. circum	*m.* two
14. con (col, com, cor)	*n.* away; from

Latin Prefixes 16-30

PREFIX	MEANING	SAMPLE WORDS
16. **ob, op**	against	*ob*loquy (a talking *against*; censure; *op*pose (set oneself *against*)
17. **per**	through, thoroughly	*per*ennial (lasting *through* the years; enduring), *per*vert (*thoroughly* turn from the right way; corrupt)
18. **post**	after	*post*war (*after* the war)
19. **pre**	before	*pre*monition (a warning *before*; forewarning)
20. **preter**	beyond	*preter*human (*beyond* what is human)
21. **pro**	forward	*pro*gressive (moving *forward*)
22. **re**	again, back	*re*vive (make alive *again*), *re*tort (hurl *back*; reply sharply)
23. **retro**	backward	*retro*gression (act of moving *backward*)
24. **se**	apart	*se*cede (move *apart*; withdraw)
25. **semi**	half	*semi*circle (*half* of a circle)
26. **sub, sup**	under	*sub*merge (put *under* or plunge into water); *sup*port (uphold)
27. **super**	above	*super*natural (*above* what is natural; miraculous)
28. **trans**	across, through	*trans*continental (extending *across* a continent), *trans*mit (send *through*)
29. **ultra**	beyond, exceedingly	*ultra*conservative (*exceedingly* conservative)
30. **vice**	in place of	*vice* president (officer acting *in place of* the president)

EXERCISE 5.3

Match each Latin prefix in column I, with the *letter* of its correct meaning in column II.

COLUMN I	COLUMN II
1. semi	*a.* against
2. ob	*b.* beyond; exceedingly
3. sub	*c.* again; back
4. trans	*d.* before
5. vice	*e.* after
6. ultra	*f.* half
7. super	*g.* apart
8. re	*h.* under
9. pro	*i.* in place of
10. post	*j.* above
11. se	*k.* forward
12. pre	*l.* across; through

EXERCISE 5.4

On your answer paper, write (1) the prefix required in column I and (2) the new word in column III. (In question 1, the prefix is *vice*, and the new word is *vice-chancellor*.)

COLUMN I	COLUMN II	COLUMN III
1. _?_ *in place of*	+ chancellor	= _?_ (*person acting in place of a chancellor*)
2. _?_ *half*	+ annual	= _?_ (*occurring every half year*)
3. _?_ *under*	+ vert turn	= _?_ (*turn under; undermine*)
4. _?_ *apart*	+ clude shut	= _?_ (*shut or keep apart; isolate*)
5. _?_ *above*	+ sede sit	= _?_ (*sit above; take the place of; replace*)
6. _?_ *forward*	+ mote move	= _?_ (*move forward; raise in rank*)

7. __?__   + durate   = __?__ (*hardened against; unyield-*
   against   *hardened*   *ing; stubborn*)

8. __?__   + ient   = __?__ *going through (not staying);*
   through   *going*   *short-lived*

9. __?__   + struct   = __?__ *pile up (an obstacle) against;*
   against   *pile up*   *hinder*

10. __?__   + calcitrant = __?__ (*kicking back; rebellious*)
    back   *kicking*

11. __?__   + pone   = __?__ (*put after; defer; delay*)
    after   *put*

12. __?__   + nationalistic = __?__ (*exceedingly nationalistic*)
    exceedingly

13. __?__   + requisite   = __?__ (*required before; necessary*
    before   *required*   *as a preliminary*)

14. __?__   + active   = __?__ (*acting backward; effective*
    backward   *in a prior time*)

15. __?__   + meate   = __?__ (*pass through*)
    through   *pass*

16. __?__   + sume   = __?__ (*take up or begin again*)
    again   *take*

17. __?__   + turb   = __?__ (*disturb thoroughly; agitate*)
    thoroughly   *disturb*

18. __?__   + natural   = __?__ (*beyond what is natural*)
    beyond

19. __?__   + gregate   = __?__ (*set apart; gather into sepa-*
    apart   *gather*   *rate groups*)

20. __?__   + marine   = __?__ (*used or existing under the*
    under   *pertaining to*   *sea's surface*)
                    the sea

EXERCISE 5.5

Using your knowledge of the Latin prefixes and the hints given below,
write the basic meaning of these sixty English words. (Your answer to
question 1 should be "carry back.")

Hint: **-port** means "carry"

1. report   3. transport   5. export
2. import   4. deport

Hint: **-ject** means "throw"

6. interject	8. object	10. inject
7. eject	9. project	

Hint: **-scribe** means "write"

11. superscribe	13. prescribe	15. subscribe
12. transcribe	14. inscribe	

Hint: **-pel** means "drive"

16. dispel	18. expel	20. repel
17. propel	19. impel	

Hint: **-voke** means "call"

21. evoke	23. provoke	25. invoke
22. convoke	24. revoke	

Hint: **-mit** means "send"

26. permit	28. transmit	30. remit
27. admit	29. emit	

Hint: **-tract** means "drag," "draw"

31. protract	33. distract	35. detract
32. subtract	34. retract	

Hint: **-duce** means "lead," "draw"

36. seduce	38. produce	40. reduce
37. induce	39. deduce	

Hint: **-cede** or **-ceed** means "go"

41. intercede	43. secede	45. recede
42. proceed	44. exceed	

Hint: **-fer** means "carry," "bring," "bear"

46. transfer	48. refer	50. defer
47. prefer	49. infer	

Hint: **-vert** means "turn"

51. avert	53. pervert	55. subvert
52. advert	54. revert	

Hint: **-pose** means "put"

56. compose	58. interpose	60. transpose
57. depose	59. propose	

Latin Roots

1. RUPT: "break," "burst"

WORD	MEANING
abrupt (*adj.*) ə-'brəpt	1. broken off; lacking in continuity; steep (*ant.* **sloping**) 2. sudden; quick and unexpected (*ant.* **leisurely; deliberate**)
corrupt (*adj.*) kə-'rəpt	changed ("broken to pieces") from good to bad; vicious
corrupt (*v.*)	change ("break to pieces") from good to bad; debase; pervert; falsify
disrupt (*v.*) dis-'rəpt	break apart; cause disorder
erupt (*v.*) i-'rəpt	burst or break out
incorruptible (*adj.*) ˌin-kə-'rəp-tə-bəl	inflexibly honest; incapable of being corrupted or bribed
interrupt (*v.*) ˌint-ə-'rəpt	break into or between; hinder; stop
rupture (*n.*) 'rəp-chə(r)	1. break; breaking 2. hostility

EXERCISE 5.6

Write the most appropriate word from group 1, *rupt*.

1. The simmering antipathy between the rival groups may __?__ into open combat.
2. The star's __?__ withdrawal from the cast took the producer by surprise.
3. Both sides had faith in the judge's honesty, for he was known to be __?__ .
4. Many homes were flooded as a result of a(n) __?__ in a water main.
5. Please don't __?__ me when I am speaking on the telephone.

2. CIDE: ''killing,'' ''killer''

bactericide (*n.*)
bak-'tir-ə-ˌsīd — substance that kills bacteria

biocide (*n.*)
'bī-ə-ˌsīd — substance that destroys living microorganisms

fratricide (*n.*)
'fra-trə-ˌsīd — act of killing (or killer of) one's brother

fungicide (*n.*)
'fən-jə-ˌsīd — substance that kills fungi or inhibits their growth

genocide (*n.*)
'jen-ə-ˌsīd — deliberate extermination of a racial or cultural group

germicide (*n.*)
'jər-mə-ˌsīd — substance that kills germs

herbicide (*n.*)
ˌ(h)ər-bə-ˌsīd — substance that kills plants

homicide (*n.*)
'häm-ə-ˌsīd — killing of one human by another

infanticide (*n.*)
in-'fant-ə-ˌsīd — act of killing (or killer of) an infant

insecticide (*n.*)
in-'sek-tə-ˌsīd — substance that kills insects

matricide (*n.*)
'ma-trə-ˌsīd — act of killing (or killer of) one's mother

patricide (*n.*)
'pa-trə-ˌsīd — act of killing (or killer of) one's father

pesticide (*n.*)
'pes-tə-ˌsīd — substance that kills rats, insects, bacteria, etc.

regicide (*n.*)
'rej-ə-ˌsīd — act of killing (or killer of) a king

sororicide (*n.*)
sə-'rȯr-ə-ˌsīd — act of killing (or killer of) one's sister

suicide (*n.*)   act of killing (or killer of) one's self
'sü-ə-ˌsīd

tyrannicide (*n.*)   act of killing (or killer of) a tyrant
tə-'ran-ə-ˌsīd

EXERCISE 5.7

Write the most appropriate word selected from group 2, *cide.*

1. The murderers planned to escape prosecution by making their deed appear like a(n) __?__ .
2. The assailant was told that he would be charged with __?__ if his victim were to die.
3. To prevent the extermination of minorities, the United Nations voted in 1948 to outlaw __?__ .
4. Claudius, in Shakespeare's HAMLET, is guilty of __?__ , for he has slain his brother.
5. The attempt at __?__ failed when the king's would-be assassins were arrested outside the palace.
6. One way to get rid of weeds is to spray them with a(n) __?__ .

3. STRING (STRICT): "bind," "draw tight"

astringent (*adj.*) ə-'strin-jənt	1. drawing (the tissues) tightly together 2. stern; austere
astringent (*n.*)	substance that shrinks tissues and checks flow of blood by drawing together blood vessels
boa constrictor (*n.*) 'bō-ə-kən-'strik-tə(r)	snake that "constricts" or crushes its prey in its coils
constrict (*v.*) kən-'strikt	draw together; render narrower; shrink (*ant.* **expand**)
restrict (*v.*) ri-'strikt	keep within limits (literally, "keep back"); confine
stricture (*n.*) 'strik-chə(r)	adverse criticism (literally, "tightening"); censure

stringent (*adj.*) 'strin-jənt	strict (literally, "binding tight"); rigid; severe
unrestricted (*adj.*) ˌən-ri-'strikt-əd	1. not confined within bounds; free 2. open to all

EXERCISE 5.8

Write the most appropriate word selected from group 3, *string* (*strict*).

1. All residents enjoy __?__ use of the pool, except children under 16, who must leave at 5 P.M.
2. Unless you __?__ your remarks to the topic on the floor, the chair will rule you "out of order."
3. Shavers use a styptic pencil or some other __?__ to check the bleeding from minor cuts.
4. Jean Valjean's sentence of five years at hard labor for stealing a loaf of bread seems an unusually __?__ punishment.
5. If you interpret a minor suggestion for improvement as a major __?__, you are being hypersensitive.

4. VOR: "eat greedily"

carnivore (*n.*) 'kär-nə-ˌvȯ(ə)r	flesh-eating animal
carnivorous (*adj.*) kär-'niv-ə-rəs	flesh-eating
devour (*v.*) di-'vau̇-ə(r)	1. eat greedily or ravenously 2. seize upon and destroy
frugivorous (*adj.*) frü-'jiv-ə-rəs	feeding on fruit
herbivore (*n.*) '(h)ər-bə-ˌvȯ(ə)r	plant-eating animal
herbivorous (*adj.*) ˌ(h)ər-'biv-ə-rəs	dependent on (literally, "eating") plants as food
insectivorous (*adj.*) ˌin-ˌsek-'tiv-ə-rəs	dependent on (literally, "eating") insects as food

omnivore (*n.*)
'äm-ni-‚vȯ(ə)r

person or animal that eats everything (both flesh and plants)

omnivorous (*adj.*)
äm-'niv-ə-rəs

1. eating everything, both plant and animal substances
2. avidly taking in everything, as an *omnivorous* reader

voracious (*adj.*)
vȯ-'rā-shəs

1. greedy in eating
2. insatiable, as a *voracious* appetite

EXERCISE 5.9

Write the most appropriate word selected from group 4, *vor*.

1. Spiders are __?__ ; their principal food is insects.
2. Have you ever watched a ravenous eater __?__ a sandwich in two or three gulps?
3. The diet of the __?__ lion includes the zebra, antelope, buffalo, and ostrich.
4. Since human beings generally obtain food from both plants and animals, they may be described as __?__ organisms.
5. The rabbit is __?__ ; it eats grass, vegetables, and even the bark of trees.
6. __?__ insects damage fruit crops.

5. *VIV: "live," "alive"*

convivial (*adj.*)
kən-'viv-ē-əl

fond of eating and drinking with friends; jovial; hospitable
(*ant.* **taciturn,** inclined to silence; **stolid,** unemotional)

revive (*v.*)
ri-'vīv

bring back to life; restore

survive (*v.*)
sər-'vīv

outlive; remain alive after
(*ant.* **perish**)

vivacious (*adj.*)
və-'vā-shəs

lively in temper or conduct
(*ant.* **languid,** lacking in vigor)

vivacity (*n.*)
və-'vas-ə-tē

liveliness of spirit

vivid (*adj.*) 'viv-əd	1. (used with things) having the vigor and spirit of life 2. sharp and clear; graphic
vivify (*v.*) 'viv-ə-ˌfī	enliven; make vivid
vivisection (*n.*) ˌviv-ə-'sek-shən	operation on a living animal for scientific investigation

EXERCISE 5.10

Write the most appropriate word selected from group 5, *viv.*

1. A business must eliminate waste if it is to __?__ in a competitive market.
2. When fashion designers can offer no new styles, they usually __?__ old ones.
3. By using carefully chosen verbs and adjectives, you can turn a dull description into a __?__ one.
4. David Copperfield found a warm welcome in the __?__ Peggotty family.
5. A few inexpensive art reproductions, cleverly arranged, can __?__ an otherwise drab wall.
6. I admire her __?__ and zest for life.

6. TORT (TORS): ''twist''

contortionist (*n.*) kən-'tȯr-shə-nəst	person who can twist his or her body into odd postures
distort (*v.*) dis-'tȯrt	1. twist out of shape; contort 2. twist out of the true meaning; misrepresent; pervert; falsify
extort (*v.*) ek-'stȯrt	wrest (money, promises, etc.) from a person by force (literally, ''twist out'')
retort (*v.*) ri-'tȯrt	reply quickly or sharply (''twist back'')
retort (*n.*)	quick, witty, or cutting reply
torsion (*n.*) 'tȯr-shən	act of twisting; twisting of a body by two opposing forces

tortuous (*adj.*)	1. full of twists or curves; winding, as a *tortuous*
'torch-ə-wəs	road
	2. tricky; crooked
torture (*v.*)	1. wrench; twist
'tor-chə(r)	2. inflict severe pain upon
torture (*n.*)	anguish of body or mind; agony

EXERCISE 5.11

Write the most appropriate word selected from group 6, *tort* (*tors*).

1. Soldiers know that if they are captured, the enemy will do its utmost to __?__ military secrets from them.
2. It is very easy to __?__ another person's ideas if you quote them out of context.
3. When teenagers are asked to help with the chores, they often __?__ that they have no time.
4. __?__ amaze us by their remarkable ability to throw their bodies into extraordinary postures.
5. Near its mouth, the Mississippi winds among numerous swamps in a(n) __?__ course to the Gulf of Mexico.

---

7. VICT (VINC): "conquer," "show conclusively"

---

convict (*v.*)	prove guilty; show conclusively to be guilty
kən-'vikt	
convict (*n.*)	person serving a prison sentence
'kän-ˌvikt	
conviction (*n.*)	1. state of having been judged guilty of an offense
kən-'vik-shən	2. strong belief
convince (*v.*)	persuade or show conclusively by argument or proof
kən-'vins	
evict (*v.*)	1. expel by legal process, as to *evict* a tenant
ē-'vikt	2. oust

evince (*v.*) ē-'vins	show clearly; disclose
invincible (*adj.*) in-'vin-sə-bəl	incapable of being conquered
vanquish (*v.*) 'vaŋ-kwish	overcome in battle; conquer
victor (*n.*) 'vik-tə(r)	winner; conqueror

EXERCISE 5.12

Write the most appropriate word selected from group 7, *vict* (*vinc*).

1. Stadium police are empowered to __?__ any spectator who creates a disturbance.
2. After the match, the __?__ shook hands with the loser.
3. Students who __?__ a talent for writing should be encouraged to contribute to the school newspaper and literary magazine.
4. Facts alone will usually not __?__ a biased person that he or she is wrong.
5. Our apparently __?__ swimming team has been neither beaten nor tied in the past two seasons.

8. FRACT (FRAG): "break"

fraction (*n.*) 'frak-shən	one or more of the equal parts of a whole; fragment
fractious (*adj.*) 'frak-shəs	apt to break out into a passion; cross; irritable (*ant.* **peaceable**)
fracture (*n.*) 'frak-chə(r)	1. break or crack 2. breaking of a bone
fragile (*adj.*) 'fraj-əl	easily broken; frail; delicate (*ant.* **tough; durable**)
fragment (*n.*) 'frag-mənt	part broken off
infraction (*n.*) in-'frak-shən	act of breaking; breach; violation, as an *infraction* of a law

refract (*v.*) ri-'frakt	bend (literally, "break back") a ray of light, a heat or sound wave, etc., from a straight course
refractory (*adj.*) ri-'frak-tə-rē	resisting; intractable; hard to manage, as a *refractory* mule (*ant.* **malleable, tractable, adaptable**)

EXERCISE 5.13

Write the most appropriate word selected from group 8, *fract* (*frag*).

1. Glassware and other __?__ materials require special packaging to prevent breakage.
2. Failure to stop at a full-stop sign is a(n) __?__ of the traffic laws.
3. X-ray diagnosis disclosed that the child had sustained no __?__ .
4. If I could find the one missing __?__ , I would be able to restore the broken vase.
5. I was criticized for not reducing the __?__ 3/12 to 1/4.

9. OMNI: "all," "every," "everywhere"

omnibus (*adj.*) 'äm-ni-bəs	covering many things at once, as an *omnibus* bill
omnibus (*n.*)	1. bus 2. book containing a variety of works by one author, as a Hemingway *omnibus*
omnifarious (*adj.*) ˌäm-nə-'far-ē-əs	of all varieties, forms, or kinds
omnific (*adj.*) äm-'nif-ik	all-creating
omnipotent (*adj.*) äm-'nip-ət-ənt	unlimited in power; almighty
omnipresent (*adj.*) ˌäm-ni-'prez-ᵊnt	present everywhere at the same time; ubiquitous
omniscient (*adj.*) äm-'nish-ənt	knowing everything

omnivorous (*adj.*) äm-'niv-ə-rəs	1. eating everything, both plant and animal substances 2. avidly taking in everything, as an *omnivorous* reader

EXERCISE 5.14

Write the most appropriate word selected from group 9, *omni*.

1. I cannot answer all questions, since I am not __?__ .
2. With his magic lamp, Aladdin was __?__ ; no feat was beyond his power.
3. Because of its __?__ uses, a scout knife is indispensable equipment for a camping trip.
4. With several desirable invitations for the same evening, I regretted that I could not be __?__ .
5. It was a conviction of the ancient Egyptians that their sun god was __?__ . They believed that he had created everything.

10. FLECT (FLEX): ''bend''

deflect (*v.*) di-'flekt	turn (''bend'') aside
flex (*v.*) 'fleks	bend, as to *flex* a limb
flexible (*adj.*) 'flek-sə-bəl	pliable (''capable of being bent''); not rigid; tractable (*ant.* **inflexible**)
flexor (*n.*) 'flek-sə(r)	muscle that serves to bend a limb
genuflect (*v.*) 'jen-yə-,flekt	bend the knee; touch the right knee to the ground, as in worship
inflection (*n.*) in-'flek-shən	change (''bend'') in the pitch or tone of a person's voice
inflexibility (*n.*) in-,flek-sə-'bil-ət-ē	rigidity; firmness
reflect (*v.*) ri-'flekt	1. throw (''bend'') back light, as from a prism 2. think

reflex (*n.*)	involuntary response ("bending back") to a stim-
're-,fleks	ulus; for example, sneezing is a *reflex*

EXERCISE 5.15

Write the most appropriate word selected from group 10, *flect* (*flex*).

1. The secretion of tears, as when a cinder enters the eye, is a(n) _?_, since it is beyond our control.
2. Copper tubing is easy to shape but it is much less _?_ than rubber hose.
3. Unable to catch the line drive, I managed to _?_ the ball toward the infield, holding the batter to a single.
4. Obedient subjects were expected to _?_ when admitted to the presence of an absolute monarch.
5. The _?_ of both sides makes an early settlement unlikely.

---

11. TEN (TIN, TENT): "hold," "keep"

---

detention (*n.*) di-'ten-shən	act of keeping back or detaining
impertinent (*adj.*) im-'pərt-ᵊn-ənt	1. not pertinent; inappropriate (*ant.* **pertinent**) 2. rude
pertinacious (*adj.*) ,pert-ᵊn-'ā-shəs	adhering ("holding") firmly to a purpose or opinion; very persistent
pertinent (*adj.*) ,pərt-ᵊn-ənt	having to do with ("holding to") the matter at hand; relevant (*ant.* **impertinent**)
retentive (*adj.*) ri-'tent-iv	tenacious; able to retain or remember
retinue (*n.*) 'ret-ᵊn-,yü	group of followers or assistants attending a distinguished person
tenacity (*n.*) tə-'nas-ət-ē	firmness in holding fast; persistence
tenancy (*n.*) 'ten-ən-sē	period of a tenant's temporary holding of real estate

tenet (*n.*) 'ten-ət	principle, belief, or doctrine generally held to be true
tenure (*n.*) 'ten-yə(r)	1. period for which an office or position is held, as: "U.S. Supreme Court Justices enjoy life *tenure*." 2. status assuring an employee a permanent position
untenable (*adj.*) ˌən-'ten-ə-bəl	incapable of being held or defended (*ant.* **tenable**)

EXERCISE 5.16

Write the most appropriate word selected from group 11, *ten* (*tin, tent*).

1. The __?__ of a member of the House of Representatives is only two years.
2. Retreating from their __?__ coastal positions, the rebels sought a more defensible foothold in the hills.
3. Your remark is not __?__; it has nothing to do with the matter we are discussing.
4. Though she can't recall names, Sylvia has a(n) __?__ memory for faces.
5. The basketball star was accompanied by a(n) __?__ of admirers.
6. Freedom of speech is one of the __?__s of democracy.

12. MON (MONIT): "warn"

admonish (*v.*) ad-'män-ish	warn of a fault; reprove; rebuke (*ant.* **commend**)
admonition (*n.*) ˌad-mə-'nish-ən	gentle reproof ("warning"); counseling against a fault or error
admonitory (*adj.*) ad-'män-ə-ˌtȯr-ē	conveying a gentle reproof
monitor (*n.*) 'män-ət-ə(r)	person or mechanical device that keeps track of, checks, or warns
monitor (*v.*) 'män-ət-ə(r)	keep track of, regulate, or control the operation of a machine or process

monument (*n.*) 'män-yə-mənt	a means of reminding us of a person or event; for example, a statue or a tomb
premonition (*n.*) ‚prē-mə-'nish-ən	forewarning; intuitive anticipation of a coming event
premonitory (*adj.*) prē-'män-ə-‚tòr-ē	conveying a forewarning

EXERCISE 5.17

Write the most appropriate word selected from group 12, *mon* (*monit*).

1. Had they heeded your __?__ to fill the gas tank, they would not have been stranded on the road.
2. I must __?__ you that you will be unable to vote if you do not register.
3. Some think that an early autumn snowstorm is a(n) __?__ of a severe winter, but you really can't tell in advance.
4. A(n) __?__ stands in the village square in memory of local veterans of foreign wars.
5. The approach of the storm was signaled by a low, __?__ rumbling from the distant hills.
6. Intensive care patients are wired to devices that __?__ their blood pressure, heart rate, and other vital body functions.

13. MAND (MANDAT): "order," "command," "commit"

countermand (*v.*) 'kaùnt-ər-‚mand	issue a contrary order
mandate (*n.*) 'man-‚dāt	1. authoritative command 2. territory administered by a trustee (supervisory nation)
mandatory (*adj.*) 'man-də-‚tòr-ē	obligatory; required by command (*ant.* **optional**)
remand (*v.*) ri-'mand	send ("order") back; recommit, as to a prison
writ of mandamus (*n.*) 'ritəvman-'dā-məs	written order from a court to enforce the performance of some public duty

EXERCISE 5.18

Write the most appropriate word selected from group 13, *mand* (*mandat*).

1. The reelected candidate regarded her huge popular vote as a _?_ from the people to continue the policies of her first term in office.
2. On learning of the colonel's ill-advised order to retreat, the general hastened to _?_ it.
3. Several prominent citizens have applied for a _?_ to compel the Mayor to publish the budget, as required by law.
4. The coach regards attendance at today's practice session as _?_ ; no one is excused.
5. Since the retrial resulted in a verdict of "guilty," the judge was obliged to _?_ the defendant to the state penitentiary.

14. CRED (CREDIT): "believe"

accredited (*adj.*)
ə-'kred-ət-id

officially authorized or recognized; provided with credentials

credence (*n.*)
'krēd-ᵊns

belief as to the truth of something

credentials (*n. pl.*)
kri-'den-shəlz

documents, letters, references, etc., that inspire belief or trust

credible (*adj.*)
'kred-ə-bəl

believable
(*ant.* **incredible**)

credit (*n.*)
'kred-ət

belief; faith; trust

credulous (*adj.*)
'krej-ə-ləs

too ready to believe; easily deceived
(*ant.* **incredulous; skeptical**)

creed (*n.*)
'krēd

summary of principles believed in or adhered to

or **credo**
'krēd-ō

discredit (*v.*)
dis-'kred-ət

1. cast doubt on; refuse to believe
2. take trust or credit away from; disgrace

discredit (*n.*) dis-'kred-ət	loss of belief or trust; damage to one's reputation; disgrace
incredible (*adj.*) in-'kred-ə-bəl	not believable
incredulity (*n.*) ˌin-kri-'d(y)ü-lət-ē	disbelief

EXERCISE 5.19

Write the most appropriate word selected from group 14, *cred(credit)*.

1. His rude behavior brought __?__ not only upon himself, but also upon his team.
2. I showed __?__ negligence in not removing the pot from the burner when the timer rang.
3. When applying for admission to college, you are likely to be asked for such __?__ as your high school transcript, standardized test scores, and letters of recommendation.
4. Gerald is too __?__ ; he will believe anything a salesperson may tell him.
5. Olga greeted the announcement that she had won the door prize with a look of baffled __?__ .
6. The diplomas and professional licenses in Dr. Green's office show that she is a(n) __?__ physician.

---

15. FID: "faith," "trust"

---

affidavit (*n.*) ˌaf-ə-'dā-vət	sworn written statement made before an authorized official
bona fide (*adj.*) 'bō-nə-ˌfīd	made or carried out in good faith; genuine
confidant (*n.*) 'kän-fə-ˌdant	(*confidante*, if a woman) one to whom secrets are entrusted
confident (*adj.*) 'kän-fəd-ənt	having faith in oneself; self-reliant; sure (*ant.* **apprehensive; diffident**)
confidential (*adj.*) ˌkän-fə-'den-shəl	communicated in trust; secret; private

diffident (*adj.*) 'dif-əd-ənt	lacking faith in oneself; timid; shy (*ant.* **confident**)
fidelity (*n.*) fə-'del-ət-ē	1. faithfulness to a trust or vow (*ant.* **perfidy; infidelity**) 2. accuracy; faithfulness of sound reproduction
fiduciary (*adj.*) fə-'d(y)ü-shē-ˌer-ē	1. held in trust (*fiduciary* property) 2. confidential (*fiduciary* duties of a trustee)
infidel (*n.*) 'in-fəd-ᵊl	one who does not accept a particular faith; unbeliever
perfidious (*adj.*) pər-'fid-ē-əs	false to a trust; faithless
perfidy (*n.*) 'pər-fəd-ē	violation of a trust; treachery; faithlessness; disloyalty (*ant.* **fidelity; fealty**)

EXERCISE 5.20

Write the most appropriate word selected from group 15, *fid*.

1. Your disclosure of secrets you were sworn to keep is unforgivable __?__ .
2. Marie looks upon her cousin Nancy as a(n) __?__ with whom she can freely discuss her personal problems.
3. At first, new motorists are usually nervous, but with experience they become more __?__ .
4. Our teacher recommends a particular translation of the ODYSSEY because of its __?__ to the original.
5. Steve was very __?__ as he mounted the platform, even though he knew his speech by heart.
6. The witness agreed to sign a(n) __?__ and, if necessary, to testify in person.
7. The trustees were sued for having used __?__ property for their own benefit.

Review Exercises

REVIEW 1: DEFINING LATIN ROOTS

Match each Latin root in column I with the *letter* of its correct meaning in column II.

COLUMN I	COLUMN II
1. CIDE	*a.* live; alive
2. VOR	*b.* break; burst
3. FLECT (FLEX)	*c.* order; command; commit
4. TORT (TORS)	*d.* bind; draw tight
5. OMNI	*e.* faith; trust
6. VICT (VINC)	*f.* warn
7. TEN (TIN, TENT)	*g.* killing; killer
8. MAND (MANDAT)	*h.* believe
9. FID	*i.* conquer; show conclusively
10. FRACT (FRAG)	*j.* bend
11. VIV	*k.* eat greedily
12. MON (MONIT)	*l.* twist
13. CRED (CREDIT)	*m.* hold; keep
14. STRING (STRICT)	*n.* all; every; everywhere

REVIEW 2: USING LATIN ROOTS

As a clue to the incomplete word, you are given some of its letters, the number of its missing letters, and its definition. On your paper, enter the complete word.

DEFINITION	WORD
1. break asunder	D I S (4)
2. germ-killing substance	G E R M I (4)
3. part broken off	(4) M E N T
4. faithfulness to a trust	(3) E L I T Y
5. one who conquers	(4) O R
6. flesh-eating	C A R N I (3) O U S

7. issue a contrary order   C O U N T E R (4)
8. forewarning   P R E (5) I O N
9. muscle that serves to bend a limb   (4) O R
10. readiness to believe on slight evidence   (4) U L I T Y
11. snake that crushes (constricts) its prey   B O A   C O N (6) O R
12. bring back to life   R E (3) E
13. adhering firmly to a purpose or opinion   P E R (3) A C I O U S
14. present everywhere at the same time   (4) P R E S E N T
15. throw (bend) back heat, light, sound, etc.   R E (5)
16. greedy in eating   (3) A C I O U S
17. breaking of a bone   (5) U R E
18. show conclusively by proof   C O N (4) E
19. killing of a human by another   H O M I (4)
20. documents inspiring trust   (4) E N T I A L S

REVIEW 3: SENTENCE COMPLETION

Write the *letter* of the word (or set of words) that best completes the sentence.

1. Circus elephants are usually __?__, but occasionally they are refractory. *a.* unmanageable   *b.* stubborn   *c.* tractable   *d.* uncooperative *e.* resisting

2. Harvey believes he is omniscient, but we are not particularly impressed by his __?__. *a.* power   *b.* knowledge   *c.* manners *d.* personality   *e.* appearance

3. The promise had been extorted and, like all promises growing out of __?__, it was __?__. *a.* ignorance . . . perfidious *b.* haste . . . untenable *c.* rumor . . . false *d.* compulsion . . . unreliable *e.* friendship . . . dependable

4. An act of regicide always has a __?__ as its victim. *a.* rebel *b.* general *c.* president *d.* prime minister *e.* monarch

5. I usually admonished my brother for distorting facts, but Mother seldom __?__ him.   *a.* reproved   *b.* encouraged   *c.* remanded *d.* praised *e.* supported

6. An omnibus bill deals with proposed legislation on __?__ problems. *a.* economic *b.* many *c.* minor *d.* transportation *e.* few

7. The rapid withdrawal of your hand from the flame was a reflex, not a(n) __?__, reaction. *a.* protective *b.* dangerous *c.* involuntary *d.* natural *e.* voluntary

8. The author read the critics' __?__ with incredulity; they were too laudatory to be __?__. *a.* censures . . . heeded *b.* strictures . . . ignored
   c. admonitions . . . challenged *d.* encomiums . . . believed
   e. rebukes . . . answered

9. It is advisable to take along plenty of sandwiches because hungry pic-
   nickers are __?__ eaters. *a.* admonitory *b.* abstemious
   c. omnifarious *d.* heterogeneous *e.* voracious

10. No one would dare to offer a bribe to an official who is known to be
    thoroughly __?__. *a.* incorruptible *b.* invincible *c.* credulous
    d. retentive *e.* convivial

REVIEW 4: ANTONYMS

Each italicized word in column I has an ANTONYM in column II. Write
the *letter* of that ANTONYM.

COLUMN I	COLUMN II
1. *perfidious* adviser	*a.* languid
2. *fragile* structure	*b.* optional
3. probably *survived*	*c.* expanded
4. *credulous* audience	*d.* peaceable
5. *confident* of the outcome	*e.* durable
6. *constricted* passageways	*f.* commended
7. *fractious* neighbors	*g.* faithful
8. *admonished* for their deed	*h.* perished
9. *vivacious* appearance	*i.* apprehensive
10. *mandatory* attendance	*j.* skeptical

REVIEW 5: SYNONYMS

Write the *letter* of the word that has most nearly the SAME MEANING
as the italicized word.

1. *fragile* flower: *a.* fragrant *b.* broken *c.* colorful *d.* frail
2. cling *tenaciously*: *a.* stubbornly *b.* dangerously *c.* hopefully
   d. timidly
3. beyond *credence*: *a.* detention *b.* doubt *c.* belief *d.* recall
4. *omnipotent* ruler: *a.* almighty *b.* wise *c.* cruel *d.* greedy
5. *mandatory* increase: *a.* deserved *b.* required *c.* temporary
   d. substantial

6. surprising *impertinence*: *a.* firmness *b.* unreliability *c.* impatience *d.* rudeness
7. *breach* of trust: *a.* atmosphere *b.* testing *c.* breaking *d.* abundance
8. *unvanquished* foe: *a.* defeated *b.* exhausted *c.* treacherous *d.* unbeaten
9. in a *fiduciary* capacity: *a.* confidential *b.* special *c.* professional *d.* important
10. refused to *genuflect*: *a.* admit *b.* kneel *c.* cooperate *d.* disclose

REVIEW 6: CONCISE WRITING

Express the thought of each sentence below in no more than four words.

1. Jim twisted the plan that we had presented out of its true meaning.
2. Laura submitted a sworn statement made before an authorized official.
3. Coughing is an act that is not subject to the control of the will.
4. Do not take roads that are full of twists and turns.
5. What is the reason that you have no faith in yourself?
6. The remark that Pat made has nothing to do with the matter at hand.
7. Sally had words of praise for our firmness in holding fast.
8. The position that we found ourselves in could not be defended.
9. George did not have anyone to whom he could entrust secrets.
10. The aim of logic is to show conclusively by means of argument or proof.

REVIEW 7: BRAINTEASERS

Write the complete word.

1. We usually listen to rumors with (3)**red**(5).
2. To everyone's surprise, the (3)**tort**(6) squeezed himself into a small metal box.
3. My brother uses a(n) (3)**ring**(3) after shaving.
4. The (3)**dent**(4) of nominees to fill important vacancies are sometimes checked not too carefully.
5. The dictator is suspected of (1)**rat**(6), though some say that he could not have murdered his own brother.
6. Elephants never hunt; they are not **car**(8).

7. Many oppose (4)**sect**(3) because they feel animals have the same right to live as humans have.

8. Some who claim to be honest turn out to be (4)**up**(1).

9. The Pilgrims had to leave their native land because they refused to surrender their (2)**nets**.

10. Foolish humans who may consider themselves (6)**tent** will soon learn that they are not gods.

REVIEW 8: COMPOSITION

Answer in two or three sentences.

1. Should the death penalty be mandatory for all persons convicted of homicide? Explain.

2. Why should we not put too much credence in the opinions of those who claim to be omniscient?

3. Discuss two precautions that might help a driver survive a collision with another vehicle.

4. Should an ordinary citizen take it upon himself or herself to admonish someone about to commit an infraction? Explain.

5. Discuss a possible result of the unrestricted use of pesticides.

REVIEW 9: ANALOGIES

Write the *letter* of the word that best completes the analogy.

1. *Matricide* is to *mother* as *genocide* is to __?__.   *a.* uncle   *b.* country   *c.* race   *d.* tyrant   *e.* general

2. *Flesh* is to *carnivorous* as *fruit* is to __?__.   *a.* omnivorous   *b.* insectivorous   *c.* vegetarian   *d.* frugivorous   *e.* agricultural

3. *Fraction* is to *whole* as *follower* is to __?__.   *a.* creed   *b.* retinue   *c.* tenure   *d.* fragment   *e.* torsion

4. *Reservation* is to *cancel* as *directive* is to __?__.   *a.* command   *b.* proclaim   *c.* flex   *d.* demand   *e.* countermand

5. *Orphan* is to *guardian* as *mandate* is to __?__.   *a.* victor   *b.* monitor   *c.* trustee   *d.* confidant   *e.* commission

16. GRAT: "pleasant," "thank," "favor"

congratulate (*v.*) kən-'grach-ə-ˌlāt	express one's pleasure to another person at that person's success
gracious (*adj.*) 'grā-shəs	pleasant; courteous; kindly (*ant.* **ungracious**)
grateful (*adj.*) 'grāt-fəl	feeling or expressing gratitude; thankful; obliged (*ant.* **ungrateful**)
gratify (*v.*) 'grat-ə-ˌfī	give or be a source of pleasure or satisfaction
gratis (*adv.*) 'grāt-əs	without charge or payment; free
gratitude (*n.*) 'grat-ə-ˌt(y)üd	thankfulness (*ant.* **ingratitude**)
gratuitous (*adj.*) grə-'t(y)ü-ət-əs	1. given freely; gratis 2. unwarranted, as a *gratuitous* remark
gratuity (*n.*) grə-'t(y)ü-ət-ē	present of money in return for a favor or service; tip
ingrate (*n.*) 'in-ˌgrāt	ungrateful ("not thankful") person
ingratiate (*v.*) in-'grā-shē-ˌāt	establish (oneself) in the favor or good graces of another

EXERCISE 5.21

Write the most appropriate word selected from group 16, *grat*.

1. I would consider myself a(n) __?__ if I did not express my gratitude to those who have helped me.
2. Some diners charge for a second cup of coffee; others provide it __?__ .
3. We were so pleased with the service that we left a generous __?__ .
4. Keeping your TV on extremely loud until three in the morning is no way to __?__ yourself with the neighbors.
5. I am sorry I was so discourteous. I shall try to be more __?__ .
6. Compliments are meant to __?__ .

17. MOR (MORT): "death"

immortal (*adj.*) im-'ȯrt-ᵊl	1. not subject to death (*ant.* **mortal**) 2. not subject to oblivion (being forgotten); imperishable (*ant.* **mortality**)
immortality (*n.*) ‚im-ȯr-'tal-ət-ē	1. eternal life 2. lasting fame
moribund (*adj.*) 'mȯr-ə-bənd	dying; near death
mortal (*adj.*) 'mȯrt-ᵊl	1. destined to die (*ant.* **mortal**) 2. human 3. causing death; fatal, as a *mortal* blow
mortal (*n.*) 'mȯrt-ᵊl	human being; person; individual
mortality (*n.*) mȯr-'tal-ət-ē	1. death rate 2. mortal nature (*ant.* **immortality**)
mortician (*n.*) mȯr-'tish-ən	undertaker
mortification (*n.*) ‚mȯrt-ə-fə-'kā-shən	shame; humiliation; embarrassment
mortify (*v.*) 'mȯrt-ə-‚fī	embarrass; shame; humiliate (literally, "make dead," "kill")
mortuary (*n.*) 'mȯr-chə-‚wer-ē	funeral home
rigor mortis (*n.*) ‚rig-ər-'mȯrt-əs	stiffness of the body that sets in several hours after death (literally, "stiffness of death")

EXERCISE 5.22

Write the most appropriate word selected from group 17, *mor* (*mort*).

1. Patrick Henry's __?__ rests on a speech ending "Give me liberty, or give me death!"
2. Infant __?__ is relatively high in nations that have few physicians and hospitals.
3. The proprietor did not realize what __?__ she caused her assistant when she scolded him in the presence of the entire staff.

4. Though the mountain climber's injury is critical, it may not be __?__ ; he has a chance of recovery.
5. The __?__ community has been given a new lease on life since the re-opening of two large factories that were shut down three years ago.

18. CORP: "body"

corporal (*adj.*) 'kȯr-p(ə-)rəl	bodily, as *corporal* punishment
corporation (*n.*) ˌkȯr-pə-'rā-shən	body authorized by law to carry on an activity with the rights and duties of a single person
corps (*n.*) 'kȯ(ə)r	1. organized body of persons 2. branch of the military, as the Marine *Corps*
corpse (*n.*) 'kȯrps	dead body
corpulent (*adj.*) 'kȯr-pyə-lənt	bulky; obese; very fat
corpus (*n.*) 'kȯr-pəs	general collection or body of writings, laws, etc.
corpuscle (*n.*) 'kȯr-pəs-əl	1. blood cell (literally, a "little body") 2. minute particle
corpus delicti (*n.*) ˌkȯr-pəs-di-'lik-ˌtī	1. facts proving that a crime has been committed 2. body of the victim in a murder case
esprit de corps (*n.*) es-ˌprēd-ə-'kȯ(ə)r	spirit of a body of persons; group spirit
habeas corpus (*n.*) ˌhā-bē-ə-'skȯr-pəs	1. writ (order) requiring a detained person to be brought before a court to investigate the legality of that person's detention (the writ begins with the words **habeas corpus,** meaning "you should have the body") 2. right of a citizen to secure court protection against illegal imprisonment
incorporate (*v.*) in-'kȯr-pə-ˌrāt	combine so as to form one body

EXERCISE 5.23

Write the most appropriate word selected from group 18, *corp.*

1. The executive in charge of sales has a(n) __?__ of able assistants.
2. Criminals were flogged or put in the stocks in olden times, but such __?__ punishment is rare today.
3. The __?__ patient was advised by a physician to try to lose weight.
4. Publishers often __?__ two or more works of an author into one volume.
5. Until the __?__ is produced, it cannot be established that a crime has been committed.
6. The residents proudly support their association; they have a fine __?__ .
7. In countries where there is no __?__, a suspect can be kept in prison without ever being brought to trial.

---

19. DUC (DUCT): "lead," "conduct," "draw"

---

aqueduct (*n.*) 'ak-wə-,dəkt	artificial channel for conducting water over a distance
conducive (*adj.*) kən-'d(y)ü-siv	tending to lead to; contributive; helpful
conduct (*v.*) kən-'dəkt	lead; guide; escort
deduction (*n.*) di-'dək-shən	1. taking away; subtraction (*ant.* **addition**) 2. reasoning from the general to the particular
duct (*n.*) 'dəkt	tube or channel for conducting a liquid, air, etc.
ductile (*adj.*) 'dək-t³l	1. able to be drawn out or hammered thin (said of metal) 2. easily led; docile
induce (*v.*) in-'d(y)üs	lead on; move by persuasion
induct (*v.*) in-'dəkt	admit ("lead in") as a member; initiate
induction (*n.*) in-'dək-shən	1. ceremony by which one is made a member; initiation 2. reasoning from the particular to the general

seduction (*n.*) si-'dək-shən	enticement; leading astray into wrongdoing
traduce (*v.*) trə-'d(y)üs	(literally, "lead along" as a spectacle to bring into disgrace); malign; slander; vilify; calumniate
viaduct (*n.*) 'vī-ə-ˌdəkt	bridge for conducting a road or railroad over a valley, river, etc.

EXERCISE 5.24

Write the most appropriate word selected from group 19, *duc* (*duct*).

1. A(n) _?_ conducts water from a source of supply to a point of distribution.
2. How much of a(n) _?_ is made from your weekly salary for taxes?
3. Though John had said that he wouldn't join, I was able to _?_ him to become a member.
4. As the train passed over the _?_, we had an excellent view of the valley below.
5. When films that exaggerate the luxury and idleness of American life are shown abroad, they _?_ our good name.

20. SECUT (SEQU): "follow"

consecutive (*adj.*) kən-'sek-yət-iv	following in regular order; successive
consequence (*n.*) 'kän-sə-ˌkwens	1. that which follows logically; result 2. importance, as a person of *consequence*
execute (*v.*) 'ek-sə-ˌkyüt	1. follow through to completion; carry out 2. put to death
inconsequential (*adj.*) in-ˌkän-sə-'kwen-shəl	of no consequence; trivial; unimportant
prosecute (*v.*) 'präs-i-ˌkyüt	1. follow to the end or until finished 2. conduct legal proceedings against; sue
sequel (*n.*) 'sē-kwəl	something that follows; continuation; consequence; outcome

sequence (*n.*) 'sē-kwəns	the following of one thing after another; succession; orderly series
sequential (*adj.*) si-'kwen-chəl	arranged in a sequence; serial

EXERCISE 5.25

Write the most appropriate word selected from group 20, *secut* (*sequ*).

1. If the vandals refuse to pay for the damage they caused, the town will __?__ them.
2. After a string of seven __?__ victories, we suffered our first loss.
3. The book about the clever detective proved so popular that the author was induced to write a(n) __?__.
4. The cards in the card catalog are arranged in strict alphabetical __?__.
5. The shortage of water during dry spells is a matter of serious __?__ in affected communities.

---

21. CUR (CURR, CURS): "run"

---

concur (*v.*) kən-'kə(r)	1. agree; be of the same opinion (literally, "run together") (*ant.* **contend**) 2. happen together; coincide
concurrent (*adj.*) kən-'kər-ənt	running together; occurring at the same time
current (*adj.*) 'kər-ənt	1. running or flowing (said of water or electricity) 2. now in progress, prevailing
curriculum (*n.*) kə-'rik-yə-ləm	course of study in a school or college
cursive (*adj.*) 'kər-siv	running or flowing (said of handwriting in which the letters are joined)
cursory (*adj.*) 'kərs-ə-rē	running over hastily; superficially done, as a *cursory* glance

discursive (*adj.*) dis-'kər-siv	wandering ("running") from one topic to another; rambling; digressive
excursion (*n.*) ik-'skər-zhən	going ("running") out or forth; expedition
incur (*v.*) in-'kə(r)	1. meet with ("run into") something undesirable 2. bring upon oneself
incursion (*n.*) in-'kər-zhən	1. a rushing into 2. hostile invasion; raid
precursor (*n.*) pri-'kər-sə(r)	forerunner; predecessor
recur (*v.*) ri-'kə(r)	happen again (literally, "run again")

EXERCISE 5.26

Write the most appropriate word selected from group 21, *cur* (*curr, curs*).

1. If you are habitually late, you will __?__ the displeasure of your employer.
2. Does your school __?__ include a course in driver training?
3. The __?__ film at the Bijou is a western; the war drama is no longer playing there.
4. A difficult passage requires much more than a(n) __?__ reading if it is to be fully understood.
5. Our conversation, as usual, was __?__ , ranging from the latest popular tunes to the prospects of our favorite teams.

22. GRESS (GRAD): "step," "walk," "go"

aggressive (*adj.*) ə-'gres-iv	disposed to attack (literally "step toward"); militant; assertive; pushing
egress (*n.*) 'ē-ˌgres	means of going out; exit (*ant.* **access**)
gradation (*n.*) grā-'dā-shən	1. a change by steps or stages 2. act of grading

grade (*n.*) 'grād	step; stage; degree; rating
gradient (*n.*) 'grād-ē-ənt	1. rate at which a road, railroad track, temperature, voltage, etc., rises ("steps" up) 2. slope
gradual (*adj.*) 'graj-ə-wəl	step-by-step; bit by bit (*ant.* **abrupt**)
graduate (*v.*) 'graj-ə-,wāt	complete all the steps of a course and receive a diploma or degree
graduated (*adj.*) 'graj-ə-,wāt-əd	arranged in regular steps, stages, or degrees
progressive (*adj.*) prə-'gres-iv	going forward to something considered better (*ant.* **reactionary; retrogressive**)
regressive (*adj.*) ri-'gres-iv	disposed to move ("step") backward; retrogressive
retrograde (*adj.*) 're-trə-,grād	1. going backward 2. becoming worse
retrogression (*n.*) ,re-trə-'gresh-ən	act of going from a better to a worse state (*ant.* **progress**)
transgress (*v.*) trans-'gres	step beyond the limits or barriers; go beyond; break a law

EXERCISE 5.27

Write the most appropriate word selected from group 22, *gress* (*grad*).

1. Learning to play an instrument is a(n) __?__ process; it cannot be achieved overnight.
2. The offenders know that they will be dealt with severely if they should __?__ again.
3. When the game ended, hordes of spectators jammed the stadium exits, making __?__ painfully slow.
4. The medical report showed __?__ rather than progress, for the patient's blood pressure had gone up.
5. In a string of __?__ pearls, the individual pearls are arranged in the order of increasing size on both halves of the string.

23. PED: "foot"

biped (*n.*) 'bī-ˌped	two-footed animal
centipede (*n.*) 'sent-ə-ˌpēd	(literally, "hundred-legged" creature); wormlike animal with one pair of legs on most of its segments
expedite (*v.*) 'ek-spə-ˌdīt	1. facilitate (literally, "extricate someone caught by the foot") 2. accelerate or speed up (*ant.* **delay**)
impede (*v.*) im-'pēd	hinder (literally, "entangle the feet"); obstruct; block (*ant.* **assist; aid**)
impediment (*n.*) im-'ped-ə-mənt	1. hindrance; obstacle (literally, "something entangling the feet") 2. defect
millipede (*n.*) 'mil-ə-ˌpēd	(literally, "thousand-legged" creature); wormlike animal with two pairs of legs on most of its segments
pedal (*n.*) 'ped-ᵊl	lever acted on by the foot
pedestal (*n.*) 'ped-əst-ᵊl	1. support or foot of a column or statue 2. foundation
pedestrian (*n.*) pə-'des-tre-ən	person traveling on foot
pedestrian (*adj.*)	commonplace or dull, as a *pedestrian* performance
velocipede (*n.*) və-'läs-ə-ˌpēd	1. child's tricycle (literally, "swift foot") 2. early form of bicycle

EXERCISE 5.28

Write the most appropriate word selected from group 23, *ped*.

1. A supervisor is expected to __?__, not impede, production.
2. It is foolhardy for a(n) __?__ to cross a busy thoroughfare against the light.

3. For a smooth stop, apply foot pressure to the brake __?__ gradually, not abruptly.
4. As a youth, Demosthenes, the famous orator, is said to have suffered from a speech __?__ .
5. At the age of six, Judy abandoned her __?__ and learned to ride a bicycle.

---

24. TACT (TANG): ''touch''

---

contact (*n.*) 'kän-ˌtakt	touching or meeting; association; connection
contiguous (*adj.*) kən-'tig-yə-wəs	touching; in physical contact; adjoining
contingent (*adj.*) kən-'tin-jənt	1. dependent on something else (literally, ''touching together'') 2. accidental
intact (*adj.*) in-'takt	untouched or uninjured; kept or left whole (*ant.* **defective**)
intangible (*adj.*) in-'tan-jə-bəl	1. not capable of being perceived by the sense of touch 2. hard to grasp or define exactly (*ant.* **tangible**)
tact (*n.*) 'takt	sensitive mental perception of what is appropriate on a given occasion (literally, ''sense of touch'')
tactful (*adj.*) 'takt-fəl	having or showing tact (*ant.* **tactless**)
tactile (*adj.*) 'tak-tᵊl	1. pertaining to the sense of touch 2. tangible
tangent (*adj.*) 'tan-jənt	touching
tangent (*n.*)	line or surface meeting a curved line or surface at one point, but not intersecting it
tangential (*adj.*) tan-'jen-chəl	merely touching; slightly connected; digressive

EXERCISE 5.29

Write the most appropriate word selected from group 24, *tact* (*tang*).

1. To discuss your admission to college in the presence of someone who has just received a rejection notice is __?__ .
2. The missing sum was found __?__ ; not a penny had been spent.
3. The Federal grant is __?__ on our raising a matching sum; if we fail to raise that sum, we will not qualify.
4. A firm's goodwill with its clients is a most valuable, though __?__ , asset.
5. If you wish to maintain __?__ with your classmates after graduation, join the Alumni Association.

---

25. PREHEND (PREHENS): "seize," "grasp"

---

apprehend (*v.*)
‚ap-ri-'hend

1. seize or take into custody
2. understand

apprehensive (*adj.*)
‚ap-ri-'hen-siv

1. quick to understand or grasp
2. fearful of what may come; anxious (*ant.* **confident**)

comprehensible (*adj.*)
‚käm-pri-'hen-sə-bəl

able to be grasped mentally; understandable (*ant.* **incomprehensible**)

comprehensive (*adj.*)
‚käm-pri-'hen-siv

including ("seizing") very much; extensive

prehensile (*adj.*)
prē-'hen-səl

adapted for seizing, as a *prehensile* claw

reprehend (*v.*)
‚rep-ri-'hend

(literally, "hold back"); find fault with; rebuke; reprimand; censure

reprehensible (*adj.*)
‚rep-ri-'hen-sə-bəl

deserving of censure; culpable

EXERCISE 5.30

Write the appropriate word selected from group 25, *prehend* (*prehens*).

1. Aggression is utterly __?__ .
2. From the observation deck at the top of the south tower of the World Trade Center, you can get a(n) __?__ view of New York City and its environs.
3. A coded message is __?__ only to those who know the code.
4. Before the curtain rose, I was __?__ about my performance, even though I had rehearsed my part many times.
5. Law enforcement officials are doing their best to __?__ the escaped convict.
6. The instructor is quick to __?__ us when we violate safety regulations.

---

26. JECT: "throw," "cast"

---

abject (*adj.*) 'ab-ˌjekt	sunk or cast down to a low condition; downtrodden; deserving contempt
conjecture (*n.*) kən-'jek-chə(r)	a guess; supposition; inference
dejected (*adj.*) di-'jek-təd	downcast ("thrown down"); discouraged; depressed
eject (*v.*) ē-'jekt	throw out or expel; evict
inject (*v.*) in-'jekt	force or introduce ("throw in") a liquid, a remark, etc.
interject (*v.*) ˌint-ər-'jekt	throw in between; insert; interpose
projectile (*n.*) prə-'jek-tᵊl	1. object (bullet, shell, etc.) designed to be shot forward 2. anything thrown forward
reject (*v.*) ri-'jekt	refuse to take; discard ("throw back") (*ant.* **accept**)
subject (*v.*) səb-'jekt	force (someone) to undergo something unpleasant or inconvenient; expose; make liable to

EXERCISE 5.31

Write the most appropriate word selected from group 26, *ject*.

1. My friend is _?_ over the damage to her new car.
2. A wise policy in buying shares of stock is to be guided by fact rather than _?_ .
3. The umpire was obliged to _?_ a player who refused to accept his decision.
4. A hypodermic syringe is used to _?_ a dose of medicine beneath the skin.
5. The mob hurled stones, bricks, bottles, eggs, and anything else that could serve as a(n) _?_ .
6. We tend to avoid rude people because we do not wish to _?_ ourselves to their insults.

27. VERT (VERS): ''turn''

aversion (*n.*) ə-'vər-zhən	feeling of repugnance toward something with a desire to turn away from it; strong dislike; antipathy
avert (*v.*) ə-'vərt	1. turn away 2. prevent; avoid
controversy (*n.*) 'kän-trə-ˌvər-sē	dispute (literally, a ''turning against''); debate; quarrel
diversion (*n.*) di-'vər-zhən	entertainment; amusement
divert (*v.*) də-'vərt	1. turn aside 2. amuse; entertain
extrovert (*n.*) 'ek-strə-ˌvərt	one more interested in matters outside the self than in one's own thoughts and feelings
inadvertently (*adv.*) ˌin-əd-'vərt-ᵊnt-lē	without turning one's mind to the matter at hand; carelessly; unintentionally
incontrovertible (*adj.*) in-ˌkän-trə-'vərt-ə-bəl	not able to be ''turned opposite'' or disputed; not open to question (*ant.* **controvertible; disputable**)

introvert (*n.*) 'in-trə-ˌvərt	one more interested in one's own thoughts and feelings than in matters outside oneself
introvert (*v.*)	turn inward
invert (*v.*) in-'vərt	turn upside down
obverse (*n.*) 'äb-ˌvərs	side turned toward the observer; therefore, the front of a coin, medal, etc. (*ant.* **reverse**)
perverse (*adj.*) pər-'vərs	turned away from what is right or good; corrupt; wrongheaded
pervert (*v.*) pər-'vərt	turn away from right or truth; give a wrong meaning to
revert (*v.*) ri-'vərt	return; go back, as: "The property will *revert* to the owner when the lease is up."
versatile (*adj.*) 'vər-sət-ᵊl	able to turn with ease from one thing to another
verse (*n.*) 'vərs	line of poetry (literally, "a turning around." After a fixed number of syllables, the poet has to "turn around" to begin a new line.)
vertigo (*n.*) 'vərt-i-ˌgō	condition in which one feels that one's surroundings are turning about; dizziness

EXERCISE 5.32

Write the most appropriate word selected from group 27, *vert* (*vers*).

1. Between Thanksgiving and Christmas most department-store employees work overtime; then they __?__ to their normal working hours.
2. The words "In God We Trust" appear above Lincoln's image on the __?__ of a cent.
3. No sooner did we settle one quarrel than we became involved in another __?__.
4. The first __?__ of Katherine Lee Bates' "America, the Beautiful" begins "O beautiful for spacious skies."
5. A(n) __?__ musician can play several instruments.
6. The proof of his guilt was so __?__ that the defendant confessed to the crime.

28. MIS (MISS, MIT, MITT): "send"

commitment (*n.*) kə-'mit-mənt	1. consignment to prison or a mental institution 2. pledge
demise (*n.*) di-'mīz	death (literally, "sending or putting down")
emissary (*n.*) 'em-ə-ˌser-ē	person sent out on a mission
emit (*v.*) ē-'mit	send out; give off
intermittent (*adj.*) ˌint-ər-'mit-ᵊnt	coming and going at intervals, as an *intermittent* fever (literally, "sending between")
missile (*n.*) 'mis-əl	weapon (spear, bullet, rocket, etc.) capable of being propelled ("sent") to hit a distant object
missive (*n.*) 'mis-iv	written message sent; a letter
remiss (*adj.*) ri-'mis	negligent (literally, "sent back"); careless; lax (*ant.* **scrupulous**)
remission (*n.*) ri-'mish-ən	period of lessening or disappearance of the symptoms of a disease
remit (*v.*) ri-'mit	1. send money due 2. forgive, as to have one's sins *remitted*

EXERCISE 5.33

Write the most appropriate word from group 28, *mis* (*miss, mit, mitt*).

1. This morning's rain was __?__ , starting and stopping several times.
2. It was my fault. I was __?__ in not writing sooner.
3. A distinguished veteran diplomat has been chosen as the President's __?__ to the international conference.
4. You must __?__ the mortgage payment by the tenth of the month.
5. My large searchlight can __?__ a powerful beam.
6. We gave you our word; we will not go back on our __?__ .
7. Three months ago, the patient's recovery seemed unlikely, but then, miraculously, there was a(n) __?__ .

29. LOCUT (LOQU): "speak," "talk"

circumlocution (*n.*) ˌsər-kəm-lō-'kyü-shən	roundabout way of speaking
colloquy (*n.*) 'käl-ə-kwē	a talking together; conference; conversation
elocution (*n.*) 'el-ə-'kyü-shən	art of speaking out or reading effectively in public
eloquent (*adj.*) 'el-ə-kwənt	speaking with force and fluency; movingly expressive
grandiloquent (*adj.*) gran-'dil-ə-kwənt	using lofty or pompous words; bombastic
interlocutor (*n.*) ˌint-ə(r)-'läk-yət-ə(r)	1. questioner 2. one who participates in a conversation
loquacious (*adj.*) lō-'kwā-shəs	talkative; garrulous
obloquy (*n.*) 'äb-lə-kwē	1. a speaking against; censure 2. public reproach (*ant.* **praise**)

EXERCISE 5.34

Write the most appropriate word selected from group 29, *locut (loqu)*.

1. "Your services will be terminated if you persist in disregarding our requirement of punctuality" is a(n) __?__. It would be more direct to say, "You will be dismissed if you come late again."
2. __?__ students who carry on noisy conversations in the library prevent others from concentrating.
3. A course in __?__ can help one to become an effective public speaker.
4. The referee held a short __?__ with the judges before announcing the winner.
5. Witnesses appearing before the investigating committee found that its chief counsel was the principal __?__; the committee members asked very few questions.

30. FER(ous): ''bearing,'' ''producing,'' ''yielding''

auriferous (*adj.*)
ȯ-ʹrif-ə-rəs

bearing or yielding gold

coniferous (*adj.*)
kō-ʹnif-ə-rəs

bearing cones, as the pine tree

odoriferous (*adj.*)
ˌōd-ə-ʹrif-ə-rəs

yielding an odor, usually fragrant

pestiferous (*adj.*)
pe-ʹstif-ə-rəs

1. infected with or bearing disease; pestilential
2. evil

proliferous (*adj.*)
prə-ʹlif-ə-rəs

producing new growth rapidly and extensively

somniferous (*adj.*)
säm-ʹnif-ə-rəs

bearing or inducing sleep

vociferous (*adj.*)
vō-ʹsif-ə-rəs

producing a loud outcry; clamorous; noisy

EXERCISE 5.35

Write the most appropriate word selected from group 30, *fer(ous)*.

1. The infant emitted so _?_ a protest when placed in the crib that his mother took him up at once.
2. A bunch of _?_ lilacs in a vase on the table gave the room an inviting fragrance.
3. Some people who have difficulty falling asleep have found that a glass of warm milk taken before retiring has a(n) _?_ effect.
4. The settlers were heartbroken to see their fields of corn and wheat devastated by swarms of _?_ locusts.
5. The seed-bearing part of pines, cedars, firs, and other _?_ trees is known as a cone.
6. _?_ weeds are a serious problem for gardeners.
7. The lucky miner struck a(n) _?_ vein.

Review Exercises

REVIEW 10: DEFINING LATIN ROOTS

Match each Latin root in column I with the *letter* of its correct meaning in column II.

COLUMN I		COLUMN II
1. MOR (MORT)	*a.*	body
2. TACT (TANG)	*b.*	step; walk; go
3. LOCUT (LOQU)	*c.*	run
4. GRAT	*d.*	bearing; producing; yielding
5. SECUT (SEQU)	*e.*	speak; talk
6. CORP	*f.*	throw
7. CUR (CURR, CURS)	*g.*	touch
8. PED	*h.*	pleasant; thank; favor
9. PREHEND (PREHENS)	*i.*	lead; conduct; draw
10. JECT	*j.*	death
11. VERT (VERS)	*k.*	send
12. FER(ous)	*l.*	turn
13. GRESS (GRAD)	*m.*	seize; grasp
14. MIS (MISS, MIT, MITT)	*n.*	foot
15. DUC (DUCT)	*o.*	follow

REVIEW 11: USING LATIN ROOTS

As a clue to the incomplete word, you are given some of its letters, the number of its missing letters, and its definition. Write the complete word.

DEFINITION	WORD
1. moved forward to something better	P R O (5) E D
2. person traveling on foot	(3) E S T R I A N
3. combine so as to form one body	I N (6) A T E
4. something that follows; continuation	(4) E L
5. artificial channel for conducting water	A Q U E (4)
6. undertaker	(4) I C I A N
7. gift of money in return for a favor	(4) U I T Y

8. producing a loud outcry   V O C I (6)
9. turning away; repugnance   A (4) I O N
10. pertaining to the sense of touch   (4) I L E
11. a speaking against; censure   O B (4) Y
12. running or flowing (handwriting)   (4) I V E
13. by steps or degrees   (4) U A L
14. a written message   (4) I V E
15. talkative   (4) A C I O U S
16. throw in between; interpose   I N T E R (4)
17. tending to lead to; contributive   C O N (3) I V E
18. person sent on a mission   E (4) A R Y
19. running together; occurring simultaneously   C O N (4) E N T
20. turning easily from one thing to another   (4) A T I L E

REVIEW 12: SENTENCE COMPLETION

Which of the two terms makes the sentence correct? Write the *letter* of your answer.

1. The __?__ speaker moved the audience deeply in her brief address. *a.* loquacious *b.* eloquent
2. Andrew is too much of an __?__; he doesn't show enough interest in what is going on around him. *a.* extrovert *b.* introvert
3. The authorities know the identity of the __?__ and expect to apprehend him soon. *a.* transgressor *b.* precursor
4. Larry's diverting account of his experiment __?__ the class. *a.* confused *b.* amused
5. The entire foreign diplomatic __?__ was present at the funeral rites for the distinguished leader. *a.* corpse *b.* corps
6. For all the kindness you have shown us, we are extremely __?__. *a.* grateful *b.* gratuitous
7. Since Emily's motion was adopted by a 12-to-2 vote, it was clear that most of the members __?__. *a.* incurred *b.* concurred
8. If you had used fewer technical terms, your explanation would have been more __?__. *a.* comprehensible *b.* comprehensive
9. The employer explained that salary increases are not automatic but __?__ on satisfactory service. *a.* contiguous *b.* contingent
10. The following is an example of __?__: "Swimmers come to the surface within seconds after a dive; when Dee didn't come up immediately, we knew she was in trouble." *a.* induction *b.* deduction

REVIEW 13: OPPOSITES

Write the word that means the OPPOSITE of the defined word by adding, dropping, or changing a prefix or a suffix. (The first answer is *inconsequential*.)

DEFINITION	WORD
1. important	consequential
2. unbelievable	incredible
3. having no tact	tactless
4. discourteous, rude	ungracious
5. disposed to move backward	regressive
6. thrown in	injected
7. yielding no odor	odorless
8. indefensible	untenable
9. having faith in oneself	confident
10. unrelated to the matter in hand	impertinent
11. front of a coin	obverse
12. capable of being corrupted	corruptible
13. a going ("running") out	excursion
14. touchable	tangible
15. reasoning from particular to general	induction
16. understandable	comprehensible
17. trust in the truth of	credit
18. faithfulness to a trust	fidelity
19. unconquered	unvanquished
20. person more interested in own thoughts than in outside matters	introvert

REVIEW 14: MEANINGS

Match the word in column I with the *letter* of its correct meaning in column II.

COLUMN I	COLUMN II
1. death rate	*a.* invert
2. turn upside down	*b.* grandiloquent
3. felicitate	*c.* retrograde
4. adapted for seizing	*d.* congratulate
5. give a wrong meaning to	*e.* mortality
6. bombastic	*f.* pervert
7. interpose	*g.* ductile
8. going backward	*h.* corpuscle
9. minute particle	*i.* interject
10. able to be hammered thin	*j.* prehensile

REVIEW 15: CONCISE WRITING

Express the thought of each sentence below in no more than four words.

1. He never appreciates a favor and he never says "thank you."
2. Is it possible for the process of growth to be speeded up?
3. The talk that you gave kept wandering from one topic to another.
4. It is important for us to have a sensitive mental perception of what is appropriate on a given occasion.
5. There are few individuals who can speak with force and fluency.
6. We drove by several people who were traveling on foot.
7. No evidence exists to prove that a crime has been committed.
8. The opinion that she has expressed is open to question.
9. You are so absorbed with your own thoughts and feelings that you pay little attention to what is going on in the world around you.
10. Some of the artificial channels that the Romans built for conducting water over a distance survive to this day.

REVIEW 16: BRAINTEASERS

Write the complete word.

1. The proprietor's purchase of a computer is (3) **t i n g e** (2) on her being able to get a loan from a bank.
2. The horse-drawn carriage was a(n) (3) **c u r** (3) of the automobile.
3. After his defeat by an unknown young newcomer, the ex-champion could not conceal his (7) **c a t** (3) .

4. A United Nations (1)**miss**(3) is being sent to help mediate the dispute between the two nations.
5. After six (5)**cut**(3) days of rain, we had severe flooding.
6. Al is a(n) (3)**rate**. I washed his car and he didn't even thank me.
7. Because of the legislator's (5)**hens**(4) conduct, the voters overwhelmingly rejected his bid for a second term.
8. Benjamin Franklin—printer, author, scientist, inventor, philosopher, and diplomat—was one of the most (3)**sat**(3) people of his time.
9. Charges against the defendant were dropped when her defense attorney presented (6)**rover**(5) evidence of her innocence.
10. Some department stores have posted signs stating that all shoplifters who are apprehended will be (5)**cute**(1).

REVIEW 17: COMPOSITION

Answer in two or three sentences.

1. If you were Mayor, how might you expedite the settlement of a labor-management controversy in your town?
2. Would you be remiss if you made an important decision on the basis of conjecture? Explain.
3. Must the gradual loss of population to the suburbs be a mortal blow to a city? Why, or why not?
4. Explain how a gratuitous remark incurred someone's displeasure.
5. Would it be a sign of retrogression or of progress for a nation to abolish the death penalty? Explain.

REVIEW 18: ANALOGIES

Write the *letter* of the word that best completes the analogy.

1. *River* is to *bridge* as *valley* is to __?__.   *a.* viaduct   *b.* mountain   *c.* pontoon   *d.* projectile   *e.* road
2. *Olfactory* is to *smell* as *tactile* is to __?__.   *a.* see   *b.* grasp   *c.* touch   *d.* hear   *e.* taste
3. *Birth* is to *demise* as *preface* is to __?__.   *a.* foreword   *b.* conclusion   *c.* footnote   *d.* introduction   *e.* outline
4. *Corpse* is to *life* as *ingrate* is to __?__.   *a.* fear   *b.* ingratitude   *c.* unkindness   *d.* dejection   *e.* gratitude
5. *Plan* is to *execution* as *outline* is to __?__.   *a.* summary   *b.* organization   *c.* killing   *d.* composition   *e.* topic

CHAPTER 6

Words From Classical Mythology and History

This chapter will teach you to use important words taken from classical (ancient Greek and Roman) mythology. The beautiful and profoundly significant myths created by the Greeks and adopted by the Romans have contributed words that an educated person is expected to know. All the words discussed below originate from myths, except the following which are based on historical fact: *Draconian, forum, laconic, Lucullan, Marathon, philippic, Pyrrhic, solon, Spartan,* and *thespian.*

Study Your New Words

WORD	MEANING AND TYPICAL USE
Adonis (*n.*) ə-'dän-əs	very handsome young man (from *Adonis*, a handsome youth loved by Aphrodite, goddess of love) Joanna's former boyfriend was not exactly handsome, but her new one is quite an *Adonis*.
aegis (*n.*) 'ē-jəs	shield or protection; auspices; sponsorship (from *aegis*, the protective shield of Zeus, king of the Greek gods) An international force under the *aegis* of the United Nations has been dispatched to the troubled area.

amazon (*n.*)
'am-ə-ˌzän

tall, strong, masculine woman (from the *Amazons*, a mythological race of women warriors)

The laborious work that pioneer women had to do would have challenged an *amazon*.

ambrosial (*adj.*)
am-'brō-zhəl

exceptionally pleasing to taste or smell; extremely delicious; excellent (from *ambrosia*, the literally "not mortal" food of the gods)

The *ambrosial* aroma of the roast whetted our appetites.

atlas (*n.*)
'at-ləs

book of maps (from *Atlas*, a giant who supported the heavens on his shoulders. The figure of Atlas supporting the world was prefaced to early map collections; hence the name *atlas*.)

For reliable information about present national boundaries, consult an up-to-date *atlas*.

auroral (*adj.*)
ə-'ror-əl

pertaining to or resembling the dawn; rosy (from *Aurora*, goddess of the dawn)

The darkness waned, and a faint *auroral* glow began to appear in the east.

bacchanalian (*adj.*)
ˌbak-ə-'nāl-yən
(or **bacchic**)

jovial or wild with drunkenness (from *Bacchus*, the god of wine)

At 2 A.M. the neighbors called the police to quell the *bacchanalian* revelry in the upstairs apartment.

Cassandra (*n.*)
kə-'san-drə

one who prophesies doom or disaster; pessimist (from *Cassandra*, who was given the power of prophecy by Apollo. When she spurned his love, he could not take back his gift, but he added the stipulation that no one would ever believe her.)
(*ant.* **Pollyanna**)

Many say we will lose, but the coach is urging us to pay no attention to those *Cassandras*.

chimerical (*adj.*)
kī-'mer-i-kəl
(or **chimeric**)

fantastic; unreal; impossible; absurd (from the *Chimera*, a fire-breathing monster with a lion's head, goat's body, and serpent's tail)

At first, Robert Fulton's plans for his steamboat were derided as *chimerical* nonsense.

Draconian (*adj.*)
drə-'kō-nē-ən
(or **draconian**)

cruel; harsh; severe; ironhanded (from *Draco*, an Athenian lawmaker who drew up a harsh code of laws)

The dictator took *Draconian* measures against those he suspected of plotting a rebellion.

echolalia (*n.*)
ˌek-ō-'lā-lē-ə

automatic and immediate repetition (echoing) of what others say (from *Echo*, a maiden who loved Narcissus. When he rejected her, she pined away until nothing was left of her but her voice.)

The *echolalia* of infants is part of the process by which they learn to speak.

Elysian (*adj.*)
i-'lizh-ən

delightful; blissful; heavenly (from *Elysium*, the mythological paradise where the brave and good dwell after death)

Students yearn for the *Elysian* leisure of the summer vacation.

eristic (*adj.*)
i-'ris-tik

prone to controversy; disputatious; argumentative (from *Eris*, the goddess of discord)

It is extremely difficult to reach an agreement with anyone who has an *eristic* temperament.

fauna (*n.*)
'fȯn-ə

animal life; animals of a particular region or period (from *Faunus*, Roman god of animals)

Our careless use of pesticides threatens to remove the bald eagle from our nation's *fauna*.

flora (*n.*)
'flȯr-ə

plant life; plants of a particular region or period (from *Flora*, Roman goddess of flowers)

Pollution is harming not only the residents of the area, but also its *fauna* and *flora*.

forum (*n.*)
'fȯr-əm

any medium or place for open discussion and expression of ideas—a public meeting, a radio or TV discussion, editorial page, etc. (from *Forum*, the marketplace and place of assembly for the people in Ancient Rome)

A dictatorship permits no *forum* where ideas can be freely and openly discussed.

hector (*v.*)
'hek-tər

bully; intimidate with threats; bluster (from *Hector*, bravest of the Trojans)

The pickets did not allow themselves to be provoked, despite the unruly crowds that gathered to *hector* them.

herculean (*adj.*)
ˌhər-kyə-'lē-ən
(or **Herculean**)

very difficult; requiring the strength of *Hercules* (a hero of superhuman strength)

Among the *herculean* tasks confronting our nation is the rebuilding of roads, bridges, and tunnels.

hermetic (*adj.*)
hər-'met-ik

airtight (from *Hermes*, messenger of the gods and reputed inventor of a magic seal to keep a vessel airtight)

To get a vitamin pill from a new bottle, you must unscrew the cap and break the *hermetic* seal.

iridescent (*adj.*)
ir-ə-'des-³nt

having colors like the rainbow (from *Iris*, goddess of the rainbow)
Children enjoy blowing *iridescent* soap bubbles.

jovial (*adj.*)
'jo-vē-əl

jolly; merry; good-humored (from *Jove*, or Jupiter, king of the Roman gods. The planet Jupiter was believed to make persons born under its influence cheerful or *jovial*.)
Our *jovial* hostess entertained us with some amusing anecdotes about her family.

labyrinthine (*adj.*)
lab-ə-'rin-thən

full of confusing passageways; intricate; complicated, like the *Labyrinth* (a fabled maze in Crete)
Out-of-towners may easily lose their way in New York City's *labyrinthine* subway passages.

laconic (*adj.*)
lə-'kän-ik

using words sparingly; terse; concise (from *Lakonikos*, meaning "Spartan." The Spartans were known for their terseness.)
All I received in response to my request was the *laconic* reply "Wait."

lethargic (*adj.*)
li-'thär-jik

unnaturally drowsy; sluggish; dull (from *Lethe*, river in Hades whose water, when drunk, caused forgetfulness of the past)
For several hours after the operation, the patient was *lethargic* because of the anesthetic.

Lucullan (*adj.*)
lü-'kəl-ən

sumptuous; luxurious (from *Lucullus*, a Roman who gave lavish banquets)
Thanksgiving dinner is almost a *Lucullan* feast.

marathon (*n.*)
'mar-ə-,thän

1. long-distance footrace of 26 miles 385 yards (from *Marathon*, where the Greeks defeated the Persian invaders in 490 B.C. The fleet-footed Pheidippides raced to Athens with the joyous news, but fell dead after announcing the victory.)
Roadrunners from all over the world compete in the annual Boston and New York City *marathons*.
2. endurance contest, as a dance *marathon*

martial (*adj.*)
'mär-shəl

pertaining to war; warlike (from *Mars*, god of war)
The Helvetians were a *martial* people who tried to conquer southern Gaul.

mentor (*n.*)
'men-,tȯ(r)

1. wise and trusted adviser (from *Mentor*, to whom Odysseus entrusted the education of his son)

The retiring supervisor was persuaded to stay on for a month as *mentor* to her successor.

2. tutor; coach

The basketball *mentor* says that our team is the best he has ever coached.

mercurial (*adj.*)
mər-'kyür-ē-əl

1. quick; vivacious; active; lively (*ant.* **saturnine**) (from *Mercury*, the Roman counterpart of *Hermes. Mercury* was the messenger of the gods, the god of commerce, eloquence, and magic, and also the patron of travelers, rogues, and thieves. His name designates a planet as well as a metal.)

The older partner is rather dull and morose, but the younger has a *mercurial* temperament that appeals to customers.

2. inconstant; unstable; capricious; subject to rapid and unpredictable mood changes

Someone with a *mercurial* disposition may at any moment turn from contentment to dissatisfaction, or from friendliness to hostility.

myrmidon (*n.*)
'mər-mə-,dän

obedient and unquestioning follower (from the *Myrmidons*, a martial tribe who accompanied Achilles to the Trojan War)

The dictator was surrounded by *myrmidons* who could be trusted to execute all orders loyally and pitilessly.

narcissistic (*adj.*)
,när-sə-'sis-tik

in love with oneself; excessively fascinated and gratified by one's own physical and mental qualities; egocentric (from *Narcissus*, a handsome youth who didn't even look at any of the many maidens who loved him. However, when he saw his own image in a pool, he fell madly in love with it. His futile longing for himself caused him such suffering that he died soon thereafter.)

Narcissistic individuals tend to overevaluate their own merits and to see no desirable qualities in others.

nectar (*n.*)
'nek-tər

something exceptionally delicious to drink (from *nectar*, the literally ''death-overcoming'' drink that made the gods immortal)

The juice of that freshly squeezed grapefruit is like *nectar*.

nemesis (*n.*)
'nem-ə-səs

1. due punishment for evil deeds (from *Nemesis*, goddess of vengeance)
   A conviction for tax evasion has been the *nemesis* of many a criminal who had previously escaped justice.
2. one who inflicts such punishment
   Napoleon crushed many opponents, but Wellington was his *nemesis*.

odyssey (*n.*)
'äd-ə-sē

any long series of wanderings or travels (from the *Odyssey*, the poem dealing with Odysseus' ten years of wandering on his way home from the Trojan War)
   A travel agent will gladly plan a year's *odyssey* to places of interest around the world.

Olympian (*adj.*)
ə-'lim-pē-ən
(or **Olympic**)
ə-'lim-pik

1. majestic; godlike; lofty (from *Mt. Olympus*, highest mountain in Greece. Its summit, obscured by clouds from human view, was the home of the gods.)
   Chief executive officers are usually given offices and staffs that are commensurate with their *Olympian* responsibilities.
2. having to do with the *Olympic Games*, an international athletic competition held every four years

paean (*n.*)
'pē-ən

song or hymn of praise, joy, or triumph (A *paean* was a hymn in praise of Apollo, the god of deliverance.)
   When the crisis was resolved, people danced in the streets and sang *paeans* of joy.

palladium (*n.*)
pə-'lād-ē-əm

safeguard or protection (from *Palladium*, the statue of Pallas Athena, which was thought to protect the city of Troy)
   The little girl habitually fell asleep clutching a battered doll, her *palladium*.

panic (*n.*)
'pan-ik

unreasoning, sudden fright that grips a multitude (from *Pan*, a god believed to cause fear)
   A *panic* ensued when someone in the crowded auditorium yelled "Fire!"

philippic (*n.*)
fə-'lip-ik

bitter denunciation; tirade (from the *Philippics*, orations by Demosthenes denouncing King Philip of Macedon)
   In an hour-long *philippic*, the legislator denounced the lobbyists opposing her bill.

plutocratic (*adj.*)
ˌplüt-ə-'krat-ik

having great influence because of one's wealth (from *Plutus*, god of wealth)

A handful of *plutocratic* investors, each owning several million shares, determined the policies of the corporation.

procrustean (*adj.*)
prə-'krəs-tē-ən
(or **Procrustean**)

cruel or inflexible in enforcing conformity (from *Procrustes*, a robber who made his victims fit the length of his bed, either stretching them if they were too short, or cutting off their legs if they were too tall)

The magistrate dispensed a *procrustean* kind of justice, imposing a fine of $200 on everyone who had received a summons, regardless of the circumstances.

protean (*adj.*)
'prōt-ē-ən

exceedingly variable; readily assuming different forms or shapes (from *Proteus*, a sea god who could readily change his shape to elude capture)

The microscopic ameba, a *protean* organism, is continually changing its shape.

Pyrrhic (*adj.*)
'pir-ik

ruinous; gained at too great a cost (from *Pyrrhus*, who suffered enormous losses in a ''victory'' over the Romans)

We won, but it was a *Pyrrhic* victory, as our leading scorer was injured and put out of action for the balance of the season.

saturnine (*adj.*)
'sat-ər-ˌnīn

heavy; dull; gloomy; morose (*ant.* **mercurial**) (from *Saturn*, father of Jupiter. Though Saturn's reign was supposedly a golden age, he has become a symbol of heaviness and dullness because the alchemists and astrologers associated his name with the metal lead.)

The research assistant was a *saturnine* scholar who said very little and smiled rarely.

siren (*n.*)
'sī-rən

1. dangerous, attractive woman (from the *Sirens*, creatures half woman and half bird, whose sweet singing lured sailors to destruction on the rocks)

The enemy employed a redhaired *siren* as a spy.
2. a woman who sings sweetly

One of the entertainers was a night-club *siren* with a melodious voice.
3. apparatus for sounding loud warnings

Emergency vehicles raced to the scene with *sirens* screaming.

solon (*n.*)
'sō-lən

legislator; wise lawgiver (from *Solon*, noted Athenian lawgiver)

Next week the *solons* will return to the capital for the opening of the legislative session.

Spartan (*adj.*)
'spärt-ᵊn

marked by self-discipline, bravery, ability to endure pain, and avoidance of comfort (from *Sparta*, a city-state in ancient Greece, whose people had the above characteristics)

The rooms had neither rugs nor sofas nor easy chairs; they were furnished with *Spartan* simplicity.

stentorian (*adj.*)
sten-'tȯr-ē-ən

very loud (from *Stentor*, a legendary herald whose voice was as loud as fifty voices)

Speak softly; you don't need a *stentorian* voice to be heard in this small room.

Stygian (*adj.*)
'stij-ē-ən

infernal; especially dark; gloomy (from *Styx*, a river of the lower world leading into Hades, or Hell)

A power failure at 11:30 P.M. plunged the city into *Stygian* blackness.

tantalize (*v.*)
'tant-ᵊl- ˌīz

excite a hope but prevent its fulfillment; tease (from *Tantalus*, who was kept hungry and thirsty in the lower world with food and water very near but just beyond his reach)

We removed the strawberry shortcake from the table so as not to *tantalize* our weight-conscious guest.

terpsichorean (*adj.*)
ˌtərp-sik-ə-'rē-ən

pertaining to dancing (from *Terpsichore*, the muse of dancing)

The reviewers lauded the ballet troupe for its *terpsichorean* artistry.

thespian (*adj.*)
'thes-pē-ən
(or **Thespian**)

pertaining to the drama or acting (from *Thespis*, reputed father of Greek drama)

If you enjoy acting in plays, join a *thespian* club.

titanic (*adj.*)
tī-'tan-ik

of enormous strength, size, or power (from the *Titans*, lawless, powerful giants defeated by Zeus)

By a *titanic* effort, our football team halted an onrush at our one-yard line.

Apply What You Have Learned

EXERCISE 6.1: MEANINGS

Write the *letter* of the best definition of the italicized word.

1. *ambrosial* fare: *a.* expensive   *b.* cut-rate   *c.* railroad   *d.* delicious
2. idle *thespians*:   *a.* musicians   *b.* actors   *c.* dancers   *d.* loafers
3. *martial* airs: *a.* matrimonial   *b.* tuneful   *c.* military   *d.* soothing
4. impassioned *philippic*:   *a.* plea   *b.* message   *c.* praise   *d.* tirade
5. *plutocratic* associates: *a.* loyal and wealthy   *b.* jovial   *c.* carefree   *d.* rich and influential
6. *Draconian* laws: *a.* democratic   *b.* ironhanded   *c.* unpopular   *d.* unenforced
7. *hermetic* compartments: *a.* rigid   *b.* tiny   *c.* airtight   *d.* labyrinthine
8. road *atlas*:   *a.* traveler   *b.* map collection   *c.* network   *d.* surface
9. endless *odyssey*:   *a.* story   *b.* wanderings   *c.* sufferings   *d.* errands
10. new *Adonis*:   *a.* lover   *b.* movie actor   *c.* myrmidon   *d.* handsome youth

EXERCISE 6.2: SENTENCE COMPLETION

Write the *letter* of the choice that best completes the sentence.

1. Photographs of __?__ celebrities decorated the walls of the dance studio.   *a.* operatic   *b.* Olympic   *c.* thespian   *d.* eristic   *e.* terpsichorean
2. The wrestler's __?__ maneuvers made it difficult for an opponent to obtain a hold.   *a.* hermetic   *b.* protean   *c.* titanic   *d.* procrustean   *e.* philippic
3. In a locker-room speech between halves, the __?__ reaffirmed his confidence in his __?__.   *a.* conductor . . . myrmidons   *b.* amazon . . . team   *c.* myrmidon . . . adherents   *d.* mentor . . . squad   *e.* conductor . . . mentors
4. Many literatures describe a paradise where the __?__ dwell in __?__ repose.   *a.* heroic . . . Stygian   *b.* unvanquished . . . bacchanalian   *c.* sirens . . . abject   *d.* perfidious . . . ambrosial   *e.* brave . . . Elysian
5. When people become __?__, their ability to reason gives way to fear.   *a.* lethargic   *b.* saturnine   *c.* panicky   *d.* Draconian   *e.* plutocratic

6. The audience laughed to see the burly actor __?__ by his puny companion's hectoring.   *a.* convinced   *b.* betrayed   *c.* tripped   *d.* intimidated   *e.* encouraged

7. The Pyrrhic victory was cause for widespread __?__.   *a.* dejection   *b.* optimism   *c.* paeans   *d.* satisfaction   *e.* promotions

8. Only a person with a __?__ voice could have been heard above the din of the angry crowd.   *a.* herculean   *b.* stentorian   *c.* jovial   *d.* laconic   *e.* titanic

9. Our __?__ host always enjoys having friends to share his Lucullan suppers.   *a.* cursive   *b.* martial   *c.* fractious   *d.* convivial   *e.* sanguine

10. Psychoanalysis can help patients recall long-forgotten experiences from the __?__ recesses of their minds.   *a.* labyrinthine   *b.* chimerical   *c.* iridescent   *d.* auroral   *e.* mercurial

EXERCISE 6.3: CONCISE WRITING

Express the thought of each sentence below in no more than four words.

1. Those who make predictions of doom and disaster are not popular.
2. Some people are inclined to be too much in love with themselves.
3. You aroused their hopes, and at the same time you made it impossible for them to realize those hopes.
4. This is not an ordinary beverage; it is exceptionally delicious.
5. Grownups should avoid the practice of automatically and instantly repeating what others say.
6. We attended a meeting at which there was open discussion and audience participation.
7. Make an effort to be sparing in your use of words.
8. Her cousin is the sort of person who likes to engage in disputes.
9. Tell us about the long series of wanderings that you were involved in.
10. Rumors can be the cause of sudden and unreasoning fright.

EXERCISE 6.4: BRAINTEASERS

Write the complete word.

1. Feeling **let**(6), the driver stopped for a short nap.
2. To lift the heavy weight that was pressing down upon the victim would have required (5)**lean** strength.

3. Sometimes, after a summer shower, a(n) (1) r i d (6) arc appears in the sky.
4. (3) m e t (2) seals help to make some products tamper-proof.
5. Larry Smith's home run in the bottom of the nineteenth inning won the game for the home team and ended the six-hour (2) r a t (3) .
6. Our (1) t e n t (5) instructor needs no microphone to be heard in our gym.
7. No one expects a(n) (2) c u l l (2) dinner to be served in a fast food restaurant.
8. Long before the first (3) o r a l light, the farmer is up and ready for the day's chores.
9. Law-abiding people breathe a sigh of relief when notorious evildoers who have never been convicted finally meet their (2) m e (3) .
10. As we kept going through the (7) t h i n e corridors, we thought we would never be able to find our way back.

EXERCISE 6.5: COMPOSITION

Answer in two or three sentences.

1. Would you be in a jovial mood after achieving a victory? Why, or why not?
2. Why is it normal for someone exploring a labyrinthine cave to be gripped with panic?
3. Of all the foods you have tasted, name one that was ambrosial, and another that was like nectar. Give reasons for your choices.
4. Are Draconian penalties an effective palladium against crime? Why, or why not?
5. Would you withdraw from an election campaign if your rival's myrmidons hectored you at every place you tried to speak? Explain.

EXERCISE 6.6: ANALOGIES

Write the *letter* of the word-pair that best expresses a relationship similar to that existing between the capitalized word-pair.

1. SOLON : LAWS
   a. atlas : maps
   b. ruler : subjects
   c. philosopher : credentials
   d. artisan : trade
   e. composer : operas

2. SIREN : BEAUTY
   a. victim : trap
   b. temptress : prey
   c. hunter : bait
   d. alarm : confidence
   e. worm : fish

3. CASSANDRA : POLLYANNA
   a. amazon : myrmidon
   b. Spartan : laconic
   c. Olympian : majestic
   d. pessimist : optimist
   e. titanic : herculean

4. NEMESIS : EVILDOER
   a. avenger : victim
   b. retribution : culprit
   c. punishment : benefactor
   d. justice : misdeed
   e. penalty : evil

5. AMAZON : STRENGTH
   a. comedienne : humor
   b. river : jungle
   c. nurse : invalid
   d. warrior : civilian
   e. servant : indifference

6. PALLADIUM : DANGER
   a. rumor : panic
   b. arena : excitement
   c. investigation : truth
   d. experience : skill
   e. vaccination : smallpox

7. MERCURIAL : CAPRICIOUS
   a. procrustean : rigid
   b. protean : uniform
   c. ethereal : earthly
   d. saturnine : hilarious
   e. narcissistic : unselfish

8. PAEAN : ECSTASY
   a. anthem : nation
   b. suffering : rejoicing
   c. lament : sorrow
   d. sadness : joy
   e. hymn : congregation

9. THESPIAN : TERPSICHOREAN
   a. painter : dancer
   b. orator : musician
   c. comedian : sculptor
   d. actress : ballerina
   e. composer : singer

10. AURORAL : DAWN
    a. fragile : care
    b. autumnal : fall
    c. visual : ear
    d. annual : season
    e. juvenile : delinquency

CHAPTER 7

Anglo-Saxon Vocabulary

About 25 percent of our modern English vocabulary comes from the language of the Angles and Saxons, Germanic tribes who invaded Britain beginning about the year 450. The Anglo-Saxons ruled until 1066, when Harold, their last king, was defeated at the Battle of Hastings by an army from France led by William, Duke of Normandy. For the next two centuries, French was England's official language, but the common people continued to use Anglo-Saxon. The basic words of English today are of Anglo-Saxon origin. They include the articles (*a, an, the*), the words for numbers, the verb *to be*, prepositions (*at, by, from, in, out, with*, etc.), conjunctions (*and, but, as, when*, etc.), many commonly used verbs (*to go, to fight, to sleep, to eat*, etc.), many commonly used nouns (*father, mother, land, house, water*, etc.), and most pronouns.

After 1066, a wealth of Latin-derived parallels for Anglo-Saxon words came into our language through French. These borrowings, and others directly from Latin, endowed English with a rich supply of synonyms and near-synonyms. For example, for the Anglo-Saxon verb *lighten*, we have (1) the synonym *relieve*, borrowed from the language of the French-speaking invaders who had earlier gotten it from Latin, and (2) the synonym *alleviate*, borrowed directly from Latin.

This brief chapter deals with (1) Anglo-Saxon elements selected to help you increase your store of words, and (2) Latin-derived synonyms and near-synonyms for Anglo-Saxon words.

Anglo-Saxon Prefixes

---

1. A-: "on," "in," "in a state of"

WORD	MEANING
aboard (*adv.*) ə-'bȯrd	on a ship, train, bus, etc. (Come *aboard*!)
aboard (*prep.*) ə-'bȯrd	on (A stowaway was *aboard* the freighter.)

    Also: **ashore, afoot**

afoul (*adj.*) ə-'faůl	in a state of entanglement (fishermen with their lines *afoul*)
afoul of (*prep.*) ə-'faů-ləv	in or into collision or entanglement with (They ran *afoul* of the law.)
aloof (*adv.*) ə-'lüf	in the state of being at a distance (I stood *aloof*.)
aloof (*adj.*) ə-'lüf	withdrawn (Join us. Don't be *aloof*.)
amiss (*adv.*) ə-'mis	in a missing-the-mark manner; wrong (Something went *amiss*.)
amiss (*adj.*) ə-'mis	wrong; imperfect; faulty (Is anything *amiss*?)
asunder (*adv.*) ə-'sən-dər	in an apart position; apart (Friends were torn *asunder*.)

    Also: **abed, adrift, afield, afire, afloat, aloft,** etc.

2. WITH-: "against," "back"

withdraw (*v.*) wi<u>th</u>-'drȯ	draw back; take back
withhold (*v.*) wi<u>th</u>-'hōld	hold back
withstand (*v.*) wi<u>th</u>-'stand	stand up against; resist
notwithstanding (*prep.*) ˌnät-wi<u>th</u>-'stan-diŋ	despite (*Notwithstanding* her inexperience, she was hired.)

3. BE- has these meanings:

a. "all around," "on all sides," "thoroughly"

beset (*v.*) bi-'set	attack on all sides; surround

  Also: **begrudge, belabor, bemuddle, besiege, besmirch,** etc.

b. "affect with," "cover with"

begrime (*v.*) bi-'grīm	cover with grime; make dirty
benighted (*adj.*) bi-'nīt-ˌəd	overtaken by darkness of night; unenlightened; intellectually or morally ignorant

  Also: **becloud, bedevil, befog, belie, bewitch,** etc.

c. "cause to be"

belittle (*v.*) bi-'lit-ᵊl	cause to be or seem little or unimportant; disparage

  Also: **becalm, bedim, bewilder,** etc.

Anglo-Saxon Suffixes and Combining Forms

---

1. -WISE: "way," "manner"

---

contrariwise (*adv.*)   on the contrary
'kän-ˌtrer-ē-ˌwīz   (*ant.* **likewise**)

nowise (*adv.*)   in no way; not at all
'nō-ˌwīz

Also: **breadthwise, lengthwise, otherwise,** etc.

---

2. -DOM: "dignity," "office," "realm," "state of being," "those having the character of"

---

earldom (*n.*)   realm or dignity of an earl
'ərl-dəm

martyrdom (*n.*)   state of being a martyr
'märt-ərd-əm

officialdom (*n.*)   those having the authority of officials; officials collec-
ə-'fish-əl-dəm   tively

Also: **dukedom, fiefdom, kingdom, serfdom, sheikdom, stardom,** etc.

---

3. -SOME has these meanings:

---

a. **"full of the thing or quality denoted in the first part of the -SOME word"**

cumbersome (*adj.*)   full of encumbrances; burdensome
'kəm-bər-səm

fulsome (*adj.*)   offensive because of excessive display or obvious
'fùl-səm   insincerity (literally, "full of fullness")

lissom(e) (*adj.*) ʹlis-əm	lithesome (literally, "full of a lithe or supple quality"); nimble
mettlesome (*adj.*) ʹmet-ᵊl-səm	full of mettle (courage); spirited
noisome (*adj.*) ʹnȯi-səm	offensive to the sense of smell (literally, "full of an annoying quality"); unwholesome
winsome (*adj.*) ʹwin-səm	full of a winning quality (literally, "full of *wynn*," the Anglo-Saxon word for *joy*); cheerful; merry

Also: **awesome, bothersome, fearsome, frolicsome, gruesome, irksome, lonesome, quarrelsome, toothsome, troublesome,** etc.

b. **"group of"**

twosome (*n.*) tü-səm	group of two

Also: **threesome, foursome,** etc.

4. -LING has these meanings:

a. **"one pertaining to or concerned with whatever is denoted in the first part of the -LING word"**

hireling (*n.*) ʹhī-ə(r)-liŋ	one whose only interest in his or her work is the *hire* (pay)
starveling (*n.*) ʹstärv-liŋ	one who is thin from lack of food
suckling (*n.*) ʹsək-liŋ	child or animal that is nursed (sucks)
yearling (*n.*) ʹyi-ə(r)-liŋ	one who is a year old

b. **"little"**

changeling (*n.*) ʹchānj-liŋ	child secretly exchanged for another in infancy (literally, "a little change")
duckling (*n.*) ʹdək-liŋ	little duck

foundling (*n.*)   infant found after being deserted by its unknown
'faun-dliŋ   parents

gosling (*n.*)   young goose
'gäz-liŋ

sibling (*n.*)   brother or sister (literally, "a little *sib*," a synonym
'sib-liŋ   for *blood relative*)

stripling (*n.*)   lad (literally, "a little strip" from the main stem)
'strip-liŋ

  Also: **fledgling, princeling, sapling,** etc.

Miscellaneous Anglo-Saxon Words

anent (*prep.*)   about; concerning; in respect to
ə-'nent

anon (*adv.*)   soon; presently
ə-'nän

behest (*n.*)   command; order
bi-'hest

beholden (*adj.*)   bound in gratitude; indebted
bi-'hōl-dən

behoove (*v.*)   be necessary for; be proper for
bi-'hüv

betimes (*adv.*)   early
bi-'tīmz

heath (*n.*)   tract of wasteland
'hēth

wane (*v.*)   decrease gradually in size
'wān

warlock (*n.*)   sorcerer or wizard
'wȯr-ˌläk

warp (*n.*)   the threads running lengthwise in the loom, crossed
'wȯrp   by the woof

wax (*v.*)
'waks

grow in size, as in "to wax and wane"

withal (*adv.*)
wi<u>th</u>-'ȯl

with it all; as well

woof (*n.*)
'wu̇f

the threads running from side to side in a woven fabric

yclept (*adj.*)
or **ycleped**
i-'klept

named; called

EXERCISE 7.1: WORD COMPLETION

Write the complete word.

1. Do not **b**(6) (*obscure, as with clouds*) the issue.
2. A **n**(6) (*offensive to the sense of smell*) odor filled the chem laboratory.
3. Jim is friendly but his uncle holds himself **a**(4) (*at a distance*).
4. Try as I might, I could not **b**(5) (*cause to be quiet*) the anxious mother.
5. In the fog, we ran **a**(4) of (*came in collision with*) a stalled car.
6. A public official should be cautious about accepting favors so as not to be **b**(7) (*bound in gratitude*) to anybody.
7. Don't you agree they make an attractive **t**(6) (*group of two*)?
8. Present your passbook to the teller whenever you deposit or **w**(7) (*take back*) funds.
9. The monarch seemed not at all displeased by the obviously **f**(6) (*offensively insincere*) compliments of his fawning subjects.
10. From her first performance, it was obvious she was destined for **s**(6) (*the state of being a star*).
11. She is an only child; she has no **s**(6) (*brother or sister*).

EXERCISE 7.2: ANGLO-SAXON SYNONYMS

Write an Anglo-Saxon synonym for the word in italics. The letters of each synonym appear in scrambled form in the parentheses. (The first answer is *behooves*.)

1. It *is necessary for* (VESHOOBE) students to be attentive.
2. She rose before dawn and retired *early* (MESBETI).

3. Nothing was said *concerning* (TENNA) the proposal to grant a pardon.
4. The witches in Shakespeare's play MACBETH usually met on the *waste-land* (TEHAH).
5. We are *indebted* (HODNEBLE) to no one.
6. The moon *grows* (XESWA) and wanes.
7. With a small stone, the *lad* (GRINPLITS) David slew the giant Goliath.
8. Richard I, *named* (PLETCY) the Lion-Hearted, was a twelfth-century king of England.
9. I'll be there *soon* (NANO).
10. The guard around the palace was doubled at the monarch's *command* (SETHEB).
11. Let us help those who are *in a state of ignorance* (THINGBEED).

EXERCISE 7.3: COMPOSITION

Answer in two or three sentences.

1. Why would it belittle someone to be called a hireling?
2. Is it likely that a person can achieve stardom without being beholden to anyone? Explain.
3. Suggest a possible solution for a particularly noisome problem that besets us today.
4. Would you be able to withstand the flatteries of fulsome admirers? Why, or why not?
5. Briefly describe a situation that resulted in tearing siblings asunder.

Latin-Derived Synonyms and Near-Synonyms for Anglo-Saxon Words

Because English has incorporated so many Latin words into its vocabulary, it often has two or more words for an idea: one from Anglo-Saxon (for example, *brotherly*) and another from Latin (for example, *fraternal*). The two words, however, are seldom exactly synonymous.

To illustrate, both *brotherly* and *fraternal* have the general meaning "pertaining to brothers." Yet, *brotherly* conveys a greater warmth of feeling than *fraternal*, which is less intimate and more formal. Thus, we speak of "brotherly love," but "fraternal organizations." This abundance of synonyms enables us to express varying shades of meaning.

In the pages that follow, Anglo-Saxon-derived adjectives, verbs, and nouns will be presented side by side with similar but not exactly synonymous Latin-derived adjectives, verbs, and nouns.

---

1. Adjectives

FROM ANGLO-SAXON	FROM LATIN
fatherly pertaining to a father (warmer than *paternal*)	**paternal** pə-'tərn-ᵊl 1. fatherly 2. inherited from or related to the father's side
motherly pertaining to a mother (warmer than *maternal*)	**maternal** mə-'tərn-ᵊl 1. motherly 2. inherited from or related to the mother's side
brotherly pertaining to a brother (more affectionate than *fraternal*)	**fraternal** frə-'tərn-ᵊl 1. brotherly 2. having to do with a *fraternal* society (a group organized to pursue a common goal in brotherly union)
daughterly pertaining to a daughter (less formal than *filial*)	**filial** 'fil-ē-əl of or befitting a daughter or son, as *filial* respect
childlike of or like a child in a good sense, as *childlike* innocence	**infantile** 'in-fən-ˌtīl of or like a very young child; babyish
childish of or like child in a bad sense, as *childish* mentality	**puerile** 'pyu̇(-ə)r-əl foolish for a grown-up to say or do, as a *puerile* remark
manly having the qualities usually considered desirable in a man, as *manly* independence	**masculine** 'mas-kyə-lən 1. denoting the opposite gender of feminine 2. having qualities appropriate to a man

virile 'vir-əl
having the physical capabilities of a male (stronger word than *masculine*)

womanly
having the qualities usually considered desirable in an adult woman, as *womanly* intuition

feminine
1. denoting the opposite gender of masculine
2. having the features, qualities, and characteristics belonging to women

devilish
like a devil; mischievous

diabolic(al)   dī-ə-'bäl-ik(-i-kəl)
very cruel; wicked; fiendish (stronger word than *devilish*)

bearish
1. like a bear; rough
2. tending to depress stock prices
3. expecting a fall in stock prices

ursine 'ər-ˌsīn
of or like a bear

bullish
1. like a bull; obstinate
2. tending to cause rises in stock prices
3. expecting a rise in stock prices

taurine 'tȯr-ˌīn
1. of or like a bull
2. relating to Taurus (a sign of the zodiac)

catlike
like a cat; stealthy

feline 'fē-ˌlīn
of or pertaining to the cat family (cat, lion, tiger, leopard, etc.); sly; stealthy

cowlike
resembling a cow
oxlike
resembling an ox

bovine 'bō-ˌvīn
1. of or like the cow or ox
2. sluggish and patient, as a *bovine* disposition

doggish
doglike

canine 'kā-ˌnīn
1. of or pertaining to the dog family (dog, wolf, jackal, etc.)
2. designating one of the four pointed teeth next to the incisors

donkeyish
like a donkey

asinine 'as-ᵊn-ˌīn
like an ass or donkey (thought to be the most stupid beast of burden); stupid; silly

fishy
like a fish in smell or taste

piscine 'pi-ˌsēn
of or like a fish

foxy
foxlike; wily; sly

vulpine 'vəl-ˌpīn
of or like a fox; crafty; cunning

goatish
goatlike; coarse; lustful

hircine 'hər-ˌsīn
goatlike, especially in smell

horsy
having to do with horses or horse
racing as *horsy* talk

equine 'ē-ˌkwīn
of or like a horse

piggish
hoggish, swinish

porcine 'pȯr-ˌsīn
of or like a pig

sheepish
1. like a sheep in timidity or
stupidity
2. awkwardly bashful or
embarrassed

ovine 'ō-ˌvīn
of or like a sheep

wolfish
characteristic of a wolf; ferocious

lupine 'lü-ˌpīn
of or like a wolf; ravenous

bloody
smeared with blood; involving
bloodshed

sanguine 'saŋ-gwən
1. having a ruddy color, as a
sanguine complexion
2. confident, as *sanguine* of
success

sanguinary 'saŋ-gwə-ˌner-ē
bloody; as a *sanguinary* battle

EXERCISE 7.4: ANALOGIES

Write the *letter* of the word or words that best completes the analogy.

1. *Canine* is to *dog* as *feline* is to __?__. *a.* ox *b.* wolf *c.* bull *d.* tiger
   e. donkey
2. *Fraternal* is to *brother* as *filial* is to __?__. *a.* son *b.* son-in-law
   c. daughter *d.* son or daughter *e.* daughter-in-law
3. *Neigh* is to *equine* as *bleat* is to __?__. *a.* horsy *b.* bashful
   c. sanguinary *d.* zodiacal *e.* ovine
4. *Mature* is to *puerile* as *intelligent* is to __?__. *a.* paternal *b.* asinine
   c. cunning *d.* porcine *e.* infantile

5. *Courageous* is to *mettle* as *sanguine* is to __?__. *a.* success *b.* despair *c.* battle *d.* complexion *e.* hope

6. *Bullish* is to *bearish* as *up* is to __?__. *a.* above *b.* under *c.* down *d.* over *e.* beyond

7. *Devilish* is to *diabolical* as *interested* is to __?__. *a.* spoiled *b.* enthusiastic *c.* ruddy *d.* cherubic *e.* clever

8. *Cow* is to *bull* as *feminine* is to __?__. *a.* masculine *b.* ferocity *c.* bovine *d.* manly *e.* virile

9. *Bear* is to *ursine* as *fox* is to __?__. *a.* vulpine *b.* taurine *c.* lupine *d.* wily *e.* stealthy

10. *Hircine* is to *goat* as *piscine* is to __?__. *a.* leopard *b.* speed *c.* lion *d.* fish *e.* swine

EXERCISE 7.5: SENTENCE COMPLETION

Write the most appropriate word from the vocabulary list below.

VOCABULARY LIST

sanguinary	canine	puerile
diabolical	bearish	feminine
lupine	filial	bullish
fraternal	vulpine	feline
sheepish	masculine	maternal

1. Joe's only response when confronted with his blunder was a __?__ (*awkwardly bashful*) grin.

2. The child followed her older sister with a kind of __?__ (*pertaining to the dog family*) devotion.

3. My cousin is selling her shares; she is no longer __?__ (*expecting a rise in stock prices*).

4. The blackmailer had devised a __?__ (*fiendish*) scheme for extorting money from his victim.

5. Some parents do not know how to cope with __?__ (*of a son or daughter*) disobedience.

6. Rarely have we witnessed such __?__ (*foolish*) behavior from a mature person.

7. The __?__ (*used to denote a female*) form of "confidant" is "confidante."

8. My __?__ (*on my mother's side*) grandfather was a Senator.

9. At the close of THE CALL OF THE WILD, the dog Buck gradually lapses into __?__ (*wolfish*) characteristics.

10. The fratricidal Battle of Gettysburg was one of the world's most __?__ (*bloody*) conflicts.

2. Verbs

FROM ANGLO-SAXON	FROM LATIN	
beget	procreate	'prō-krē-ˌāt
	generate	'jen-ə-ˌrāt
begin	originate	ə-'rij-ə-ˌnāt
	initiate	in-'ish-ē-ˌāt
behead	decapitate	di-'kap-ə-ˌtāt
bless	consecrate	'kän-sə-ˌkrāt
bow, stoop	condescend	ˌkän-di-'send
	prostrate	'präs-ˌtrāt
break	disintegrate	dis-'int-ə-ˌgrāt
	invalidate	in-'val-ə-ˌdāt
chew	masticate	'mas-tə-ˌkāt
curse	execrate	'ek-sə-ˌkrāt
drink	imbibe	im-'bīb
eat	devour	di-'vaủ(ə)r
	consume	kən-'süm
flay, fleece, skin	excoriate	ek-'skȯr-e-ˌāt
free	emancipate	i-'man-sə-ˌpāt
	liberate	'lib-ə-ˌrāt
frighten	intimidate	in-'tim-ə-ˌdāt
lie	prevaricate	pri-'var-ə-ˌkāt
lighten	relieve	ri-'lēv
	alleviate	ə-'lē-vē-ˌāt
sail	navigate	'nav-ə-ˌgāt
shorten	abridge	ə-'brij
	abbreviate	ə-'brē-vē-ˌāt
show	demonstrate	'dem-ən-ˌstrāt
soothe	assuage	ə-'swāj
	pacify	'pas-ə-ˌfī
spit	expectorate	ek-'spek-tə-ˌrāt
steal	peculate	'pek-yə-ˌlāt
strengthen	corroborate	kə-'räb-ə-ˌrāt
	invigorate	in-'vig-ə-ˌrāt
sweat	perspire	pər-'spī-ə(r)

take (for oneself)	appropriate	ə-prō-prē-ˌāt
think	cogitate	ˈkäj-ə-ˌtāt
	ratiocinate	ˌrat-ē-ˈōs-ᵊn-ˌāt
twinkle, sparkle	scintillate	ˈsint-ᵊl-ˌāt
understand	comprehend	ˌkäm-pri-ˈhend
withstand	resist	ri-ˈzist
	oppose	ə-ˈpōz
worship	venerate	ˈven-ə-ˌrāt
	revere	ri-ˈvi-ə(r)
yield	capitulate	kə-ˈpich-ə-ˌlāt
	succumb	sə-ˈkəm

EXERCISE 7.6: LATIN-DERIVED SYNONYMS

Replace the italicized Anglo-Saxon word with a Latin-derived synonym from the verb list just presented.

1. Tell the truth. Don't *lie.*
2. The young acrobat gave a *sparkling* performance.
3. Your opponents will *flay* you if you accuse them without proof.
4. We cannot *understand* how you can be intimidated by such a small dog.
5. Don't gulp down your food; take the time to *chew* it.
6. At the end of the play, Macbeth is *beheaded* by Macduff.
7. *Spitting* in a public place is an offense punishable by a fine.
8. I am not afraid of you; you can't *frighten* me.
9. Sir Toby Belch's excessive *drinking* got him into trouble with his niece.
10. We shall evict those who have illegally *taken* our homes and our land.

3. Nouns

FROM ANGLO-SAXON		FROM LATIN
blessing	benediction	ˌben-ə-ˈdik-shən
breach	infraction	in-ˈfrak-shən
	rupture	ˈrəp-chə(r)
burden	obligation	ˌäb-lə-ˈgā-shən
curse	execration	ˌek-sə-ˈkrā-shən

	malediction	ˌmal-ə-'dik-shən
fire	conflagration	ˌkän-flə-'grā-shən
food	nutriment	'n(y)ü-trə-mənt
greed	avarice	'av-(ə-)rəs
heaven	firmament	'fər-mə-mənt
home	domicile	'däm-ə-ˌsīl
	residence	'rez-əd-əns
mirth	hilarity	hil-'ar-ət-ē
name	appellation	ˌap-ə-'lā-shən
oath	affirmation	ˌaf-ə(r)-'mā-shən
shame	ignominy	'ig-nə-ˌmin-ē
shard	fragment	'frag-mənt
smear	vilification	ˌvil-ə-fə-'kā-shən
snake	reptile	'rep-tᵊl
sorrow	contrition	kən-'trish-ən
	remorse	ri-'mȯrs
speed	velocity	və-'läs-ət-ē
	celerity	sə-'ler-ət-ē
strength	impregnability	im-ˌpreg-nə-'bil-ət-ē
theft	larceny	'lars-ə-nē
	peculation	ˌpek-yə-'lā-shən
thread	filament	'fil-ə-mənt
threat	menace	'men-əs
truth	verity (of things)	'ver-ət-ē
truthfulness	veracity (of persons)	və-'ras-ət-ē
wedding	nuptials	'nəp-shəlz

EXERCISE 7.7: SENTENCE COMPLETION

Which of the two terms makes the sentence correct?

1. It is a well-known __?__ that the early bird catches the worm.   *a.* verity   *b.* veracity
2. The guillotine was an instrument of __?__.   *a.* capitulation   *b.* decapitation
3. It was difficult to carry the __?__ crowbar.   *a.* lissome   *b.* cumbersome
4. Cats, leopards, and tigers belong to the __?__ family.   *a.* feline   *b.* canine

5. Dan's brawl with the umpire was a serious __?__ of the rules of the game. *a.* fragment *b.* breach
6. Shares of stock are relatively cheaper in a __?__ market. *a.* bullish *b.* bearish
7. If you have attended regularly and done the assignments, you should feel __?__ of passing. *a.* sanguinary *b.* sanguine
8. Do not interfere in matters that are not your concern, or you will be called __?__. *a.* meddlesome *b.* mettlesome
9. The hungry hiker __?__ his sandwiches quickly. *a.* consumed *b.* imbibed
10. The drowning woman was saved by a __?__ of 16. *a.* yearling *b.* stripling

EXERCISE 7.8: BRAINTEASERS

Write the complete word.

1. The Rock of Gibraltar is a symbol of **(6)nab(5)**.
2. How can we forgive those who feel no **(3)or(2)** for their misdeeds?
3. The hunger striker drank some water but refused **(2)trim(3)**.
4. We have no faith in the **(1)era(4)** of a prevaricator.
5. There was not a cloud in the **fir(6)**.
6. The thief looked so innocent that one would not have thought him capable of **(1)arc(3)**.
7. Light travels at a much higher **(4)city** than sound.
8. There is no **(2)no(4)** in defeat if one has done one's best.
9. "The Father of His Country" is an **(3)ell(5)** conferred on George Washington by his fellow Americans.
10. The vase fell and shattered into a hundred **(1)hard(1)**.

EXERCISE 7.9: CONCISE WRITING

Express the thought of each sentence below in no more than four words.

1. She paid no attention to her brothers and her sisters.
2. Many of those who invest are expecting a fall in the price of stocks.
3. Your friend had an awkwardly bashful grin on his face.
4. Their praise was offensive because it obviously was not sincere.
5. Don't do or say things that are foolish for a grown-up to do or say.
6. The ones who had been digging were covered with grime.

7. The plan that you are presenting is full of encumbrances.
8. Who are the individuals who took our bicycles for their own personal use?
9. The remarks that they made caused us to seem little and unimportant.
10. Those who have the authority of officials often move at a slow pace.

EXERCISE 7.10: COMPOSITION

Answer in two or three sentences.

1. How serious a menace are drivers who imbibe? Why?
2. Under what circumstances, if any, might it be forgiveable for an individual to appropriate a vacant domicile? Explain.
3. Why do some candidates stoop to vilification in the closing hours of a political campaign?
4. Should the shortage of jail space influence judges in sentencing those who have committed larceny but no other infractions? Explain.
5. Under what circumstances would it be ignominy to capitulate? Explain.

CHAPTER 8

French Words in English

English has never hesitated to adopt useful French words. Any French expression that describes an idea better than the corresponding English expression may sooner or later be incorporated into English. The process has been going on for centuries.

This chapter will teach you how to use some of the more important French words and expressions that are today part of an educated person's English vocabulary.

1. Terms Describing Persons

WORD	MEANING AND TYPICAL USE
au courant (*adj.*) ˌō-ˌku-ˈräⁿ	well-informed; up-to-date By reading reviews, you can keep *au courant* with the latest in literature, films, television, and the theater.
blasé (*adj.*) blä-ˈzā	tired of pleasures; bored After a while, Edna had had her fill of mountain scenery, and when the guide pointed out some additional peaks, she reacted in a *blasé* manner.
bourgeois (*adj.*) ˈbürzh-ˌwä	1. having to do with the middle class 2. concerned with petty, materialistic interests; lacking in culture or refinement At first, the aristocrat firmly opposed his daughter's prospective marriage into a *bourgeois* family.
chic (*adj.*) ˈshēk	stylish You looked very *chic* in your new outfit.

216

clairvoyant (*adj.*)
kler-'voi-ənt

clear-sighted; unusually perceptive
    If General Braddock had listened to George Washington, his *clairvoyant* young subordinate, he would not have been caught in an ambush.

complaisant (*adj.*)
kəm-'plāz-ᵊnt

willing to please; obliging; amiable
    We were sorry to hear that the Reeds were moving because they had been very *complaisant* neighbors.

debonair (*adj.*)
ˌdeb-ə-'ne(ə)r

courteous, gracious, and charming
    The headwaiter was *debonair* with the guests but firm with the waiters.

gauche (*adj.*)
'gōsh

lacking social grace; crude; tactless; awkward
    It would be *gauche* for a host or hostess to begin eating before their guests have been served.

maladroit (*adj.*)
ˌmal-ə-'droit

unskillful; clumsy
(*ant.* **adroit**)
    Our new supervisor is clever in many matters in which his predecessor was *maladroit*.

naive (*adj.*)
nä-'ēv

simple in nature; artless; ingenuous
    You are *naive* if you believe implacable foes can be reconciled easily.

nonchalant (*adj.*)
ˌnän-shə-'länt

without concern or enthusiasm; indifferent
    I am amazed that you can be so *nonchalant* about the coming test when everyone else is so worried.

EXERCISE 8.1

Write the most appropriate word or expression from group 1.

1. Some advertising is so exaggerated that only a(n) __?__ person would believe it.
2. If every meal were a banquet, we should soon greet even the most delicious food with a(n) __?__ expression.
3. Read a good daily newspaper to keep __?__ with what is going on in the world.
4. The cuts on Ralph's face show that he is __?__ in the use of his razor.
5. Unlike her discourteous predecessor, the new office manager is quite __?__ .

2. Terms for Persons

attaché (*n.*)
ˌat-ə-ˈshā
member of the diplomatic staff of an ambassador or minister
We were unable to see the ambassador, but we spoke to one of the *attachés*.

bourgeoisie (*n.*)
ˌbürzh-wä-ˈzē
the middle class
A strong *bourgeoisie* contributes to a nation's prosperity.

chargé d'affaires (*n.*)
ˈshär-ˌzhäd-ə-ˈfe(ə)r
temporary substitute for an ambassador
Whom did the President designate as *chargé d'affaires* when he recalled the ambassador?

concierge (*n.*)
kōⁿˈsyerzh
doorkeeper; custodian; janitor
We had notified the *concierge* that we were expecting visitors, and he admitted them as soon as they arrived.

confrere (*n.*)
ˈkōⁿ-ˌfre(ə)r
colleague; co-worker; comrade
The attorney introduced us to his *confrere*, Mr. Quinones; they share the same office.

connoisseur (*n.*)
ˌkän-ə-ˈsər
expert; critical judge
To verify the gem's value, we consulted a *connoisseur* of rare diamonds.

coterie (*n.*)
ˈkōt-ə-rē
set or circle of acquaintances; clique
Helen won't bowl with us; she has her own *coterie* of bowling friends.

debutante (*n.*)
ˈdeb-yu̇-ˌtänt
young woman who has just had her *debut* (first introduction into society)
The *debutante's* photograph was at the head of the society page.

devotee (*n.*)
ˌdev-ə-ˈtē
zealous follower; ardent adherent of something or someone; fan
Eva is a *devotee* of the guitar.

elite (*n.*)
ā-ˈlēt
group of individuals thought to be superior; aristocracy; choice part
Fred likes to consider himself a member of the intellectual *elite*.

émigré, *masc.* (*n.*)
ʹem-i-ˌgrā
(**émigrée,** *fem.*)

refugee; person who has fled (*emigrated*) from his or her native land because of political conditions
A committee was formed to find housing and employment for the anxious *émigrés.*

entourage (*n.*)
ˌän-tu̇-ʹräzh

group of attendants, assistants, or associates accompanying a person
Several dignitaries were at the airport to welcome the Prime Minister and his *entourage.*

entrepreneur (*n.*)
än-trə-prə-ʹnər

one who assumes the risks and management of a business
What *entrepreneur* will invest capital unless there is some prospect of a profit?

envoy (*n.*)
ʹen-ˌvȯi

diplomatic agent or messenger
The President's *envoy* to the conference has not yet been chosen.

fiancé, *masc.* (*n.*)
ˌfē-än-ʹsā
(**fiancée,** *fem.*)

person engaged to be married
Madeline introduced Mr. Cole as her *fiancé.*

gendarme (*n.*)
ʹzhän-ˌdärm

armed police officer, especially in France and other European countries
The chargé d'affaires requested that extra *gendarmes* be posted outside the embassy.

gourmand (*n.*)
ʹgu̇(ə)r-ˌmänd

person excessively fond of eating and drinking; glutton
The food was so good that I ate more than I should have. I behaved like a *gourmand.*

gourmet (*n.*)
ʹgu̇(ə)r-ˌmā

connoisseur in eating and drinking
Valerie can recommend a good restaurant; she is a *gourmet.*

ingenue (*n.*)
ʹan-jə-ˌnü

actress playing the role of a naive young woman; naive young woman
She was as simple and pretty as a film *ingenue.*

maître d'hôtel (*n.*)
ˌmā-trə-dō-ʹtel
or **maître d'**

headwaiter
The *maître d'hôtel* supervises the waiters.

martinet (*n.*)
ˌmärt-ᵊn-ʹet

person who enforces very strict discipline
Our dean is an understanding counselor, not a *martinet.*

nonpareil (*n.*)
nän-pǝ-'rel

person of unequalled excellence; paragon
Few can compare with Stella as a speller. Her classmates regard her as the *nonpareil.*

nouveaux riches (*n. pl.*)
ˌnü-vō-'rēsh

persons newly rich
An unexpected inheritance lifted him into the ranks of the *nouveaux riches.*

parvenu, *masc.* (*n.*)
'pär-vǝ-ˌn(y)ü
(**parvenue,** *fem.*)

person suddenly risen to wealth or power who lacks the proper social qualifications; upstart
When the entrepreneur first moved into the exclusive area, his aristocratic neighbors regarded him as a *parvenu.*

protégé, *masc.* (*n.*)
'prōt-ǝ-ˌzhā
(**protégée,** *fem.*)

person under the care of another
The veteran infielder passed on numerous fielding hints to his young *protégé.*

raconteur (*n.*)
ˌrak-än-'tǝr

person who excels in telling stories, anecdotes, etc.
Mark Twain was an excellent *raconteur.*

valet (*n.*)
'val-ǝt

manservant who attends to the personal needs of his employer, as by taking care of his employer's clothes
That morning, the old gentleman got dressed without the help of his *valet.*

EXERCISE 8.2

Write the most appropriate word or expression from group 2.

1. After a particularly unpleasant quarrel with her __?__, Rita considered breaking their engagement.
2. Between the nobles on one extreme and the peasants on the other, a middle class known as the __?__ emerged.
3. The __?__ brushed his employer's clothes.
4. Sherlock Holmes collaborated on the case with his __?__, Dr. Watson.
5. Louise can relate an anecdote better than I; she is a fine __?__ .
6. Though the food was delicious, Ed refused a second helping; he is no __?__ .
7. If I were a(n) __?__, I would be able to tell whether the cheese in this salad is imported or domestic.
8. When the young attorney was elected to a seat on the board of directors, some of the veteran members considered her a(n) __?__ .

9. A man who flees his native land to escape political oppression is a(n) __?__ .

10. Though the Allens are friendly with everyone, they have rarely visited with anyone outside their tightly knit __?__ .

---

3. Terms for Traits or Feelings of Persons

---

aplomb (*n.*)
ə-'pləm

absolute confidence in oneself; poise; self-possession
    At the public hearing, the mayor met all challenges with his customary *aplomb*.

éclat (*n.*)
ā-'klä

brilliancy of achievement
    The violinist performed with rare *éclat*.

élan (*n.*)
ā-'lä^n

enthusiasm; eagerness for action
    Because the cast had rehearsed with such *élan*, the director had few apprehensions about the opening-night performance.

ennui (*n.*)
än-'wē

feeling of weariness and discontent; boredom; tedium
    You too might suffer from *ennui* if you had to spend months in a hospital bed.

esprit de corps (*n.*)
es-,prēd-ə-'kȯ(ə)r

feeling of union and common interest pervading a group; devotion to a group or to its ideals
    The employees showed extraordinary *esprit de corps* when they volunteered to work Saturdays for the duration of the crisis.

finesse (*n.*)
fə-'nes

skill and adroitness in handling a difficult situation
    The adroit prosecutor conducted the cross-examination with admirable *finesse*.

legerdemain (*n.*)
,lej-ərd-ə-'mān

sleight of hand; artful trick
    By a feat of *legerdemain*, the magician produced a rabbit from her hat.

malaise (*n.*)
ma-'lāz

vague feeling of bodily discomfort or illness
    After the late, heavy supper, he experienced a feeling of *malaise*.

noblesse oblige (*n.*)
nō-,bles-ə-'blēzh

principle that persons of high rank or birth are obliged to act nobly

In the olden days, kings and other nobles, observing the principle of *noblesse oblige,* fought at the head of their troops.

rapport (*n.*)   relationship characterized by harmony, confor-
ra-'pȯ(ə)r   mity, or affinity
      A common interest in gardening brought Molly and Loretta into closer *rapport.*

sangfroid (*n.*)   coolness of mind or composure in difficult circum-
'säⁿ-frwä   stances; equanimity
      The quarterback's *sangfroid* during the last tense moments of the game enabled him to call the winning play.

savoir faire (*n.*)   knowledge of just what to do; tact
ˌsav-ˌwär-'fe(ə)r   You need both capital and *savoir faire* to be a successful entrepreneur.

EXERCISE 8.3

Write the most appropriate word or expression from group 3.

1. Joel is tactful; he has plenty of __?__ .
2. Your physician may help you obtain some relief from the __?__ that accompanies a severe cold.
3. Instead of reducing their subordinates' salaries, the executives cut their own compensation substantially, according to the principle of __?__ .
4. To do card tricks, you have to be good at __?__ .
5. If you are bored, try reading detective stories; they help to overcome __?__ .

4. Terms Dealing With Conversation and Writing

adieu (*n.*)   good-bye; farewell
ə-'d(y)ü   On commencement day we shall bid *adieu* to our alma mater.

au revoir (*n.*)   good-bye till we meet again
ˌȯr-əv-'wär   Since I hope to see you again, I'll say *au revoir* rather than adieu.

billet-doux (*n.*)
͵bil-ā-'dü

love letter
A timely *billet-doux* patched up the lovers' quarrel.

bon mot (*n.*)
bōⁿ-'mō

clever saying; witty remark
The jester Yorick often set the table a-roaring with a well-placed *bon mot*.

brochure (*n.*)
brō-'shu̇(ə)r

pamphlet; treatise
This helpful *brochure* explains the procedures for obtaining a driver's license.

canard (*n.*)
kə-'närd

false rumor; absurd story; hoax
It took a public appearance by the monarch to silence the *canard* that he had been assassinated.

cliché (*n.*)
klē-'shā

trite or worn-out expression
Two *clichés* that we can easily do without are ''first and foremost'' and ''last but not least.''

entre nous (*adv.*)
͵än-trə-'nü

between us; confidentially
The Wildcats expect to win, but *entre nous* their chances are not too good.

mot juste (*n.*)
mō-zhu̅e̅st

the exactly right word
To improve your writing, try to find the *mot juste* for each idea. Also, avoid clichés.

nom de plume (*n.*)
͵näm-di-'plüm

pen name; pseudonym
Benjamin Franklin used the *nom de plume* ''Silence Dogood'' when he submitted essays to his brother's newspaper.

précis (*n.*)
'prā-sē

brief summary
Include only the essential points when you write a *précis*.

repartee (*n.*)
͵rep-ər-'tē

skill of replying quickly, cleverly, and humorously; witty reply
Dorothy Parker was known for her *repartee*.

résumé (*n.*)
'rez-ə-͵mā

1. brief account of personal, educational, and professional qualifications and experience submitted by an applicant for a position
Martha sent copies of her *résumé* to fourteen prospective employers.
2. summary
The teacher asked us to write a *résumé* of the last act.

riposte (*n.*)
ri-'pōst

1. quick retort or repartee
   When Dan was criticized for his error, his *riposte* was "All of us make mistakes."
2. in fencing, a quick return thrust after a parry
   The fencing instructor showed us how to defend ourselves against *ripostes*.

tête-à-tête (*n.*)
ˌtāt-ə-'tāt

private conversation between two persons
   Before answering, the witness had a *tête-à-tête* with his attorney.

EXERCISE 8.4

Write the most appropriate word or expression from group 4.

1. There are valuable hints on safe driving in this sixteen-page __?__ .
2. Avoid the expression "old as the hills"; it is a(n) __?__ .
3. Investigation proved the story was unfounded; it was just a(n) __?__ .
4. The manager went out to the mound for a brief __?__ with his faltering pitcher.
5. Everyone supposes this diamond is genuine, but __?__ it's only an imitation.

5. Terms Dealing With Situations

bête noire (*n.*)
ˌbāt-nə-'wär

object or person dreaded; bugbear
   He enjoyed all his subjects except mathematics, his *bête noire*.

carte blanche (*n.*)
'kärt-'blä^nsh

full discretionary power; freedom to use one's own judgment
   Ms. Mauro gave her assistant *carte blanche* in managing the office while she was away.

cause célèbre (*n.*)
ˌkōz-sā-'lebrᵊ

famous case in law that arouses considerable interest; an incident or situation attracting much attention
   The trial of John Peter Zenger, a *cause célèbre* in the eighteenth century, helped to establish freedom of the press in America.

contretemps (*n.*)
'kän-trə-₊täⁿ

inopportune occurrence; embarrassing situation or mishap

The proctor arrived late but that wasn't the only *contretemps*; the examination sent to our room was not the one we were supposed to take.

cul-de-sac (*n.*)
₊kəl-di-'sak

blind alley

Painting proved to be a *cul-de-sac* for Philip Carey, as he had no real talent.

debacle (*n.*)
di-'bäk-əl

collapse, overthrow; rout

The *debacle* at Waterloo signaled the end of Napoleon's power.

fait accompli (*n.*)
₊fā-ta-kōⁿ-'plē

thing already done

A reconciliation between the bitter foes, once thought an impossibility, may soon become a *fait accompli*.

faux pas (*n.*)
(')fō-'pä

misstep or blunder in conduct, manners, speech, etc.

One of the guests got no dessert because Dolores had committed the *faux pas* of serving herself too generous a helping.

impasse (*n.*)
'im-₊pas

deadlock; predicament affording no escape; impassable road

The judge was informed that the jury had reached an *impasse* and could deliberate no further.

liaison (*n.*)
'lē-ə-₊zän

bond; linking up; coordination of activities

By joining the alumni association, graduates can maintain their *liaison* with the school.

mélange (*n.*)
mā-'läⁿzh

mixture; medley; potpourri

The last amateur show was a *mélange* of dramatic skits, acrobatics, ballet, popular tunes, and classical music.

mirage (*n.*)
mə-'räzh

optical illusion

The sheet of water we thought we saw on the road ahead turned out to be only a *mirage*.

EXERCISE 8.5

Write the most appropriate word or expression from group 5.

1. Your flippant remark to Mrs. Lee about her ailing son was a(n) _?_ .
2. The inhabitants of the remote Eskimo village had practically no _?_ with the outside world.
3. Mr. Briggs never concerned himself with hiring or dismissing employees, having given his plant manager _?_ in these matters.
4. Despite seventeen hours of continuous deliberations, the weary negotiators still faced a(n) _?_ over wages.
5. Alice's position turned out to be a(n) _?_ , since it offered no opportunity for advancement.

Review Exercises

REVIEW 1: MEANINGS

Match each word or expression in column I with the *letter* of its correct meaning in column II.

	COLUMN I		COLUMN II
1.	refugee	a.	devotee
2.	till we meet again	b.	debacle
3.	well-informed	c.	bête noire
4.	partisan	d.	concierge
5.	brief summary	e.	sangfroid
6.	hoax	f.	nom de plume
7.	bugbear	g.	émigré
8.	rout	h.	précis
9.	love letter	i.	au revoir
10.	equanimity	j.	canard
11.	doorkeeper	k.	au courant
12.	pen name	l.	billet-doux

REVIEW 2: SENTENCE COMPLETION

On your answer page, enter the *letter* of the choice that best completes the sentence.

1. In serving the soup, the __?__ waitress spilled some of it on the guest of honor.
   a. chic *b.* maladroit *c.* debonair
2. Monotonous repetition usually brings on __?__ .
   a. ennui *b.* éclat *c.* savoir faire
3. I'll be glad to give my opinion, but you must realize I am no __?__ .
   a. raconteur *b.* martinet *c.* connoisseur
4. A bibliophile is usually a __?__ of good literature.
   a. protégée *b.* devotee *c.* repartee
5. We made a right turn into the next street, but it proved to be a __?__ .
   a. mélange *b.* cul-de-sac *c.* canard

6. The President was represented at the state funeral in Paris by a special __?__.
   a. ingenue b. bourgeoisie c. envoy
7. We had a __?__ over a couple of ice-cream sodas.
   a. bête noire b. tête-à-tête c. mirage
8. Do not commit the __?__ of seating Frank next to Rhoda because they are not on speaking terms.
   a. faux pas b. impasse c. riposte
9. Today, my biology teacher began with a __?__ of yesterday's lesson.
   a. rapport b. résumé c. brochure
10. Because of her excellent training, she has developed remarkable __?__ at the piano.
    a. sangfroid b. élan c. finesse
11. The launch of the space shuttle was delayed by one __?__ after another.
    a. mirage b. contretemps c. brochure
12. It would be __?__ to come to an employment interview in a jogging suit.
    a. chic b. complaisant c. gauche

REVIEW 3: BRAINTEASERS

Write the complete word.

1. The celebrity was surrounded by a **cot**(4) of admirers.
2. She was as nervous as a(n) (4)**tan**(2) at a coming-out party.
3. You don't have to be so strict. Don't be a(n) (5)**net**.
4. No further progress is possible. We are at a(n) (2)**pass**(1).
5. They get along poorly. There is little **rap**(4) between them.
6. A(n) (1)**lair**(6) person could have seen that trouble was coming.
7. A conceited person who has no talent often thinks that he or she is the (3)**par**(3).
8. To be a food columnist, you must be a writer and a(n) (4)**met**.
9. Most of our school's intellectual (1)**lit**(1) is in the Honor Society.
10. She enjoys opera, and she is also a(n) (2)**vote**(1) of the ballet.

REVIEW 4: COMPOSITION

Answer in two or three sentences.

1. Can a naive entrepreneur succeed in business? Why, or why not?
2. Describe a situation in which it might not be a faux pas to give someone else carte blanche to make decisions for you.

3. Is it normal for employees who consider themselves in a cul-de-sac to show ennui? Explain.

4. How would a club's esprit de corps be affected if its president were a martinet?

5. Why must you have rapport with your audience to succeed as a raconteur?

---

6. Terms Dealing With History and Government

coup d'etat (*n.*)
ˌküd-ə-ˈtä
or **coup**
ˈkü

sudden violent, or illegal overthrow of a government
Napoleon seized power by a *coup d'etat.*

demarche (*n.*)
dā-ˈmärsh

course of action, especially one involving a change of policy
Hitler's attack on Russia, shortly after his pact with Stalin, was a stunning *demarche.*

détente (*n.*)
dā-ˈtänt

a relaxing, as of strained relations between nations
An effective world disarmament treaty should bring a *détente* in international tensions.

entente (*n.*)
än-ˈtänt

understanding or agreement between governments
Canada and the United States have a long-standing *entente* on border problems.

laissez-faire (*n.*)
ˌles-ˌā-ˈfe(ə)r

absence of government interference or regulation
Adam Smith believed a policy of *laissez-faire* toward business would benefit a nation.

lettre de cachet (*n.*)
ˌle-trə-də-ˌka-ˈshā

sealed letter obtainable from the King of France (before the Revolution) ordering the imprisonment without trial of the person named in the letter
Dr. Manette was imprisoned through a *lettre de cachet.*

premier (*n.*)
ˌprē-mē-ər

prime minister
A *premier* can be forced out of office at any time by a vote of no confidence.

rapprochement (*n.*)
ˌrap-ˌrōsh-ˈmä^n

establishment or state of cordial relations; coming together

The gradual *rapprochement* between these two nations, long traditional enemies, cheered all Europeans.

regime (*n.*)   system of government or rule
rā-'zhēm   The coup d'etat brought to power a *regime* that restored civil liberties to the oppressed people.

EXERCISE 8.6

Write the most appropriate word or expression from group 6.

1. Do you favor strict regulation of business or a policy of __?__ ?
2. The tyrannical ruler was eventually overthrown by a(n) __?__ .
3. The newly elected officials will face many problems left by the outgoing __?__ .
4. Before 1789, a French nobleman could have an enemy imprisoned without trial by obtaining a(n) __?__ .
5. Hopes for world peace rose sharply with reports of a(n) __?__ in the strained relations between the two major powers.

---

7. Terms Dealing With the Arts

---

avant-garde (*n.*)   experimentalists or innovators in any art
ˌäv-ˌän-'gärd   Walt Whitman was no conservative; his daring innovations in poetry place him in the *avant-garde* of nineteenth-century writers.

bas-relief (*n.*)   carving or sculpture in which the figures project only
ˌbä-ri-'lēf   slightly from the background
          The ancient Greek Parthenon is famed for its beautiful sculpture in *bas-relief*.

baton (*n.*)   stick with which a conductor beats time for an or-
ba-'tän   chestra or band
          A downbeat is the downward stroke of the conductor's *baton*, denoting the principally accented note of a measure.

chef d'oeuvre (*n.*)   masterpiece in art, literature, etc.
shā-'dəvrə   Many connoisseurs regard HAMLET as Shakespeare's *chef d'oeuvre*.

denouement (*n.*)
͵dā-nü-'mäⁿ

solution ("untying") of the plot in a play, story, or complex situation; outcome; end

In the *denouement* of GREAT EXPECTATIONS, Pip's benefactor is identified as the escaped convict whom Pip had once befriended.

encore (*n.*)
'än-͵kȯ(ə)r

repetition of a performance (or the rendition of an additional selection) in response to the demand from an audience

In appreciation of the enthusiastic applause, the vocalist sang an *encore*.

genre (*n.*)
'zhän-rə

1. kind; sort; category

The literary *genre* to which Virginia Woolf contributed most is the novel.

2. style of painting depicting scenes from everyday life

Painters of *genre* choose scenes from everyday life as their subject matter.

musicale (*n.*)
͵myü-zi-'kal

social gathering, with music as the featured entertainment

Last night's *musicale* at the White House featured entertainment by a popular folk singer.

palette (*n.*)
'pal-ət

thin board (with a thumb hole at one end) on which an artist lays and mixes colors

After a few strokes on the canvas, an artist reapplies the brush to the *palette* for more paint.

repertoire (*n.*)
'rep-ə(r)-͵twär

1. stock of plays, operas, roles, compositions, etc., that a company or performer is prepared to perform

The guitarist apologized for not playing the requested number, explaining that it was not in his *repertoire*.

2. collection

Whenever I hear a good joke, I add it to my *repertoire*.

vignette (*n.*)
vin-'yet

short verbal description; small, graceful literary sketch

James Joyce's DUBLINERS offers some unforgettable *vignettes* of life in Dublin at the turn of the century.

EXERCISE 8.7

Write the most appropriate word or expression from group 7.

1. After studying poetry, we turned our attention to another __?__, short stories.
2. A novel with a suspenseful plot makes the reader impatient to get to the __?__.
3. If audience reaction is favorable, Selma is prepared to play a(n) __?__.
4. Beethoven's NINTH SYMPHONY is regarded by many as his __?__.
5. By diligent study, the singer added several new numbers to his __?__.

8. Terms Dealing With Food

a la carte (*adv.*)
ˌal-ə-ˈkärt

according to the bill of fare; dish by dish; with a stated price for each dish
   If you order *a la carte*, you select whatever you wish from the bill of fare, paying only for the dishes ordered.

a la mode (*adj.*)
ˈal-ə-ˈmōd

1. according to fashion; stylish
   Most shoppers buy only the latest fashions because they want their clothes to be *a la mode*.
2. with ice cream
   We enjoy apple pie *a la mode*.

aperitif (*n.*)
ˌap-ˌer-ə-ˈtēf

alcoholic drink taken before a meal as an appetizer
   Select a nonalcoholic appetizer, such as tomato juice, if you do not care for an *aperitif*.

bonbon (*n.*)
ˈbän-ˌbän

piece of candy
   For St. Valentine's Day, we gave Mother a heart-shaped box of delicious *bonbons*.

consommé (*n.*)
ˌkän-sə-ˈmā

clear soup; broth
   Ask the waiter if we may order some *consommé* instead of the *soup du jour*.

croissant (*n.*)
ˌkwä-ˈsäⁿ

rich, flaky crescent-shaped roll
   Croissants are more tasty than ordinary rolls.

cuisine (*n.*)
kwi-ˈzēn

style of cooking or preparing food
   This restaurant specializes in French *cuisine*.

demitasse (*n.*)
'dem-ē-ˌtas

small cup for, or of, black coffee
Aunt Dorothy always takes cream with her coffee; she is not fond of *demitasse*.

entrée (*n.*)
'än-trā

main dish at lunch or dinner
We had a choice of the following *entrées*: roast beef, fried chicken, or baked mackerel.

filet (*n.*)
fi-'lā

slice of meat or fish without bones or fat
Because they contain no bones or excess fat, *filets* are more expensive than ordinary cuts of meat.

hors d'oeuvres (*n. pl.*)
ȯr-'dərvz

light food served as an appetizer before the regular courses of a meal
Malcolm purchased olives, celery, and anchovies for the *hors d'oeuvres*.

pièce de résistance (*n.*)
pē-ˌes-də-rə-ˌzē-'stäns

1. main dish
If you eat too much of the introductory dishes, you will have little appetite for the *pièce de résistance*.
2. main item of any collection, series, program, etc.
The preliminaries were followed by the *pièce de résistance*, the title bout.

soup du jour (*n.*)
ˌsüp-də-'zhu̇r

special soup served in a restaurant on a particular day
Often, the only soup a restaurant offers is the *soup du jour*.

table d'hôte (*n.*)
ˌtäb-əl-'dōt

complete meal of several courses offered in a hotel or restaurant at a fixed price
If you order the *table d'hôte*, you pay the fixed price for the entire dinner, even if you do not have some of the dishes.

EXERCISE 8.8

Write the most appropriate word or expression from group 8.

1. Before dinner, our hostess brought in a large tray of appetizing __?__ .
2. Though this chef's style of cooking is quite interesting, it cannot compare with my grandmother's __?__ .
3. When I do not care to have a complete dinner, I order a couple of dishes __?__ .

4. My little sister was so fond of candy that she had to be restricted to one __?__ after each meal.

5. If you like flounder without fishbones, order __?__ of flounder.

6. We would have had some split pea soup, but unfortunately it was not the __?__ .

---

9. Terms Dealing With Dress

---

bouffant (*adj.*)
bü-'fänt

puffed out; full
    Corridors and stairways would have to be widened considerably if all women were to wear *bouffant* skirts.

boutique (*n.*)
bü-'tēk

small shop specializing in fashionable clothes
    Rhoda found her outfit in a midtown *boutique*.

chemise (*n.*)
shə-'mēz

loose-fitting, sacklike dress
    Though more comfortable than most other dresses, the *chemise* has often been ridiculed for its shapelessness.

coiffure (*n.*)
kwä-'fyü(ə)r

style of arranging the hair; headdress
    Sally's *coiffure* was created for her by my sister's hair stylist.

corsage (*n.*)
kȯr-'säzh

small bouquet worn by a woman
    Holly *corsages* are often worn at Christmas.

cravat (*n.*)
krə-'vat

necktie
    He wore a light blue shirt and a navy blue *cravat*.

ensemble (*n.*)
än-'säm-bəl

complete costume of harmonious clothing and accessories
    Her red blouse, black skirt, and matching red slippers made an attractive *ensemble*.

flamboyant (*adj.*)
flam-'bȯi-ənt

flamelike; very ornate; showy
    To add a touch of bright color to his outfit, Jack wore a *flamboyant* scarf.

toupee (*n.*)
tü-'pā

wig
    The actor's blond hair was cleverly concealed by a grey *toupee*.

vogue (*n.*)
'vōg

fashion; accepted style
    Fashions change rapidly; today's style may be out of *vogue* tomorrow.

EXERCISE 8.9

In each blank, insert the most appropriate word from group 9.

1. The excessive heat made George untie his __?__ and unbutton his shirt collar.
2. After trying several elaborate hairstyles, Marie has returned to a simple __?__ .
3. On your visit to Mount Vernon in Virginia, you will see furniture styles that were in __?__ in George and Martha Washington's time.
4. It was easy to identify the guest of honor because of the beautiful __?__ at her shoulder.
5. The gowns in the dress salon include sedate blacks, as well as __?__ reds and golds.

---

10. Miscellaneous Terms

---

ambience (*n.*) äⁿ-'byäns	surrounding atmosphere; environment We enjoyed the restaurant for its food, as well as its *ambience*; never had we dined in pleasanter surroundings.

ambience (*n.*)
äⁿ-'byäns

surrounding atmosphere; environment
    We enjoyed the restaurant for its food, as well as its *ambience*; never had we dined in pleasanter surroundings.

apropos (*adv.*)
ˌap-rə-'pō

by the way; incidentally
    We'll meet you at the station. *Apropos*, when does your train arrive?

apropos (*adj.*)

appropriate; relevant; pertinent
    So far, none of your comments are *apropos*; everything you have said is off the topic.

avoirdupois (*n.*)
ˌav-ərd-ə-'pȯiz

weight; heaviness
    Dieters constantly check their *avoirdupois*.

bagatelle (*n.*)
ˌbag-ə-'tel

trifle
    Pay attention to important matters; don't waste time on *bagatelles*.

coup de grace (*n.*)
ˌküd-ə-'gräs

decisive finishing blow
    We won, 5-1, thanks to Pat. He administered the *coup de grace* by homering with the bases loaded.

en route (*adv.* or *adj.*)
äⁿ-'rüt

1. on the way
    My friends are *en route*; they will be here shortly.

2. along the way
We left before breakfast but stopped for an early lunch *en route*.

etiquette (*n.*)
'et-i-kət

conduct and manners of polite society
According to the rules of *etiquette*, a person should not come to a party to which he or she has not been invited.

facade (*n.*)
fə-'säd

face or front of a building, or of anything
The patient's cheerful smile was just a *facade*; actually, she was suffering from ennui.

fete (*n.*)
'fāt

festival; entertainment; party
Our block party last year was a memorable *fete*.

fete (*v.*)

honor with a fete
Retiring employees are often *feted* at a special dinner.

foyer (*n.*)
'foi(-ə)r

entrance hall; lobby
Let's meet in the *foyer* of the public library.

milieu (*n.*)
mēl-'yə

environment; setting
David found it much easier to make friends in his new *milieu*.

parasol (*n.*)
'par-ə-ˌsȯl

umbrella for protection against the sun
In summer when you stroll on the boardwalk in the noonday sun, it is advisable to take along a *parasol*.

par excellence (*adj.*)
ˌpär-ˌek-sə-'lä^{n}s

above all others of the same sort (follows the word it modifies)
Charles Dickens was a raconteur *par excellence*.

passé (*adj.*)
pa-'sā

old-fashioned; behind the times; outmoded
Recently bought equipment may quickly become *passé*, thanks to the rapid pace of technological innovation.

pince-nez (*n.*)
pa^{n}s-'nā

eyeglasses clipped to the nose by a spring
Since they are held in place by a spring that pinches the nose, *pince-nez* may not be as comfortable as ordinary eyeglasses.

premiere (*n.*)
pri-'mye(ə)r

first performance
The second performance was even better than the *premiere*.

queue (*n.*)
'kyü

line of persons waiting their turn
The *queue* at the box office was so long that I decided to come back another time.

raison d'être (*n.*)
ˌrā-ˌzōⁿ-'detrᵊ

reason or justification for existing
Apparently, Alice lives just for dancing; it is her *raison d'être*.

rendezvous (*n.*)
'rän-di-ˌvü

1. meeting place fixed by prior agreement
We agreed to meet after the test at the handball courts, our usual *rendezvous*.
2. appointment to meet at a fixed time and place
Our *rendezvous* with the coach and captain of the visiting team was set for 2 P.M.

silhouette (*n.*)
ˌsil-ə-'wet

shadow; outline
I knew Jonah was coming to let me in because I recognized his *silhouette* behind the curtained door.

sobriquet (*n.*)
or **soubriquet**
'sō-bri-ˌkā

nickname
Andrew Jackson was known by the *sobriquet* ''Old Hickory.''

souvenir (*n.*)
'sü-və-ˌni(ə)r

reminder; keepsake; memento
The Yearbook, in time to come, will be a treasured *souvenir* of high school days.

tour de force (*n.*)
ˌtü(ə)rd-ə-'fȯrs

feat of strength, skill, or ingenuity
The sixty-yard run was the *tour de force* that won the game for us.

vis-à-vis (*prep.*)
ˌvē-zə-'vē

face to face; opposite
At the banquet table, I had the good fortune to sit *vis-à-vis* an old friend.

EXERCISE 8.10

Write the most appropriate word or expression from group 10.

1. Carmela brought me a print of the Lincoln Memorial as a(n) __?__ of her visit to Washington.
2. Paul mounts the scale morning and night to check his __?__ .
3. After class, my friends gather at our __?__ outside the pizza parlor.
4. Agnes is a mimic __?__ ; no one else in our club can do impersonations as well as she.

5. Because of his flaming hair, Harvey is popularly known by the ___?___ "Red."

6. The small merchants in our area are fearful that the opening of another shopping mall will be the ___?___ for them.

7. Our club is planning a(n) ___?___ in honor of the outgoing president.

8. On the first day in a new school, arriving students find themselves in a bewildering ___?___ .

9. I did not recognize the hotel because its ___?___ and foyer had been modernized since I was last there.

10. Winning the league pennant is an outstanding achievement, but going on to capture the World Series in four straight victories is an even greater ___?___ .

11. When the film had its premiere at our local theater, the ___?___ stretched half way around the block.

12. Blanche, we're glad to see you. ___?___, how is your brother?

Review Exercises

REVIEW 5: MEANINGS

Match each word or expression in column I with the *letter* of its correct meaning in column II.

COLUMN I	COLUMN II
1. piece of candy	*a.* silhouette
2. nickname	*b.* coup d'etat
3. relaxing of strained relations	*c.* consommé
4. full; puffed out	*d.* coup de grace
5. style of cooking	*e.* apropos
6. masterpiece	*f.* bonbon
7. shadow	*g.* chef d'oeuvre
8. weight	*h.* cuisine
9. decisive finishing stroke	*i.* avoirdupois
10. sudden overthrow of a regime	*j.* sobriquet
11. relevant	*k.* détente
12. broth	*l.* bouffant

REVIEW 6: MORE MEANINGS

Write the *letter* of the choice that correctly defines the italicized word or expression.

1. prosperous *bourgeoisie*   *a.* elite   *b.* entrepreneur   *c.* middle class   *d.* citizenry   *e.* officialdom
2. *flamboyant* jacket   *a.* debonair   *b.* warm   *c.* sanguinary   *d.* showy   *e.* stylish
3. happy *denouement*   *a.* ending   *b.* vignette   *c.* milieu   *d.* event   *e.* episode
4. sudden *demarche*   *a.* détente   *b.* reversal   *c.* entrée   *d.* discovery   *e.* aggression
5. attitude of *laissez-faire*   *a.* boredom   *b.* equanimity   *c.* eagerness   *d.* cordiality   *e.* noninterference
6. enduring *entente*   *a.* influence   *b.* understanding   *c.* bitterness   *d.* cause célèbre   *e.* entrance

7. serve *hors d'oeuvres*   *a.* entrée   *b.* appetizers   *c.* desserts   *d.* pièce de résistance   *e.* table d'hôte

8. join the *avant-garde*   *a.* gendarmes   *b.* protégés   *c.* devotees   *d.* underground   *e.* innovators

9. welcome *encore*   *a.* cancellation   *b.* delay   *c.* repetition   *d.* refund   *e.* improvement

10. flavor *par excellence*   *a.* new   *b.* unsurpassed   *c.* spicy   *d.* mild   *e.* inferior

11. has become *passé*   *a.* popular   *b.* fashionable   *c.* outmoded   *d.* unnecessary   *e.* acceptable

12. delayed *en route*   *a.* for a short time   *b.* before departure   *c.* somewhere   *d.* on arrival   *e.* on the way

REVIEW 7: SENTENCE COMPLETION

Complete the sentence by writing the correct word or expression selected from the vocabulary list below.

VOCABULARY LIST

coiffure	chargé d'affaires	regime
au courant	pièce de résistance	raison d'être
envoy	éclat	avant-garde
genre	bagatelle	nouveaux riches
laissez-faire	facade	souvenir

1. At one time or another, some hobby or interest becomes so important to us that it is practically our only _?_ (*reason for existence*).

2. This piece of driftwood is a(n) _?_ (*something that serves as a reminder*) of last summer's camping trip.

3. The reason you were not ready is that you spent too much time on a mere _?_ (*unimportant, trifling matter*).

4. What _?_ (*style of arranging the hair*) is most in vogue today?

5. The _?_ (*persons who had newly become rich*) felt ill at ease in their new social milieu.

6. In her letters Susan kept me _?_ (*up to date*) about events in my old neighborhood.

7. The _?_ (*main number on the program*) of the musicale was a medley of Gilbert and Sullivan airs.

8. It is an unwise parent who follows a policy of _?_ (*absence of interference*) in bringing up children.

9. The United States has encouraged nations everywhere to install a democratic __?__ (*system of government or rule*).
10. The __?__ (*ambassador's substitute*) has had years of experience in the diplomatic service.

REVIEW 8: BRAINTEASERS

Write the complete word.

1. Don't change your hairstyle. We like your present (4)**fur**(1).
2. Is (2)**let** of sole on today's menu?
3. The matter is of little importance. It is a mere **bag**(6).
4. They enjoy simple cooking; they don't care for fancy (3)**sin**(1).
5. Only the (2)**cad**(1) has been renovated. The interior is unchanged.
6. We didn't stick to the topic. Little that was said was (1)**prop**(2).
7. Residents complain that the park has become a **rend**(6) for drug traffickers.
8. A(n) (4)**boy**(3) ensemble is not for a conservative dresser.
9. The **rap**(10) between the rivals suggests that an era of harmony may be beginning.
10. We were told that the tune we had asked for was, regrettably, not in the band's (2)**pert**(4).

REVIEW 9: CONCISE WRITING

Express the thought of each sentence below in no more than four words.

1. We went into a small shop that specializes in fashionable clothes.
2. The line of persons waiting their turn kept getting longer and longer.
3. People who travel on foot sometimes carry umbrellas for protection against the sun.
4. We arranged an appointment to meet at a fixed time and place.
5. The loose-fitting sacklike dress that she wore is not expensive.
6. What is the time at which the first performance will be presented?
7. Sometimes, people who assume the risks and management of a business go bankrupt.
8. Give us full discretionary power to use our own judgment.
9. The vague feeling of illness that I was having is gone.
10. Do you know anyone who is fond of eating and drinking to excess?

REVIEW 10: COMPOSITION

Answer in two or three sentences.

1. Who are more likely to have trouble with their avoirdupois, gourmands or gourmets? Explain.
2. Though the hazards of overexposure to the sun have been widely publicized, parasols do not seem to be in vogue. Why?
3. Suppose you are eager to attend a premiere, but when you get there you find a queue stretching around the block. Would you stay or leave? Explain.
4. Why do so many émigrés from totalitarian regimes seek to settle in our country? Give two important reasons.
5. Why is it advisable to know what the pièce de résistance is going to be before having any of the hors d'oeuvres?

REVIEW 11: ANALOGIES

Write the *letter* of the expression that best completes the analogy.

1. *Parasol* is to *sun* as *variety* is to __?__ .
   a. queue b. fete c. ennui d. sky e. souvenir
2. *Regime* is to *revolutionists* as *custom* is to __?__ .
   a. elite   b. connoisseurs   c. devotees   d. avant-garde
   e. conservatives
3. *Scene I* is to *climax* as *hors d'oeuvres* is to __?__ .
   a. entrée b. cuisine c. bonbon d. chef d'oeuvre e. bagatelle
4. *Passé* is to *a la mode* as *apropos* is to __?__ .
   a. appropriate b. stylish c. outmoded d. irrelevant e. pertinent
5. *Bottle* is to *neck* as *hotel* is to __?__ .
   a. facade b. cul-de-sac c. foyer d. suburb e. table d'hôte
6. *Nourished* is to *food* as *au courant* is to __?__ .
   a. exercise b. drink c. news d. rest e. rumor
7. *Star* is to *understudy* as *ambassador* is to __?__ .
   a. coterie b. valet c. entrepreneur d. chargé d'affaires e. protégé
8. *Bas-relief* is to *sculpture* as *genre* is to __?__ .
   a. palette b. painter c. sculptor d. baton e. painting
9. *Faux pas* is to *embarrassment* as *détente* is to __?__ .
   a. rapprochement b. impasse c. cul-de-sac d. pièce de résistance
   e. encore
10. *Ice* is to *thaw* as *hostility* is to __?__ .
    a. coup de grace b. détente c. coup d'etat d. tour de force
    e. denouement

CHAPTER *9*

Italian Words in English

The Italian impact on English is especially important because Italy's rich contributions to the arts have profoundly influenced our cultural life. It is no wonder, then, that many English words that deal with music, painting, architecture, sculpture, and other arts are Italian loanwords.

1. Words for Singing Voices

(arranged in order of increasing pitch)

WORD	MEANING
basso (*n.*) 'bas-ō	lowest male voice; bass (pronounced bās)
baritone (*n.*) 'bar-ə-ˌtōn	male voice between bass and tenor
tenor (*n.*) 'ten-ə(r)	adult male voice between baritone and alto
alto (*n.*) 'al-tō	1. highest male voice 2. lowest female voice, the contralto
contralto (*n.*) kən-'tral-tō	lowest female voice
mezzo-soprano (*n.*) ˌmet-sō-sə-'pran-ō	female voice between contralto and soprano
soprano (*n.*) sə-pran-ō	highest singing voice in women and boys

coloratura (*n.*)
ˌkəl-ə-rə-'t(y)ür-ə

1. ornamental passages (runs, trills, etc.) in vocal music
2. soprano who sings such passages, i.e., a *coloratura* soprano

falsetto (*n.*)
fȯl-'set-ō

1. unnaturally high-pitched male voice
2. artificially high voice

EXERCISE 9.1

Write the most appropriate word from group 1.

1. For her superb rendering of ornamental passages, the __?__ was wildly acclaimed.
2. The lowest singing voice is *contralto* for women and __?__ for men.
3. Yodeling is a form of singing that requires frequent changes from the natural voice to a(n) __?__ .
4. Since Oscar's singing voice is between baritone and alto, he is classified as a(n) __?__ .
5. The highest singing voice is soprano for women and __?__ for men.

2. Words for Tempos (Rates of Speed) of Musical Compositions

(arranged in order of increasing speed)

grave (*adv.* or *adj.*)
'gräv-ā

slow (the slowest tempo in music)

largo (*adv.* or *adj.*)
'lär-gō

slow and dignified; stately

adagio (*adv.* or *adj.*)
ə-'däj-ō

slow; in an easy, graceful manner

lento (*adv.* or *adj.*)
'len-ˌtō

slow

andante (*adv.* or *adj.*)
än-'dän-ˌtā

moderately slow, but flowing

moderato (*adv.* or *adj.*)
‚mäd-ə-'rät-ō

in moderate time

allegro (*adv.* or *adj.*)
ə-'leg-rō

brisk; quick; lively

vivace (*adv.* or *adj.*)
vē-'väch-ā

brisk; spirited

presto (*adv.* or *adj.*)
'pres-tō

quick

prestissimo (*adv.* or *adj.*)
pre-'stis-ə-‚mō

at a very rapid pace

EXERCISE 9.2

Write the most appropriate word from group 2.

1. Music marked __?__ moves more rapidly than one marked *presto*.
2. The slowest tempo in music, __?__, is used in the opening measures of Beethoven's SONATE PATHÉTIQUE.
3. A ballad with a(n) __?__ tempo has to be sung at a moderately slow but flowing pace.
4. The __?__ movement of Dvořák's NEW WORLD SYMPHONY is played in a slow and dignified manner.
5. The term __?__ over the opening notes of SWEET GEORGIA BROWN indicates that this tune should be played neither rapidly nor slowly, but in moderate time.

3. Words for Dynamics (Degrees of Loudness)

crescendo (*adv.*, *adj.*, or *n.*)
kri-'shen-dō

gradually increasing (or a gradual increase) in force or loudness (*ant.* **decrescendo**)

decrescendo (*adv.*, *adj.*, or *n.*)
‚dā-krə-'shen-dō

gradually decreasing (or a gradual decrease) in force or loudness (*syn.* **diminuendo**; *ant.* **crescendo**)

dolce (*adv.* or *adj.*)
'dōl-chā

soft; sweet

forte (*adv.* or *adj.*) 'fȯr-ˌtā	loud (*ant.* **piano**)
fortissimo (*adv.* or *adj.*) fȯr-'tis-ə-ˌmō	very loud (*ant.* **pianissimo**)
pianissimo (*adv.* or *adj.*) ˌpē-ə-'nis-ə-ˌmō	very soft (*ant.* **fortissimo**)
piano (*adv.* or *adj.*) pē-'än-ō	soft (*ant.* **forte**)
sforzando (*adv.* or *adj.*) sfȯrt-'sän-dō	accented

EXERCISE 9.3

Write the most appropriate word from group 3.

1. The word __?__ designates a familiar musical instrument, as well as a musical direction meaning "soft."
2. Ravel's BOLERO rises to a dramatic climax by a gradual increase in loudness; few pieces have such an electrifying __?__ .
3. When a chord is to be played with a strong accent, the composer marks it with the term __?__ .
4. Mendelssohn's SCHERZO has a __?__ ending; it has to be played very softly.
5. A degree of loudness higher than *forte* is __?__ .

4. Words for Musical Effects

a cappella (*adv.* or *adj.*) ˌäk-ə-'pel-ə	(literally, "in chapel or church style") without musical accompaniment, as to sing *a cappella*, or an *a cappella* choir
arpeggio (*n.*) är-'pej-ō	1. production of the tones of a chord in rapid succession, rather than at the same time. (Normally, the tones of a chord are played simultaneously.) 2. a chord thus played
legato (*adv.* or *adj.*) li-'gät-ō	smooth and connected

pizzicato (*adv.* or *adj.*) ˌpit-si-ˈkät-ō	by means of plucking the strings instead of using the bow
staccato (*adv.* or *adj.*) stə-ˈkät-ō	with breaks between successive notes; disconnected; abrupt
tremolo (*n.*) ˈtrem-ə-ˌlō	rapid (''trembling'') repetition of a tone or chord, without apparent breaks, to express emotion
vibrato (*n.*) vē-ˈbrät-ō	slightly throbbing or pulsating effect, adding warmth and beauty to the tone

EXERCISE 9.4

Write the most appropriate word or expression from group 4.

1. By plucking the strings with the fingers, a violinist achieves a(n) __?__ effect.
2. In Tchaikovsky's 1812 OVERTURE, the rapid and prolonged repetition of two tones produces a ''trembling'' emotion-stirring effect known as __?__ .
3. Some beginning piano students strike all the correct notes but fail to achieve a smooth and connected effect because they do not play them __?__ .
4. It is surely much easier to play the tones of a chord simultaneously than to play them as a(n) __?__ .
5. In Schubert's AVE MARIA, the notes are smoothly connected, but in his MARCHE MILITAIRE they are mainly __?__ .

---

5. Words Dealing With Musical Compositions

---

aria (*n.*) ˈär-ē-ə	air, melody, or tune; especially, an elaborate, accompanied melody for a single voice in an opera
bravura (*n.*) brə-ˈv(y)ùr-ə	1. piece of music requiring skill and spirit in the performer 2. display of daring or brilliancy
cantata (*n.*) kən-ˈtät-ə	story or play set to music to be sung by a chorus, but not acted

concerto (*n.*)
kən-'chert-ō
long musical composition for one or more principal instruments with orchestral accompaniment

duet (*n.*)
d(y)ü-'et
1. piece of music for two voices or instruments
2. two singers or players performing together; duo

finale (*n.*)
fə-'nal-ē
close or termination, as the last section of a musical composition

intermezzo (*n.*)
͵int-ər-'met-sō
1. short musical or dramatic entertainment between the acts of a play
2. short musical composition between the main divisions of an extended musical work
3. short, independent musical composition

libretto (*n.*)
lə-'bret-ō
text or words of an opera or other long musical composition

opera (*n.*)
'äp-(ə)-rə
play mostly sung, with costumes, scenery, action, and music

oratorio (*n.*)
͵or-ə-'tor-ē-͵ō
musical composition, usually on a religious theme, for solo voices, chorus, and orchestra

scherzo (*n.*)
'skert-sō
light or playful part of a sonata or symphony

solo (*n.*)
'sō-lō
1. piece of music for one voice or instrument
2. anything done without a partner

sonata (*n.*)
sə-'nät-ə
piece of music (for one or two instruments) having three or four movements in contrasted rhythms but related tonality

trio (*n.*)
'trē-ō
1. piece of music for three voices or instruments
2. three singers or players performing together

tutti (*adv.*)
'tüt-ē
all (a direction for all the instruments and/or voices to perform together)

tutti (*n.*)
'tüt-ē
section of a musical composition performed by all the performers

EXERCISE 9.5

Write the most appropriate word from group 5.

1. To perform in a(n) __?__, one must be gifted both as a singer and as an actor.
2. Roberta refuses to do a solo, but she is willing to join with someone else in a(n) __?__.
3. From the opening selection to the __?__, we enjoyed the concert thoroughly.
4. Though there is orchestral accompaniment in a piano __?__, the pianist is the principal performer.
5. The selection you played is unfamiliar to me, but its light and playful character leads me to believe that it's a(n) __?__.
6. Not a single instrument in the orchestra is silent in a passage marked __?__.

6. Words Dealing With Arts Other Than Music

cameo (*n.*) 'kam-ē-ˌō	1. carved gem with a design higher and of a different color than its background (*ant.* **intaglio**) 2. brief role, usually limited to a single scene, by a prominent actor or actress 3. brief passage of exceptionally fine writing
campanile (*n.*) ˌkam-pə-'nē-lē	bell tower
canto (*n.*) 'kan-ˌtō	one of the chief divisions of a long poem
chiaroscuro (*n.*) kē-ˌär-ə-'sk(y)ů(ə)r-ō	1. distribution and treatment of light and shade in painting or sketching 2. painting or drawing that uses only light and shade
cupola (*n.*) 'kyü-pə-lə	1. rounded roof; dome 2. small dome or tower on a roof
fresco (*n.*) 'fres-ˌkō	1. art of painting with watercolors on damp fresh plaster 2. picture or design so painted

intaglio (*n.*)
in-'tal-yō

design engraved by making cuts in a surface
(*ant.* **cameo**)

majolica (*n.*)
mə-'jäl-i-kə

enameled Italian pottery richly decorated in
colors

mezzanine (*n.*)
'mez-ᵊn-ˌēn

intermediate story in a theater between the main
floor and the first balcony

mezzotint (*n.*)
'met-sō-ˌtint

picture engraved on copper or steel by polishing
or scraping away parts of a roughened surface

patina (*n.*)
'pat-ə-nə

film or incrustation, usually green, on the surface of old bronze or copper

portico (*n.*)
'pōrt-i-ˌkō

roof supported by columns, forming a porch or
a covered walk

rialto (*n.*)
rē-'al-tō

1. marketplace
2. theater district of a town

rotunda (*n.*)
rō-'tən-də

1. round building, especially one with a dome
or cupola
2. large round room, as the *rotunda* of the Capitol

stucco (*n.*)
'stək-ō

plaster for covering exterior walls of buildings

tempera (*n.*)
'tem-pə-rə

method of painting in which the colors are
mixed with white of egg or other substances, instead of oil

terra-cotta (*n.*)
'ter-ə-'kät-ə

1. kind of hard, brownish-red earthenware,
used for vases, statuettes, etc.
2. dull brownish-red color

torso (*n.*)
'tȯr-sō

1. trunk or body of a statue without head, arms,
or legs
2. human trunk

EXERCISE 9.6

Write the most appropriate word from group 6.

1. Because it is a large round room, the __?__ of the Capitol in Washington, D.C., is ideal for an impressive ceremony.
2. The __?__ my aunt wears has a carved ivory head raised on a light brown background.
3. A(n) __?__ actually becomes a part of the wall on whose damp, fresh plaster it is painted.
4. The head of the statue was discovered not far from the place where its __?__ had been found.
5. An antique increases in artistic value when its surface becomes incrusted with a fine natural __?__ .
6. The white of egg or a similar substance is used for mixing colors in __?__ painting.
7. Read the fifth __?__ of Dante's INFERNO for a stirring account of the lovers Paolo and Francesca.
8. The __?__ applied to exterior walls of buildings is a mixture of portland cement, sand, and lime.
9. In the morning we heard the sound of bells coming from the __?__ , a tall structure right next to the church.
10. The main building and the annex are connected by a(n) __?__ that facilitates traffic between the two, especially in bad weather.
11. A half hour before curtain time, the sidewalks of the __?__ are thronged with theatergoers.

7. Words Dealing With Persons

buffo (*n.*)
ˈbü-fō
male singer who plays a comic role in an opera; buffoon; clown

cognoscente (*n.*)
ˌkän-yō-ˈshent-ē
person who has a superior knowledge and understanding of a particular field; expert; connoisseur

dilettante (*n.*)
ˌdil-ə-ˈtänt(-ē)
person who follows some art or science as an amusement or in a trifling way

diva (*n.*)
ˈdē-və
principal female singer in an opera; prima donna

impresario (*n.*)
,im-prə-'sär-ē-,ō

organizer, or director of an opera or ballet company or a concert series; manager; promoter

inamorata (*n.*)
in-,am-ə-'rät-ə

woman who loves or is loved

inamorato (*n.*)
in-,am-ə-'rät-ō

man who loves or is loved

maestro (*n.*)
mä-'e-strō

1. eminent conductor, composer, or teacher of music
2. master in any art

mountebank (*n.*)
'maún-ti-,baŋk

boastful pretender; charlatan; quack

politico (*n.*)
pə-'lit-i-,kō

politician

prima donna (*n.*)
,prim-ə-'dän-ə

1. principal female singer in an opera
2. high-strung, vain, or extremely sensitive person

simpatico, *m.* (*adj.*)
sim-'pät-i-,kō
(**simpatica,** *f.*)

possessing attractive qualities; appealing; likable; congenial

virtuoso (*n.*)
,vər-chə-'wō-sō

one who exhibits great technical skill in an art, especially in playing a musical instrument

EXERCISE 9.7

Write the most appropriate word or expression from group 7.

1. All eyes were riveted on the __?__ as he raised his baton to begin the concert.
2. She hopes one day to take up the cello as a serious student rather than as a(n) __?__ .
3. The versatile young musician has won fame not only as a conductor and composer, but as a(n) __?__ at the piano.
4. The gentleman sent a St. Valentine's greeting to his __?__ .
5. The owner is unpleasant to deal with, but the manager is very __?__ .
6. An event like a parade or a marathon needs a skillful and devoted __?__ to organize and direct it.
7. The __?__ in tonight's opera has won acclaim for his portrayal of comic roles.

8. Words for Situations Involving Persons

dolce far niente (*n.*) delightful idleness
'dol-chē-ˌfär-nē-'ent-ē

fiasco (*n.*) crash; complete or ridiculous failure
fē-'as-kō

imbroglio (*n.*) 1. difficult situation
im-'brōl-yō 2. complicated disagreement

incognito (*adv.*) with one's identity concealed
ˌin-ˌkäg-'nēt-ō
incognito (*n.*) disguised state

vendetta (*n.*) feud for blood revenge
ven-'det-ə

9. Words Dealing With Food

antipasto (*n.*) appetizer consisting of fish, meats, etc.; hors d'oeuvres
ˌant-i-'pas-tō

Chianti (*n.*) a dry, red Italian wine
ke-'änt-ē

gusto (*n.*) liking or taste; hearty enjoyment
'gəs-ˌtō

pasta (*n.*) 1. wheat paste or dough—either dried, as for spaghetti
'päs-tə or macaroni, or used fresh, as for ravioli
2. dish of cooked pasta

pizza (*n.*) large, flat pie of bread dough spread with tomato pulp,
'pēt-sə cheese, meat, anchovies, etc.

10. Miscellaneous Common Words

alfresco (*adj.* or *adv.*) in the open air; outdoor
al-'fres-kō

brava (*interj.*) 'bräv-ə	(used to applaud a woman performer) well done; excellent
bravo (*interj.*) 'bräv-ō	(used to applaud a performance or a male performer) well done; excellent
gondola (*n.*) 'gän-də-lə	1. boat used in the canals of Venice 2. cabin attached to the underpart of an airship
grotto (*n.*) 'grät-ō	cave
piazza (*n.*) pē-'az-ə	1. open square in an Italian town 2. veranda or porch
portfolio (*n.*) pȯrt-'fō-lē-ˌō	1. briefcase 2. position or duties of a cabinet member or minister of state
salvo (*n.*) 'sal-vō	1. simultaneous discharge of shots 2. burst of cheers, as a *salvo* of applause
sotto voce (*adv.* or *adj.*) ˌsät-ō-'vō-chē	under the breath; in an undertone; privately, as a *sotto voce* remark

EXERCISE 9.8

Write the most appropriate word or expression from groups 8–10.

1. My old briefcase can hold more books and papers than this new __?__ .
2. The host filled his guests' wineglasses from a freshly opened bottle of __?__ .
3. The complicated disagreement about this year's budget is similar to the __?__ we had about last year's budget.
4. Philip's cold prevented him from eating his dinner with his usual __?__ .
5. The playwright attended the premiere __?__ so that he would not be recognized.
6. Because of the ridiculous failure of the first performance, they have canceled tonight's show to avoid a repetition of that __?__ .
7. At last the feuding parties have ended their __?__ .
8. I did not hear what the mother said to the daughter, for they conferred __?__ .
9. The tourist relies on the taxicab in New York City and on the __?__ in Venice.

10. While in prison, Edmond Dantès learned of an immense fortune concealed in an underground __?__ on the island of Monte Cristo.

11. When the diva completed her first aria, the audience sprang to its feet and shouted "__?__."

12. We had a delightful __?__ lunch at a sidewalk cafe.

Review Exercises

REVIEW 1: MEANINGS

Match each word or expression in column I with the *letter* of its correct meaning in column II.

COLUMN I	COLUMN II
1. rialto	*a.* trunk
2. canto	*b.* diva
3. cognoscente	*c.* promoter
4. grotto	*d.* division
5. buffo	*e.* hors d'oeuvres
6. sforzando	*f.* cave
7. torso	*g.* square
8. antipasto	*h.* connoisseur
9. piazza	*i.* dough
10. impresario	*j.* marketplace
11. prima donna	*k.* stressed
12. pasta	*l.* clown

REVIEW 2: SENTENCE COMPLETION

Write the *letter* of the choice that correctly completes the sentence.

1. A (an) __?__ choir performs without accompaniment.
   a. a capella *b.* cantata

2. A __?__ is a musical composition requiring an entire orchestra, but featuring a solo instrument such as the piano or violin.
   a. sonata *b.* concerto

3. When Ulysses returned __?__ to his palace, he was recognized by his dog Argus.
   a. incognito *b.* falsetto

4. The anchored fleet welcomed the chief of state with a thunderous _?_ .
   a. salvo *b.* staccato

5. An impression made from an _?_ results in a raised image.
   a. imbroglio *b.* intaglio

6. The overworked executive longed for the _?_ of a Caribbean cruise.
   a. sotto voce *b.* dolce far niente

7. The orchestra and balcony seats are sold out, but a few _?_ tickets are available.
   a. mezzanine *b.* mezzotint

8. To achieve a smooth and flowing effect, I was advised to play the first two measures _?_ .
   a. tremolo *b.* legato

9. For an example of a crescendo from pianissimo all the way to _?_, listen to Grieg's IN THE HALL OF THE MOUNTAIN KING.
   a. prestissimo *b.* fortissimo

10. A _?_ sketch achieves its effects principally by its treatment of light and shade.
    a. chiaroscuro *b.* terra-cotta

REVIEW 3: BRAINTEASERS

Write the complete word.

1. While the spaghetti was boiling, our hostess served a delicious **(4)past(1)**.

2. The **(1)rot(2)** had once been used to store stolen treasure.

3. Have you ever heard of the **vend(4)** between the Hatfields and the McCoys?

4. Over the years a(n) **(2)tin(1)** had formed on the surface of the copper vessel.

5. Responding to the **(5)end(1)** of applause, the violinist returned for an encore.

6. Though exhausted from crying, the child continued to punctuate the silence with occasional **(4)cat(1)** sobs.

7. The ill-matched challenger's bid ended in a(n) **(2)as(2)** in the opening seconds of the first round.

8. The **mount(5)** convinced gullible customers that his snake oil would cure their aches and pains.

9. My uncle paints as a(n) **(5)tan(2)**, not as a serious artist.

10. The **(2)her(2)** movement of that symphony is light and playful.

REVIEW 4: CONCISE WRITING

Express the thought of each sentence below in no more than four words.

1. The plotters arrived wearing disguises, so that they would not be recognized.

2. This is a painting in watercolors that was done on damp fresh plaster.

3. Is the section of the theater between the main floor and the first balcony crowded?

4. They met the person who is doing the organizing and the promoting.

5. We sang without the accompaniment of any musical instrument whatsoever.

6. People respect someone who has a superior knowledge and understanding of a particular field.

7. Play these notes by plucking the strings, instead of using the bow.

8. This is the district in which the theaters of the city are concentrated.

9. Here is a piece of music for two voices or instruments.

10. The conversation that we took part in was conducted in an undertone.

REVIEW 5: COMPOSITION

Answer in two or three sentences.

1. Explain why most people usually eat pizza with gusto.

2. Would a virtuoso enjoy being called a dilettante by a music critic? Explain.

3. Who contributes more to the success of an opera, the composer of the music, or the author of the libretto? Explain.

4. Why is an action taken on the advice of a mountebank likely to end in a fiasco?

5. What does a salvo of applause for the prima donna—even before she has sung a single note—tell us about the audience?

REVIEW 6: ANALOGIES

1. DESSERT : ANTIPASTO
   a. grave : prestissimo
   b. basso : soprano
   c. entrée : hors d'oeuvres
   d. play : denouement
   e. finale : overture

2. STAR : FILM
   a. composer : sonata
   b. soloist : concerto
   c. aria : vocalist
   d. drama : protagonist
   e. actor : cast

3. COGNOSCENTE : DILETTANTE
   a. uncle : aunt
   b. professional : amateur
   c. odor : aroma
   d. ignoramus : connoisseur
   e. artist : patron

4. INCOGNITO : IDENTITY
   a. novel : pen name
   b. masquerade : disguise
   c. pseudonym : authorship
   d. fiction : real
   e. anonymous : known

5. TORSO : STATUE
   a. trunk : tree
   b. dismember : intact
   c. shard : vase
   d. atom : nucleus
   e. violinist : orchestra

6. PATINA : AGE
   a. film : camera
   b. hair : baldness
   c. blush : embarrassment
   d. mold : cheese
   e. tarnish : silver

7. LENTO : TEMPO
   a. gondola : canal
   b. papers : portfolio
   c. Chianti : meal
   d. piano : volume
   e. allegro : loudness

8. ROTUNDA : EDIFICE
   a. gondola : canal
   b. pizza : dough
   c. sole : fish
   d. stucco : wall
   e. portico : columns

9. BUFFO : ZANY
   a. entrepreneur : risky
   b. mediator : partial
   c. mentor : knowledgeable
   d. prevaricator : truthful
   e. diplomat : tactless

10. PASTA : NOURISHMENT
    a. uncertainty : rumor
    b. instruction : enlightenment
    c. shelter : domicile
    d. beverage : thirst
    e. ignorance : superstition

CHAPTER *10*

Spanish Words in English

It should not surprise you that English has adopted many Spanish words. For centuries Spain governed many areas of this continent, including Florida and our vast Southwest. Despite the disintegration of the Spanish Empire, Spanish today is spoken in Mexico, virtually all of Central and South America (except Brazil), the Caribbean, the Philippines, and numerous other regions. As one of the world's principal languages, Spanish continues to exert its influence on English.

1. Words for Persons

WORD	MEANING
aficionado (*n.*) ə-ˌfis-ē-ə-'näd-ō	devoted follower of some sport or art; fan; devotee
caballero (*n.*) ˌkab-ə-'ler-ō	1. gentleman or gallant 2. horseman
Chicano (*n.*) chi-'kän-ō	American of Mexican descent
conquistador (*n.*) kȯŋ-'kēs-tə-ˌdȯ(r)	conqueror
desperado (*n.*) ˌdes-pə-'räd-ō	bold, reckless criminal

duenna (*n.*)
d(y)ü-'en-ə

elderly woman chaperon of a young lady; governess

gaucho (*n.*)
'gaü-chō

Argentine cowboy of mixed Spanish and Indian descent

grandee (*n.*)
gran-'dē

1. nobleman of the highest rank
2. person of eminence

hidalgo (*n.*)
hid-'al-gō

nobleman of the second class (not so high as a *grandee*)

junta (*n.*)
'hün-tə

1. council for legislation or administration
2. group of military officers controlling a government after a coup d'etat
3. junto

junto (*n.*)
'jənt-ō

group of persons joined for a common purpose; clique; group of plotters

Latino (*n.*)
la-'tēn-ō

Latin American; native of any western-hemisphere country where a Latin-derived language (Spanish, Portuguese, French) is spoken

Latino (*adj.*)
la-'tēn-ō

Latin-American; characteristic of Latinos

macho (*n.*)
'mä-ˌchō

man who exhibits **machismo** (strong sense of masculine pride); overly assertive, domineering, virile male

macho (*adj.*)
'mä-ˌchō

characterized by exaggerated masculinity; overly assertive, domineering, virile, etc.

matador (*n.*)
'mat-ə-ˌdȯ(r)

bullfighter assigned to kill the bull

mestizo (*n.*)
me-'stē-zō

man or person of mixed American Indian and European ancestry

peon (*n.*)
'pē-ˌän

1. common laborer
2. worker kept in service to repay a debt

picador (*n.*)
'pik-ə-ˌdȯ(r)

rider on horseback who irritates the bull with a lance

picaro (*n.*)
'pē-kä-ˌrō

adventurous rogue or vagabond

renegade (*n.*)
'ren-i-ˌgād

1. apostate (deserter) from a religion, party, etc.
2. turncoat; traitor

señor (*n.*) sān-'yȯ(r)	Spanish or Spanish-speaking man; gentleman; Mr.; Sir
señora (*n.*) sān-'yōr-ə	married Spanish or Spanish-speaking woman; lady; Mrs.; Madam
señorita (*n.*) ˌsān-yə-'rēt-ə	unmarried Spanish or Spanish-speaking woman; young lady; girl; Miss
toreador (*n.*) 'tȯr-ē-ə-ˌdȯ(r)	bullfighter, usually mounted
torero (*n.*) tə-'rer-ō	bullfighter on foot
vaquero (*n.*) vä-'ker-ō	herdsman; cowboy

EXERCISE 10.1

Write the most appropriate word from group 1.

1. The onetime Democrat who joined the Republican Party was regarded as a(n) __?__ by some of his former Democratic colleagues.
2. In the Old West, it was common for a stagecoach to be robbed by a(n) __?__ .
3. A(n) __?__ is a nobleman of higher rank than a hidalgo.
4. Anyone who lacks an education or a skilled trade may earn little more than the wages of a(n) __?__ .
5. The average fan attends two or three games a season, but the __?__ goes to many more.
6. Hernando Cortes was the __?__ who engineered the conquest of Mexico and destroyed the highly advanced civilization of the Aztecs.
7. The __?__ was chaperoned by her duenna.
8. The ruler ordered the arrest of all members of the __?__ involved in the plot against his regime.
9. The __?__ who risks his life to kill the bull is idolized by his aficionados, but not by animal lovers.
10. Mexican Americans are proud of their fellow __?__ Cesar Chavez for his contributions to the American labor movement.
11. For a long time, women were denied the right to vote because of a(n) __?__ belief that they were weak and inferior.
12. The band played __?__ music, like cha-chas, mambos, and sambas.

2. Miscellaneous Words

adobe (*n.*)
ə-'dō-bē

1. brick of sun-dried clay or mud
2. structure made of such bricks

bolero (*n.*)
bə-'ler-ō

1. Spanish dance in ¾ time, with sharp turns, stamping, sudden pauses, and one arm arched over the head
2. music for this dance
3. loose waist-length jacket worn open at the front

bonanza (*n.*)
bə-'nan-zə

1. accidental discovery of a rich mass of ore
2. something yielding a rich return

bravado (*n.*)
brə-'väd-ō

1. boastful behavior
2. pretense of bravery

cabana (*n.*)
kə-'ban-(y)ə

beach shelter resembling a cabin

castanets (*n. pl.*)
ˌkas-tə-'nets

hand instruments clicked together to accompany music or dancing

fiesta (*n.*)
fē-'es-tə

saint's day celebrated with processions and dances; any festival or holiday

flotilla (*n.*)
flō-'til-ə

small fleet; fleet of small vessels

hacienda (*n.*)
ˌ(h)äs-ē-'en-də

1. large estate or ranch; plantation
2. main house in such an estate

incommunicado (*adv.*)
ˌin-kə-ˌmyü-nə-'käd-ō

deprived of communication with others, as a prisoner held *incommunicado*

mantilla (*n.*)
man-'tē-(y)ə

1. woman's light scarf or veil
2. cloak or cape

olio (*n.*)
'ō-lē-ˌō

mixture; hodgepodge; medley

patio (*n.*)
'pat-ē-ˌō

paved outdoor dining or lounging area adjacent to a house

peccadillo (*n.*)
ˌpek-ə-'dil-ō

slight offense

pimento (*n.*)
or **pimiento**
pǝ-'ment-ō

thick-fleshed pepper used for stuffing olives and as a source of paprika

poncho (*n.*)
'pän-chō

1. blanketlike cloak with a slit in the middle for the head, used mainly in Spanish America
2. similar garment made of waterproof material and used chiefly as a raincoat

pueblo (*n.*)
pü-'eb-lō

Indian village of southwestern U.S. built of adobe or stone

siesta (*n.*)
sē-'es-tǝ

short rest or nap, especially at midday

tortilla (*n.*)
tȯr-'tē-(y)ǝ

thin, flat, round corn cake

EXERCISE 10.2

Write the most appropriate word from group 2.

1. Have you ever seen graceful Spanish dancers do the bolero to the accompaniment of clicking __?__?
2. For every prospector who struck a(n) __?__, there were countless others whose finds were disappointing.
3. Taking a bribe is not a(n) __?__. It is a serious infraction of ethics.
4. You may be surprised to learn that a house made of __?__ can last for more than a hundred years.
5. The ruffian's defiant challenge turned out to be mere __?__, for when someone offered to fight him, he backed down.
6. Our Latino neighbors celebrate a(n) __?__ by wearing brightly colored costumes and by singing and dancing.
7. By midafternoon, the whole __?__ of fishing vessels had returned to port with the day's catch.
8. A gaucho uses his __?__ both as a blanket and a cloak.
9. In regions where the afternoon heat is unbearably intense, one often takes a(n) __?__ before resuming work.
10. __?__s are made of cornmeal.
11. There were no plain olives on the shelves, only olives stuffed with __?__.
12. Shall we stay indoors, or would you prefer to sit on the __?__?

3. Additional Miscellaneous Words

arroyo (*n.*) ə-'ròi-ō	watercourse; small, often dry, gully
barrio (*n.*) 'bär-ē-ˌō	Spanish-speaking neighborhood
bodega (*n.*) bō-'dä-gə	small grocery store
bronco (*n.*) 'bräŋ-kō	half-wild pony
burro (*n.*) 'bər-ō	small donkey used as a pack animal
canyon (*n.*) 'kan-yən	deep valley with high, steep slopes, often with a stream flowing through it, as the Colorado River in the Grand Canyon
indigo (*n.*) 'in-di-ˌgō	1. plant yielding a blue dye 2. deep violet-blue color
mañana (*adv.*) mən-'yän-ə	tomorrow; in the indefinite future
mesa (*n.*) 'mā-sə	flat-topped, rocky hill with steeply sloping sides
mustang (*n.*) 'məs-ˌtaŋ	bronco
pampas (*n. pl.*) 'pam-pəz	vast, treeless, grassy plains, especially in Argentina
sierra (*n.*) sē-'er-ə	ridge of mountains with an irregular, serrated (saw-toothed) outline
sombrero (*n.*) səm-'brer-ō	broad-rimmed, high-crowned hat of felt or straw
taco (*n.*) 'täk-ō	fried, folded tortilla stuffed with chopped meat, cheese, shredded lettuce, etc.

EXERCISE 10.3

Write the most appropriate word from group 3.

1. A Hopi village was secure against enemy attacks because it was built on top of a steeply sloping, flat-topped __?__ .
2. The blue dye formerly obtained from __?__ can now be made artificially.
3. Do today's work today; don't put it off to __?__ .
4. In desert areas of Mexico and of our own Southwest, the __?__ is used for carrying heavy loads.
5. The __?__ in Argentina are famous for their cattle, corn, and wheat.
6. Most __?__s are open late for the convenience of people who may need groceries.
7. At first, the newly arrived Latino immigrants lived in the __?__ of a large American city.
8. Some of us like hamburgers for lunch; others prefer __?__s.

Review Exercises

REVIEW 1: MEANINGS

Write the *letter* of the word or expression in each group that has the *same meaning* as the italicized word.

1. *duenna*   *a.* duet   *b.* junta   *c.* chaperon   *d.* twosome   *e.* fiancé
2. *indigo*   *a.* hill   *b.* sugar   *c.* clay   *d.* native   *e.* violet-blue
3. *peccadillo*   *a.* pepper   *b.* groundhog   *c.* alligator   *d.* petty officer   *e.* slight offense
4. *olio*   *a.* grease   *b.* mixture   *c.* fuel   *d.* page   *e.* noise
5. *macho*   *a.* reckless   *b.* domineering   *c.* excessive   *d.* roguish   *e.* eminent
6. *aficionado*   *a.* zeal   *b.* connoisseur   *c.* fan   *d.* trifler   *e.* fictional hero
7. *conquistadors*   *a.* discoverers   *b.* conquests   *c.* explorers   *d.* conquerors   *e.* bullfighters
8. *renegade*   *a.* infidel   *b.* desperado   *c.* rogue   *d.* villain   *e.* turncoat
9. *arroyo*   *a.* dart   *b.* gully   *c.* mesa   *d.* waterfall   *e.* bronco
10. *siesta*   *a.* holiday   *b.* sojourn   *c.* fiesta   *d.* nap   *e.* sierra

REVIEW 2: SENTENCE COMPLETION

Write the *letter* of the choice that best completes the sentence.

1. A section of Fifth Avenue will be closed to traffic tomorrow for a day-long __?__ .
   a. siesta *b.* bonanza *c.* bolero *d.* fiesta *e.* vendetta
2. To maintain anonymity, the leader of the junto employed a __?__ .
   a. lackey *b.* grandee *c.* pseudonym *d.* poncho *e.* peon
3. __?__ are Argentine cowboys who inhabit the __?__ .
   a. Gauchos . . . pampas *b.* Caballeros . . . mesas *c.* Desperadoes
   . . . sierras *d.* Vaqueros . . . pueblos *e.* Picaros . . . adobes
4. A famous painting by Murillo depicts a smiling señorita looking down
   from a window with her mantilla-clad __?__ by her side.
   a. protégé *b.* aficionado *c.* duenna *d.* grandee *e.* fiancé
5. Benedict Arnold was the American __?__ whose plot to surrender West
   Point resulted in a __?__ .
   a. patriot . . . vendetta *b.* renegade . . . coup d'etat *c.* grandee
   . . . junto *d.* turncoat . . . fiasco *e.* apostate . . . détente
6. One cannot dine alfresco __?__ .
   a. on the patio *b.* in the canyon *c.* on the mesa *d.* in the hacienda
   e. on the pampas
7. As a rule, a __?__ does not offend anyone.
   a. macho *b.* desperado *c.* picaro *d.* caballero *e.* renegade
8. At the airport, we talked with some Chicanos from __?__ .
   a. Spain *b.* Arizona *c.* Quebec *d.* Peru *e.* Portugal
9. The filling of a taco resembles but is not the same as the topping of
   a(n) __?__ .
   a. croissant *b.* aperitif *c.* pizza *d.* tortilla *e.* bonbon
10. When you hear a(n) __?__ , you are listening to Latino music.
    a. foxtrot *b.* waltz *c.* polka *d.* rumba *e.* lindy

REVIEW 3: BRAINTEASERS

Write the complete word.

1. A friend of ours has a **cab**(3) at the beach.
2. Occasionally, a **mat**(4) is gored by an enraged bull.
3. Several customers in the **bode**(2) were waiting to be served.
4. Her face was partly veiled by a(n) (1)**ant**(4).
5. How many vessels were there in the (1)**lot**(4)?

6. When the guests arrived, there was no one at the (4)**e n d** (1) .
7. Reckless driving must not be treated as a(n) (5)**d i l l** (1) .
8. There were fewer than a dozen conspirators in the (1)**u n t o** .
9. The blouse was pale yellow, and the slacks were deep (2)**d i g** (1) .
10. Before dismounting, the (2)**b a l l** (3) removed his sombrero.

REVIEW 4: CONCISE WRITING

Express the thought of each sentence below in no more than four words.

1. Wear your loose jacket that comes up to the waist and is open at the front.
2. This is an investment that will pay you very rich returns.
3. I took a short nap in the middle of the day.
4. Males who have an exaggerated sense of masculinity often behave in a boastful way.
5. Hector was the bullfighter who was assigned to kill the bull.
6. Elena respected the elderly lady who was acting as her chaperon.
7. They were held without being given an opportunity to get in touch with anyone, or even to make a telephone call.
8. The dancers used hand instruments that they clicked together to accompany the music.
9. Some were wearing tall-crowned hats that had very wide brims.
10. The group of military officers who engineered the coup d'etat and took over the government lacks experience.

REVIEW 5: COMPOSITION

Answer in two or three sentences.

1. Suppose a security guard is discovered taking a siesta while on duty. Should the matter be treated as a peccadillo? Explain.
2. Why would it be wrongheaded for someone to exhibit his machismo when confronted by armed desperados?
3. Why is a fiesta usually a bonanza for local merchants? Explain.
4. Explain why a poncho is extremely valuable not only to a gaucho on the pampas, but to campers and hikers everywhere.

5. Why might the members of a junto hesitate to admit a renegade from a rival party?

REVIEW 6: ANALOGIES

Write the *letter* of the word pair that best expresses a relationship similar to that existing between the capitalized word-pair.

1. MATADOR : SWORD
   - *a.* gaucho : poncho
   - *b.* picador : lance
   - *c.* torero : horse
   - *d.* desperado : loot
   - *e.* toreador : bull

2. BONANZA : MINER
   - *a.* legacy : heir
   - *b.* crop : farmer
   - *c.* diploma : student
   - *d.* jackpot : gambler
   - *e.* bull's-eye : sharpshooter

3. ADOBE : PUEBLO
   - *a.* settlement : Indian
   - *b.* cabana : beach
   - *c.* terra-cotta : clay
   - *d.* seaport : flotilla
   - *e.* concrete : turnpike

4. OLIO : INGREDIENT
   - *a.* concerto : instrument
   - *b.* medley : tune
   - *c.* potpourri : confusion
   - *d.* entrée : dessert
   - *e.* aria : opera

5. SIERRA : CANYON
   - *a.* zenith : nadir
   - *b.* arroyo : mesa
   - *c.* indigo : red
   - *d.* grandee : hidalgo
   - *e.* monarch : retinue

6. MACHO : ASSERTIVE
   - *a.* cognoscente : uninformed
   - *b.* martinet : inflexible
   - *c.* dipsomaniac : abstemious
   - *d.* renegade : loyal
   - *e.* peon : prosperous

7. PONCHO : RAIN
   - *a.* sombrero : shade
   - *b.* mentor : guidance
   - *c.* antitoxin : immunity
   - *d.* taco : nourishment
   - *e.* parasol : sun

CHAPTER *11*

Sample Vocabulary Questions in Pre-College Tests

Vocabulary questions play a prominent and decisive role in pre-college tests. You will probably take one or more of these tests in high school if you expect to apply for college admission or college scholarship awards. Naturally, you will want to familiarize yourself with the types of vocabulary questions you are likely to encounter on such tests. For your guidance, therefore, this chapter will present officially released sample vocabulary questions for two widely administered pre-college examinations:

1. The Preliminary Scholastic Aptitude Test/National Merit Scholarship Qualifying Test (PSAT/NMSQT)
2. The Scholastic Aptitude Test (SAT)

1. The PSAT/NMSQT

The sample vocabulary questions and explanations that follow are from the 1991 PSAT/NMSQT *Student Bulletin*, published by the College Entrance Examination Board and the Educational Testing Service, which have graciously granted permission to reprint this material.

Sample Questions with Explanations

Antonyms (Opposites)

Antonym questions measure the extent and depth of your vocabulary. The words tested are ones that you are likely to find in your reading both in and out of school, although some may not be the kind you use in everyday speech.

These are the directions you will see on the test:

Each question below consists of a word in capital letters, followed by five lettered words or phrases. Choose the word or phrase that is most nearly opposite in meaning to the word in capital letters. Since some of the questions require you to distinguish fine shades of meaning, consider all the choices before deciding which is best.

EXAMPLE:

GOOD: (A) sour   (B) bad   (C) red   (D) hot   (E) ugly

This sample question is very easy, but thinking about it may help you with other antonym questions. Remember that you are looking for the *best* answer given. Begin by eliminating **hot** and **red** because they don't have much to do with GOOD.

If you think that **sour** is the opposite of GOOD, you could ask yourself, "What is the opposite of **sour**?" You can eliminate **sour** because the opposite of **sour** is "sweet," not GOOD. And you can eliminate **ugly** because the opposite of **ugly** is "handsome," or "pretty," or "beautiful."

Of course, the correct answer is (B). GOOD and **bad** are precise opposites. You probably did not have to go through this process to answer such an easy question, but you may want to try it when you are working on harder antonym questions.

1. RETRIEVE: **(A) lose (B) believe (C) ask (D) strip (E) move**

Some questions in the verbal section of the PSAT/NMSQT require that you have only a general understanding of the words being tested. To RE-TRIEVE an object means to get it back again. You had an object, a ball or book, in your possession once but misplaced it or lost it. Then, you **re-trieved** it. The opposite meaning of RETRIEVE is (A) **lose.** (B) **believe** means to have faith in something, not to regain an object. (C), (D), and (E) have obvious definitions, none of which is the opposite of RETRIEVE.

2. FRIVOLITY: **(A) notoriety (B) dissonance (C) seriousness
   (D) firm denial (E) mild manner**

Sometimes it may help you to think of other forms of a word when you are looking for its opposite. In this case, **frivolous** is a more common form of the word FRIVOLITY. You probably know that **frivolous** means silly or lacking in seriousness. Be sure to look at all of the choices; don't take the first one that you think is right. In this question, both (C) and (E) may seem correct to you at first. However, a better opposite for (E) **mild man-ner** would be excitability or tempestuousness. The closest opposite for FRIVOLITY is solemn manner, or **seriousness**; therefore, choice (C) is the correct answer.

HINTS FOR ANTONYMS

1. Since you may have to distinguish between shades of meaning, be sure you read all the choices before you decide which is correct.
2. Choose the word that is *most nearly opposite* the word in CAPITAL letters.
3. Words often have several meanings, but only one meaning of a word has to be the ''opposite'' for that word to be the correct choice.
4. Most people can work faster on antonyms than on any other part of the test. However, don't go so fast that you make careless errors.

Sentence Completions

Sentence completion questions measure your ability to choose a word or words that fit logically with the other parts of a sentence. The sentences, taken from published material, cover a wide variety of topics of the sort you are likely to have encountered in school or in your general reading. Your understanding of the sentences will not depend on specialized knowledge in science, literature, social studies, or any other field.

These are the directions you will see on the test:

Each sentence below has one or two blanks, each blank indicating that something has been omitted. Beneath the sentence are five lettered words or sets of words. Choose the word or set of words that, when inserted in the sentence, <u>best</u> fits the meaning of the sentence as a whole.

EXAMPLE:

Although its publicity has been ----, the film itself is intelligent, well-acted, handsomely produced, and altogether ----.

(A) tasteless . . respectable   (B) extensive . . moderate
(C) sophisticated . . amateur   (D) risqué . . crude
(E) perfect . . spectacular

In many sentences with two blanks, one blank will be easier to figure out than the other. The blank in the first part of this sentence could be filled in with almost any description. The publicity could be **tasteless, extensive,** or any of the other choices given.

To get started on this question you should look at the second part of the sentence. The second blank is the last word of a list, so the word that fills the blank should fit with the other words in the list. **Intelligent, well-acted,** and **handsomely produced** are all complimentary, so the word that goes into the blank should also be complimentary.

Of the choices for the second word, **crude** and **amateur** are certainly not compliments, so you can eliminate (C) and (D). **Moderate** might be a compliment in some situations, but it does not work as well as **respectable** or **spectacular.** To decide which of these two is correct, you have to go back to the first part of the sentence.

Look for signals. The word **Although** is a signal that the first part of the sentence will contrast with the second part. Which word in the first part will make you surprised to read the second part? If the publicity were **perfect,** it wouldn't be much of a surprise to find out that the film itself was **spectactular. Tasteless** publicity, on the other hand, contrasts strongly with a **respectable** film and therefore fits the logic of the sentence.

The whole sentence works best with choice (A).

3. **With each retelling, the description the witness gave of the accident drifted further from reality, and the whole episode appeared more and more ----.**

   (A) persuasive   (B) venerable   (C) sarcastic   (D) fictitious
   (E) infallible

Look for a *key word* or *phrase.* The word or phrase that best fills the blank is determined logically by the other parts of the sentence. ''Drifted further from reality'' indicates that the missing word should mean unreal. If the description ''drifted further from reality,'' then the episode did not become more **persuasive** (A), or **venerable** (B), which means worthy of respect. **Infallible** (E) means incapable of error. Choice (C) **sarcastic** means an unpleasant or mocking tone. None of these choices fits the blank as well as (D) **fictitious,** which means not real.

4. **Edgar wrote the conclusion to the novel with such ––– that we began to suspect he was not an artist but a remarkable ––– processing plots and characters with mechanical efficiency.**

    **(A) emotion . . computer (B) awkwardness . . prodigy
    (C) hesitation . . wizard (D) dispatch . . automaton (E) difficulty
    . . plagiarist**

Look for parts of the sentence that influence what words logically fill the blanks. The phrase ''processing plots and characters with mechanical efficiency'' controls the blanks. Find a word for the second blank that describes mechanical efficiency. The second words in (A) **computer** and (D) **automaton** describe machine-like behavior. (The second words in (B), (C), and (E) are inappropriate beause they do *not* describe machine-like behavior.) Now try both terms from choice (A). ''Edgar wrote with such **emotion** that he seemed like a **remarkable computer** . . .'' **Emotion** and mechanical efficiency do not work together. Now try (D). ''Edgar wrote with such **dispatch** that he seemed like a **remarkable automaton** . . .'' Since **dispatch** means with speed or mechanical efficiency, (D) is correct. Both **dispatch** and **automaton** support the idea of mechanical efficiency.

HINTS FOR SENTENCE COMPLETIONS

1. When you have to fill in two words, make sure *both* make sense in the sentence. Wrong answer choices often include one correct and one incorrect word.

2. Don't try to figure out both words at once. Narrow down the choices for one word, then use the other word to help you make your final decision.

3. Before you mark your answer, read the complete sentence with your choice filled in to be sure it makes sense.

Analogies

Analogy questions test your ability to see a relationship in a pair of words, to understand the ideas expressed in the relationship, and to recognize a similar relationship in another pair of words.

These are the directions you will see on the test:

Each question below consists of a related pair of words or phrases, followed by five lettered pairs of words or phrases. Select the lettered pair that best expresses a relationship similar to that expressed in the original pair.

EXAMPLE:

YAWN:BOREDOM::   (A) dream:sleep   (B) anger:madness
(C) smile:amusement   (D) face:expression   (E) impatience:rebellion

---

The first step in answering an analogy question is to figure out the exact relationship between the words in CAPITAL letters. Many people find that it helps to *make up a short sentence that states the relationship*: "A YAWN is a physical sign or facial expression of BOREDOM." The second step is to look for the pair of words among the answer choices that fits your sentence best.

Choice (A), **dream:sleep**, is not correct. A **dream** is something you do when you **sleep**, but is not a "sign" or "expression" of **sleep** as closed eyes or a snore might be. In (B), **anger** means strong displeasure and **madness** refers to rage or insanity, but neither word is a "sign" or "expression" of the other. Choice (C), **smile:amusement**, fits the sentence since "a **smile** is a physical sign and a facial expression of **amusement**." Before you mark your answer, however, check the other choices. The words in (D) do not have the same relationship as YAWN and BOREDOM. You show an **expression** on your **face**, but your **face** is not a "sign" of an **expression**. In choice (E), **impatience** may lead to **rebellion** or be characteristic of a rebellious person, but **impatience** is not a "sign" or "expression" of **rebellion**. The choice that *best* expresses a relationship similar to the one between YAWN and BOREDOM is (C).

5. SQUABBLE:FIGHT::   (A) enlightenment:novel   (B) glimmer:blaze
(C) drink:tavern   (D) ship:port   (E) quiet:sound

First, make up a sentence stating the relationship between the pair of words in capital letters. A SQUABBLE is a small or not very serious FIGHT. Now, look for a pair of words among the choices that has the same or nearly the same relationship. **Enlightenment** may come from a **novel**, but it is not a kind of novel. **Glimmer** is a faint, or small, **blaze**, but check the other choices to see if another pair might fit even more closely than (B). Is **drink** a small **tavern**? No. Is **ship** a small **port**? No. Is **quiet** a small **sound**? No. **Quiet** is the absence of **sound**. A SQUABBLE is a small or not very serious FIGHT just as a **glimmer** is a small or not very serious **blaze**. (B) is the correct answer.

6. LIAR : MENDACIOUS :: (A) culprit : naive (B) heretic : bogus
(C) dupe : illusory (D) seer : prophetic (E) resident : nomadic

A pair of words may have more than one relationship. Since MENDACIOUS means "given to deception or falsehood," you could say that "a LIAR indulges in the MENDACIOUS" is the relationship of the first pair of words above. Using this same rationale, you could then say of (C) "a **dupe** may indulge in the **illusory**," or of (D) "A **seer** indulges in the **prophetic**." However, since there can be only one correct answer, and since when you use the relationship given above it appears that you have two answers, you must return to the first pair of words and restate the rationale. Try "a LIAR is by definition MENDACIOUS." If you check the words in the dictionary, you will see that this new rationale is a correct one. Applying this rationale to the choices, you see that it fits only choice (D); "a **seer** is by definition **prophetic**" is the same relationship as "a LIAR is by definition MENDACIOUS." You could not say, **using** this rationale, that "a **dupe** is by definition **illusory**." The correct answer is choice (D), **seer : prophetic**.

HINTS FOR ANALOGIES

1. First make up a sentence that shows how the two words in CAPITAL letters work together. Then see what pair of words among the choices works best in your sentence.

2. Remember that you are not looking for words that are similar to the words in CAPITAL letters or that have the same meaning. Don't look for a relationship between the first word in CAPITAL letters and the first word in each of the choices. Look for a *pair* of words with the same relationship between them as the *pair* in CAPITAL letters.

3. Many words have more than one meaning, and many pairs of words have more than one relationship between them. You may have to try a few relationships before you find the one that helps you choose the best answer.

4. If you can eliminate two or three answer choices with the first relationship you find, you may be able to select the *best* answer by defining the relationship more precisely rather than by trying an entirely different one.

Sample Questions from PSAT/NMSQT Practice Test—Section 1

Each question below consists of a word in capital letters, followed by five lettered words or phrases. Choose the word or phrase that is most nearly <u>opposite</u> in meaning to the word in capital letters. Since some of the questions require you to distinguish fine shades of meaning, consider all the choices before deciding which is best.

Example:

GOOD: (A) sour   (B) bad   (C) red   (D) hot   (E) ugly

1. BIND: (A) lend   (B) seek   (C) free   (D) measure   (E) level
2. PENALIZE: (A) respect   (B) reward   (C) befriend (D) correct   (E) release
3. EXAGGERATE: (A) comply   (B) adapt   (C) specialize   (D) minimize (E) familiarize
4. ELEGANT: (A) coarse   (B) manual   (C) illegitimate   (D) large (E) possible
5. BLOAT: (A) divide   (B) fade   (C) soften   (D) dilute   (E) shrink
6. ENTERPRISING: (A) unexpected   (B) appropriate   (C) well preserved   (D) without initiative   (E) in need of protection
7. GRAPHIC: (A) inconvenient   (B) unjustified   (C) not vivid   (D) not satisfactory   (E) not tolerable
8. TRIFLING: (A) mistaken   (B) hidden   (C) confused   (D) tactless (E) significant

Each sentence below has one or two blanks, each blank indicating that something has been omitted. Beneath the sentence are five lettered words or sets of words. Choose the word or set of words that, when inserted in the sentence, <u>best</u> fits the meaning of the sentence as a whole.

Example:

Although its publicity has been ——, the film itself is intelligent, well-acted, handsomely produced, and altogether ——.

(A) tasteless . . respectable   (B) extensive . . moderate   (C) sophisticated . . amateur   (D) risqué . . crude   (E) perfect . . spectacular

21. He writes like a man crossing a minefield—every word a --- step.

    (A) rhythmical (B) weary (C) militant (D) brazen (E) hesitant

22. Some Native American organizations recently have been successful in defending legal land rights previously protected only by tradition and unenforced ---.

    (A) debts (B) chronicles (C) testimony (D) outposts
    (E) treaties

23. Although many women in politics are not feminists, research --- that there is a pronounced --- women's rights on the part of officeholders who are women.

    (A) denies . . interest in (B) supports . . neglect of (C) confirms . . concern for (D) obscures . . need for (E) refutes . . consciousness of

24. As a scientist, Dr. Conti makes only --- predictions, for she does not believe that science can ever absolutely foretell the future.

    (A) unquestionable (B) explicit (C) categorical (D) conditional
    (E) negative

25. The architects agree that it would be --- to reconstruct the mansion exactly because the few existing records provide only --- information about the structure.

    (A) difficult . . unavailable (B) efficient . . historical
    (C) impossible . . sketchy (D) important . . reclassified
    (E) pointless . . detailed

Each question below consists of a related pair of words or phrases, followed by five lettered pairs of words or phrases. Select the lettered pair that best expresses a relationship similar to that expressed in the original pair.

Example:

YAWN : BOREDOM :: (A) dream : sleep (B) anger : madness
(C) smile : amusement (D) face : expression (E) impatience : rebellion

31. CUT:CHISEL::   (A) eat:plate   (B) act:stage   (C) kick:mule
(D) gore:bull   (E) dig:shovel
32. BABY CARRIAGE:INFANT::   (A) bus:bus driver   (B) taxi:passenger
(C) wheelchair:nurse   (D) horse:groom   (E) car:auto mechanic
33. FLOWER:BOUQUET::   (A) blouse:suit   (B) dog:animal
(C) finger:arm   (D) cow:herd   (E) nail:hammer
34. LOCKER ROOM:ATHLETE::   (A) barracks:soldier
(B) ballroom:debutante   (C) dressing room:actor   (D) concert
hall:pianist   (E) reformatory:delinquent
35. MORTIFY:EMBARRASSMENT::   (A) disillusion:fantasy
(B) infuriate:anger   (C) chide:confusion   (D) assuage:pain
(E) alienate:empathy
36. GREENHOUSE:PLANTS::   (A) incubator:chicks
(B) smokehouse:meats   (C) refrigerator:ice   (D) hold:cargo
(E) vault:jewels

ANSWER KEY FOR
PSAT/NMSQT PRACTICE TEST
SECTION 1

1. C	21. E	31. E
2. B	22. E	32. B
3. D	23. C	33. D
4. A	24. D	34. C
5. E	25. C	35. B
6. D		36. A
7. C		
8. E		

2. The SAT

The following vocabulary questions and explanations are reprinted with permission from *Taking the SAT*, a 1991–1992 booklet published by the College Entrance Examination Board and the Educational Testing Service.

Sample Questions and Explanations

Antonyms (opposites)

Antonym questions primarily test the extent of your vocabulary. The vocabulary used in the antonym questions includes words that you are likely to come across in your general reading, although some words may not be the kind you use in everyday speech.

Directions: Each question below consists of a word in capital letters, followed by five lettered words or phrases. Choose the word or phrase that is most nearly opposite in meaning to the word in capital letters. Since some of the questions require you to distinguish fine shades of meaning, consider all the choices before deciding which is best.

Example:
GOOD: (A) sour (B) bad (C) red (D) hot (E) ugly

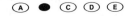

You can probably answer this example without thinking very much about the choices. However, most of the antonyms in the verbal section require more careful analysis. When you work on antonym questions, remember that:

1. Among the five choices offered, you are looking for the word that means the *opposite* of the given word. Words that have exactly the same meaning as the given word are not included among the five choices.

2. You are looking for the *best* answer. Read all of the choices before deciding which one is best, even if you feel sure you know the answer. For example:

   SUBSEQUENT: (A) primary (B) recent (C) contemporary
   (D) prior (E) simultaneous

Subsequent means "following in time or order; succeeding." Someone working quickly might choose (B) *recent* because it refers to a past action and *subsequent* refers to an action in the future. However, choice (D) *prior* is the best answer. It is more nearly the opposite of *subsequent* than is *recent*.

3. Few words have exact opposites, that is, words that are opposite in all of their meanings. You should find the word that is *most nearly* opposite. For example:

**FERMENTING: (A) improvising   (B) stagnating   (C) wavering
(D) plunging   (E) dissolving**

Even though *fermenting* is normally associated with chemical reactions, whereas *stagnating* is normally associated with water, *fermenting* means "being agitated," and *stagnating* means "being motionless." Therefore, choice (B) *stagnating* is the best of the five choices.

4. You need to be flexible. A word can have several meanings. For example:

DEPRESS: (A) force   (B) allow   (C) clarify   (D) elate   (E) loosen

The word *depress* can mean "to push down." However, no word meaning "to lift up" is included among the choices. Therefore, you must consider another meaning of *depress*, "to sadden or discouarge." Option (D) *elate* means "to fill with joy or pride." The best answer is (D) *elate*.

5. You'll often recognize a word you have encountered in your reading but have never looked up in the dictionary. If you don't know the dictionary meaning of a word but have a sense of how the word should be used, try to make up a short phrase or sentence using the word. This may give you a clue as to which choice is an opposite, even though you may not be able to define the word precisely.

**INCUMBENT: (A) conscious   (B) effortless   (C) optional
(D) improper   (E) irrelevant**

You may remember *incumbent* used in a sentence such as "It is incumbent upon me to finish this." If you can think of such a phrase, you may be able to recognize that *incumbent* means "imposed as a duty" or "obligatory." Of the five choices, (A), (B), and (D) are in no way opposites of *incumbent* and you can easily eliminate them. Choice (E) means "not pertinent" and choice (C) means "not compulsory." Although choice (E) may look attractive, choice (C) *optional* is more nearly an exact opposite to *incumbent*. Choice (C), therefore, is the answer.

Hints for Antonyms:

Answering antonyms depends on knowing the uses as well as the meanings of words, so just memorizing word lists is probably of little value. You're more likely to improve your performance on antonyms and other kinds of verbal questions by doing things that help you to think about words and the way they are used. So, it would be a good idea to:

- Read books or magazines on subjects with which you're not already familiar. This will give you an idea of how familiar words can have different meanings in different contexts.
- Use a dictionary when you come across words that you don't understand. This will help to broaden your vocabulary and could improve your performance on the tests.

Analogies

Analogy questions test your ability to see a relationship in a pair of words, to understand the ideas expressed in the relationship, and to recognize a similar or parallel relationship.

Directions: Each question below consists of a related pair of words or phrases, followed by five lettered pairs of words or phrases. Select the lettered pair that <u>best</u> expresses a relationship similar to that expressed in the original pair.

Example:
YAWN:BOREDOM:: **(A) dream:sleep** **(B) anger:madness** **(C) smile:amusement** **(D) face:expression** **(E) impatience:rebellion**

Ⓐ Ⓑ ● Ⓓ Ⓔ

The first step in answering an analogy question is to establish a precise relationship between the original pair of words (the two capitalized words). In the example above, the relationship between *yawn* and *boredom* can best be stated as "(first word) is a physical sign of (second word)," or "(first word) is a facial expression of (second word)."

The second step in answering an analogy question is to decide which of the five pairs given as choices best expresses a similar relationship. In the example above, the answer is choice (C): a (smile) is a physical sign of (amusement), or a (smile) is a facial expression of (amusement). None of the other choices shares a similar relationship with the capitalized pair of words: a *dream* is something that occurs when you are asleep, but it is not usually thought of as being a sign of *sleep* as, for example, closed eyes or a snore might be; *anger* denotes strong displeasure and *madness* can refer to rage or insanity, but neither word is a physical sign of the other; an *expression* is something that appears on a *face*, but a *face* is not a sign of an *expression*; *impatience* may lead to *rebellion* or be characteristic of a rebellious person, but *impatience* is not a physical sign of *rebellion*.

For the analogy below, state the relationship between the original pair of words and then decide which pair of words from choices (A) to (E) has a similar or parallel relationship.

> **SUBMISSIVE : LED ::   (A) wealthy : employed**
> **(B) intolerant : indulged   (C) humble : humiliated**
> **(D) incorrigible : taught   (E) inconspicuous : overlooked**

The relationship between *submissive* and *led* can be expressed as "to be submissive is to be easily led." Only choice (E) has the same relationship: "to be inconspicuous is to be easily overlooked." To be *intolerant* is not to be easily *indulged*, to be *humble* is not to be easily *humiliated*, and to be *incorrigible* (or incapable of being reformed) is not to be easily *taught*. With regard to choice (A), the statement "to be wealthy is to be easily employed" is an expression of opinion and not an expression of the relationship between the words according to their dictionary meanings.

You may want to practice describing precise verbal relationships. Below are some examples of the kinds of relationships that could be used.

> **SONG : REPERTOIRE: (A) score : melody   (B) instrument : artist**
> **(C) solo : chorus   (D) benediction : church   (E) suit : wardrobe**

The best answer is choice (E). The relationship between the words can be expressed as "several (first word) make up a (second word)." Several (songs) make up a (repertoire) as several (suits) make up a (wardrobe).

> **REQUEST : ENTREAT ::   (A) control : explode   (B) admire : idolize**
> **(C) borrow : steal   (D) repeat : plead   (E) cancel : invalidate**

The best answer is choice (B). Although both of the capitalized words have similar meanings, they express different degrees of feeling; to (entreat) is to (request) with strong feeling as to (idolize) is to (admire) with strong feeling. To answer analogy questions, you must think carefully about the precise meanings of words. For instance, if you thought the word "entreat" meant only "to ask" instead of "to ask urgently," you would have trouble establishing the correct relationship between *request* and *entreat*.

FAMINE : STARVATION ::   (A) deluge : flood
(B) drought : vegetation   (C) war : treaty   (D) success : achievement
(E) seed : mutation

The best answer is (A). The relationship can be stated as (famine) results in (starvation) as a (deluge) results in a (flood). None of the other pairs of words expresses a causal relationship. (C) is close, since a *treaty* often follows a *war*, but we do not think of a war "causing" a treaty in the same way that a famine "causes" starvation.

AMPLIFIER : HEAR ::   (A) turntable : listen   (B) typewriter : spell
(C) platter : eat   (D) camera : feel   (E) microscope : see

The best answer is choice (E). An (amplifier) magnifies in order to help a person (hear) in the same way that a (microscope) magnifies in order to help a person (see). Note that, in (A), while a *turntable* is part of a larger mechanism that allows a person to *listen*, the choice is not as good an answer as (E) because a *turntable* does not magnify anything. Choice (D) is also wrong for a similar reason: a *camera* produces pictures that may make a person *feel* something, but a *camera* does not magnify in order to help a person *feel*.

Some choices may have relationships that are close but not parallel to the relationship in the original pair. However, the correct answer has *most nearly* the same relationship as the original pair. Look at the following:

KNIFE : INCISION ::   (A) bulldozer : excavation   (B) tool : operation
(C) pencil : calculation   (D) hose : irrigation   (E) plow : agriculture

On the most general level, the relationship between *knife* and *incision* is that the object indicated by the first word is used to perform the action indicated by the second word. Since "a (knife) is used to make an (incision)," "a (bulldozer) is used to make an (excavation)," and "a (hose) is used for (irrigation)," there appear to be two correct answers. You need to go back and state the relationship more precisely. Some aspect of the relationship between the original pair exists in only one of the choices. A more precise relationship between *knife* and *incision* could be expressed as: "a knife cuts into something to make an incision" and "a bulldozer cuts into something to make an excavation." This relationship eliminates *hose : irrigation* as a possible answer. The best answer is choice (A).

Remember that a pair of words can have more than one relationship. For example:

PRIDE : LION ::   (A) snake : python   (B) pack : wolf   (C) rat : mouse
(D) bird : starling   (E) dog : canine

A possible relationship between *pride* and *lion* might be that "the first word describes a characteristic of the second (especially in mythology)." Using this reasoning, you might look for an answer such as *wisdom:owl*, but none of the given choices has that kind of relationship. Another relationship between *pride* and *lion* is "a group of lions is called a pride"; therefore, the answer is (B) *pack:wolf*, since "a group of wolves is called a pack."

Hints for Analogies

State the relationship between the two capitalized words in a sentence or phrase as clearly as you can. Next, find the pair of words that has the most similar or parallel relationship. Don't be misled by choices that merely suggest a vague association. Be sure that you can identify a specific relationship.

Always compare the relationship between the pair of capitalized words with the relationship between the pair of words in each of the choices. Don't try to set up a relationship between the first word in the original pair and the first word in each of the five choices.

Think carefully about the meanings of words. The words in analogy questions are used according to their dictionary definitions or meanings closely related to their dictionary definitions. The better you know the precise meanings of words, the less trouble you'll have establishing the correct relationships between them.

Don't be misled by relationships that are close but not parallel to the relationship in the original pair. The correct answer has a relationship that is most nearly parallel to the relationship between the capitalized words.

Sentence Completion Questions

Sentence completion questions test your ability to recognize relationships among parts of a sentence. In sentence completion questions, you have to know the meanings of the words offered as choices and you also have to know how to use those words properly in the context of a sentence. The sentences are taken from published material and cover a wide variety of topics. You'll find that, even if you're not familiar with the topic of a sentence, there's enough information in the sentence for you to find the correct answer from the context of the sentence itself.

Directions: Each sentence below has one or two blanks, each blank indicating that something has been omitted. Beneath the sentence are five lettered words or sets of words. Choose the word or set of words that, when inserted in the sentence, <u>best</u> fits the meaning of the sentence as a whole.

Example:
Although its publicity has been ———, the film itself is intelligent, well-acted, handsomely produced, and altogether ———.
(A) tasteless . . respectable   (B) extensive . . moderate   (C) sophisticated . . amateur   (D) risqué . . crude   (E) perfect . . spectacular

The word *although* suggests that the publicity gave the wrong impression of the movie, so look for two words that are more or less opposite in meaning. Also, the second word has to fit in with "intelligent, well-acted, handsomely produced." Choices (D) and (E) are not opposites. The words in choice (B) are somewhat opposite in meaning, but do not logically fulfill the expectation set up by the word *although.* Choice (C) can't be the correct answer, even though *sophisticated* and *amateur* are nearly opposites, because an "intelligent, well-acted, handsomely produced" film isn't amateurish. Only choice (A), when inserted in the sentence, makes a logical statement.

For a better understanding of sentence completion questions, read the following sample questions and explanations.

Nearly all the cultivated plants utilized by the Chinese have been of ——— origin; even rice, though known in China since Neolithic times, came from India.

   (A) foreign   (B) ancient   (C) wild   (D) obscure   (E) common

To answer this question, you need to consider the entire sentence—the part that comes after the semicolon as well as the part that comes before it. If you only consider the first part of the question, all five choices seem plausible. The second part of the sentence adds a specific example—that rice came to China from India. This idea of origin supports and clarifies the "origin" mentioned in the first part of the sentence and eliminates (C), (D), and (E) as possible answers. The mention of Neolithic times makes (B) harder to eliminate, but the sentence is not logical when (B) is used to fill in the blank because the emphasis in the second part of the sentence—country of origin—is inconsistent with that in the first—age. Only choice (A) produces a sentence that is logical and consistent.

The excitement does not --- but --- his senses, giving him a keener perception of a thousand details.

(A) slow .. diverts (B) blur .. sharpens (C) overrule .. constricts (D) heighten .. aggravates (E) forewarn .. quickens

Since the sentence has two blanks to be filled, you must make sure that both words make sense in the sentence. If you look for grammatical clues within the sentence, you will see that the word *but* implies that the answer will involve two words that are more or less opposite in meaning. If you keep this in mind, you can eliminate all of the choices except for (B) *blur .. sharpens.* Only the words in choice (B) imply opposition. Also, "sharpens his senses" is consistent with the notion that he has a "keener perception of a thousand details."

They argue that the author was determined to --- his own conclusion, so he --- any information that did not support it.

(A) uphold .. ignored (B) revise .. destroyed (C) advance .. devised (D) disprove .. distorted (E) reverse .. confiscated

The logic of the sentence makes it fairly easy to eliminate choices (B), (D), and (E). The first word in choice (A), *uphold,* and the first word in (C), *advance,* seem all right. However, the second word in choice (C), *devised,* does not make sense in the sentence. Why would an author who wished to advance his theory devise information that did not support it? Only choice (A) makes a logically consistent sentence.

She is a skeptic, --- to believe that the accepted opinion of the majority is generally ---.

(A) prone .. infallible (B) afraid .. misleading (C) inclined .. justifiable (D) quick .. significant (E) disposed .. erroneous

The words to be inserted in the blank spaces in the question above must result in a statement that is consistent with the definition of a skeptic. Since a skeptic would hardly consider the accepted opinion of the majority as *infallible, justifiable,* or *significant,* you can eliminate choices (A), (C), and (D). A skeptic would not be afraid that the accepted opinion of the majority is misleading; a skeptic would believe that it was. Therefore, choice (B) is not correct. Only choice (E), *disposed .. erroneous* makes a logical sentence.

Hints for Sentence Completions

- ✓ Read the entire sentence carefully; make sure you understand the ideas being expressed.
- ✓ Don't select an answer simply because it is a popular cliché or "sounds good."
- ✓ In a question with two blanks, the right answer must correctly fill <u>both</u> blanks. A wrong answer choice often includes one correct and one incorrect word.
- ✓ After choosing an answer, read the entire sentence to yourself and make sure that it makes sense.
- ✓ Consider all the choices; be sure you haven't overlooked a choice that makes a better and more accurate sentence than your choice does.

Sample Questions from SAT Practice Test— Section 1

Each question below consists of a word in capital letters, followed by five lettered words or phrases. Choose the word or phrase that is most nearly <u>opposite</u> in meaning to the word in capital letters. Since some of the questions require you to distinguish fine shades of meaning, consider all the choices before deciding which is best.

Example:

GOOD: (A) sour (B) bad (C) red (D) hot (E) ugly

1. DRENCH: (A) extend (B) heat (C) search (D) dry out
   (E) pull apart
2. STIMULATE: (A) record (B) suppress (C) criticize
   (D) assemble (E) illuminate
3. CIVIL: (A) rude (B) inefficient (C) shy (D) lazy (E) proud
4. RUPTURE: (A) immensity (B) clamor (C) dejection
   (D) scrutiny (E) union
5. GROUNDLESS: (A) familiar (B) symmetrical (C) well-founded
   (D) deeply appreciated (E) carefully executed

Each sentence below has one or two blanks, each blank indicating that something has been omitted. Beneath the sentence are five lettered words or sets
of words. Choose the word or set of words that, when inserted in the sentence, <u>best</u> fits the meaning of the sentence as a whole.

Example:

Although its publicity has been ---, the film itself is intelligent, well-acted,
handsomely produced, and altogether ---.
(A) tasteless . . respectable   (B) extensive . . moderate   (C) sophisticated
. . amateur   (D) risqué . . crude   (E) perfect . . spectacular

● Ⓑ Ⓒ Ⓓ Ⓔ

11. Scientists have discovered that our sense of smell is surprisingly
    ---, capable of distinguishing thousands of chemical odors.

    (A) rigid   (B) inert   (C) erratic   (D) keen   (E) innate

12. With these --- sites as evidence, it would be --- to draw definite
    conclusions as to the places typically selected as settlements by the
    people of the Neolithic age.

    (A) imperfect . . feasible
    (B) few . . unsound
    (C) complete . . ridiculous
    (D) abundant . . presumptuous
    (E) scattered . . prudent

Each question below consists of a related pair of words or phrases, followed
by five lettered pairs of words or phrases. Select the lettered pair that <u>best</u>
expresses a relationship similar to that expressed in the original pair.

Example:

YAWN : BOREDOM ::   (A) dream : sleep   (B) anger : madness
(C) smile : amusement   (D) face : expression   (E) impatience : rebellion

Ⓐ Ⓑ ● Ⓓ Ⓔ

16. NUTRIENTS : FOOD ::   (A) oxygen : air   (B) earth : plants
    (C) diet : health   (D) disease : symptom   (E) moon : night
17. LIE : UNTRUTHFUL ::   (A) steal : punished   (B) exaggerate : retold
    (C) proofread : erroneous   (D) pardon : forgiving   (E) pray : kneeling
18. SHELL : WALNUT ::   (A) coating : candy   (B) peel : banana
    (C) icing : cake   (D) loaf : bread   (E) root : tree
19. RENOVATE : BUILDING ::   (A) revoke : contract
    (B) rejuvenate : age   (C) restore : painting   (D) repeat : sentence
    (E) relinquish : possession

Section 3

Each question below consists of a word in capital letters, followed by five lettered words or phrases. Choose the word or phrase that is most nearly <u>opposite</u> in meaning to the word in capital letters. Since some of the questions require you to distinguish fine shades of meaning, consider all the choices before deciding which is best.

Example:

GOOD: (A) sour (B) bad (C) red (D) hot (E) ugly

1. EXCESS: (A) response (B) modification (C) concealment
   (D) shortage (E) slenderness
2. DETESTABLE: (A) measurable (B) mature (C) agreeable
   (D) expensive (E) colorful
3. PREDETERMINED: (A) not encountered before (B) not decided
   in advance (C) not essential (D) imperfect (E) undesirable
4. COINCIDE: (A) diverge (B) hesitate (C) intend (D) remove
   (E) excite
5. VAPORIZE: (A) decrease (B) progress (C) immobilize
   (D) condense (E) dilute
6. DRAWBACK: (A) festivity (B) proposal (C) tabulation
   (D) sketch (E) asset

Each sentence below has one or two blanks, each blank indicating that something has been omitted. Beneath the sentence are five lettered words or sets of words. Choose the word or set of words that, when inserted in the sentence, <u>best</u> fits the meaning of the sentence as a whole.

Example:

Although its publicity has been ---, the film itself is intelligent, well-acted, handsomely produced, and altogether ---.
(A) tasteless . . respectable (B) extensive . . moderate (C) sophisticated
. . amateur (D) risqué . . crude (E) perfect . . spectacular

16. The athlete's insistence on self-discipline had become ---; rarely, it seemed, did he allow himself even a minor indulgence.

    (A) dilatory (B) obsessive (C) spontaneous (D) infectious
    (E) unemotional

17. All female red *Colobus* monkeys leave their natal troops, but because these females are ---- by young females from other troops, the practice has little effect on troop size and composition.

(A) joined   (B) replaced   (C) ignored   (D) influenced   (E) rejected

---

Each question below consists of a related pair of words or phrases, followed by five lettered pairs of words or phrases. Select the lettered pair that <u>best</u> expresses a relationship similar to that expressed in the original pair.

Example:

YAWN:BOREDOM::   (A) dream:sleep   (B) anger:madness
(C) smile:amusement   (D) face:expression   (E) impatience:rebellion

---

36. HAMMER:CARPENTER::   (A) stone:mason   (B) brush:painter
(C) music:violinist   (D) suspect:detective   (E) bracelet:jeweler
37. EXPEL:SCHOOL::   (A) deny:entrance   (B) banish:country
(C) reject:offer   (D) extricate:safety   (E) abandon:enemy
38. SALUTATION:LETTER::   (A) greeting:conversation
(B) message:telegram   (C) goodwill:feeling   (D) address:location
(E) agreement:debate
39. PEPPER MILL:GRINDING::
(A) scale:weighing   (B) grease:moving   (C) detergent:scrubbing
(D) engine:fueling   (E) spice:seasoning
40. FACTION:POLITICS::   (A) geography:history   (B) war:peace
(C) sect:religion   (D) taxes:income   (E) duel:honor

ANSWER KEY FOR SAT PRACTICE TEST

SECTION 1			SECTION 3		
1. D	11. D	16. A	1. D	16. B	36. B
2. B	12. B	17. D	2. C	17. B	37. B
3. A		18. B	3. B		38. A
4. E		19. C	4. A		39. A
5. C			5. D		40. C
			6. E		

CHAPTER 12

Dictionary of Words Taught in This Text

The following pages contain a partial listing of the words presented in this book. The words included are those likely to offer some degree of difficulty. The definitions given have in many cases been condensed.

The numeral following a definition indicates the page on which the word appears. Roman type (e.g., **abhor,** 26) is used when the word appears as a main entry. Italic type (e.g., **abase,** *68*) is used when the word appears as a subentry, such as a definition or a synonym of the main entry.

Use this dictionary as a tool of reference and review. It is a convenient means of restudying the meanings of words that you may have missed in the exercises. It is also a useful device for a general review before an important vocabulary test. Bear in mind, however, that you will get a fuller understanding of these words from the explanations and exercises in the foregoing chapters.

abase: lower *68*

abhor: utterly detest; loathe; hate 26

abhorrent: loathsome, repugnant 26

abiogenesis: spontaneous generation 116

abject: deserving contempt; sunk to a low condition 67, 176

aboard: on a ship, train, bus, *etc.*; on or into 200

abridge: shorten 211

abrupt: broken off; sudden 144, *172*

abstemious: sparing in eating and drinking 79

abstinent: sparing in eating and drinking *79*

absurd: ridiculous *60, 90*

abysmal: profound; immeasurably great 67

abyss: bottomless, immeasurably deep space 67

a cappella: without musical accompaniment 246

access: way of entering *171*

acclaim: welcome with approval 57

acclivity: upward slope 65

accredited: officially authorized or recognized 157

acme: highest point 65

acquit: pronounce not guilty 34

acrid: sharp in smell or taste 71

acrophobia: fear of being at a great height   99

adagio: slow; in an easy, graceful manner   244

adherent: supporter; follower   *218*

adieu: good-bye   222

adjacent: lying near or next to   83

admonish: warn of a fault   26, 155

admonitory: conveying a gentle rebuke   155

adobe: brick of sun-dried clay or mud; structure made of such bricks   262

adolescent: growing from childhood to adulthood   75

adolescent: teenager   75

Adonis: very handsome young man   187

adulation: excessive praise   47

aegis: shield or protection; sponsorship   187

affidavit: sworn written statement made before an authorized official   158

affirmation: oath   213

aficionado: devoted follower of some sport or art; fan; devotee   259

afoul: in a state of entanglement   200

aggressive: disposed to attack   171

agoraphobia: fear of open spaces   99

à la carte: dish by dish, with a stated price for each dish   232

alacrity: cheerful willingness   65

a la mode: according to fashion; stylish   232

alfresco: in the open air; outdoor   253

allegro: quick   245

aloof: withdrawn   200

alto: highest male voice; lowest female voice (contralto)   243

altruism: unselfish concern for others   94

amazon: tall, strong, masculine woman   188

ambience: surrounding atmosphere   235

ambrosial: exceptionally pleasing to taste or smell   26, 188

ameliorate: become better; improve   7

amiss: wrong; imperfect; faulty   200

amoral: without sense of moral responsibility   106

amorphous: shapeless; without definite form; unorganized   91, 106, 129

amphibious: able to live both on land and in water   116

analogy: likeness in some respects between things otherwise different   87

anarchy: total absence of rule or government; confusion   107, 126

anatomy: dissection of plants or animals for the purpose of studying their structure; structure of a plant or animal   118

andante: moderately slow, but flowing   244

anemia: lack of a normal number of red blood cells   107

anent: about; concerning; in respect to   204

anesthesia: loss of feeling or sensation resulting from ether, chloroform, novocaine, etc.   107

anesthetic: drug that produces anesthesia   107

Anglophile: supporter of England or the English   101

Anglophobe: one who dislikes England or the English   100

Anglophobia: dislike of England or the English   100

anguish: extreme pain   45

anhydrous: destitute of water   107

anomalous: not normal; abnormal   107

anomaly: deviation from the common rule   107

anon: soon; presently   204

anonymous: nameless; of unknown or unnamed origin   107

anoxia: deprivation of oxygen   107

antediluvian: antiquated; belonging to the time before the Biblical Flood   75

anthropology: science dealing with the origin, races, customs, and beliefs of man   114

anthropomorphic: attributing human form or characteristics to beings not human, especially gods   129

antibiotic: antibacterial substance produced by a living organism   116

anticlimax: abrupt decline from the

important to the trivial;
comedown 67

antidote: remedy for a poison or
evil 54

antipasto: appetizer consisting of fish,
meats, etc.; hors d'oeuvres 253

antipathy: strong dislike 128

antipodes: parts of the earth (or their
inhabitants) diametrically
opposite 119

anxious: fearful of what may
come *175*

apathy: lack of feeling, emotion, interest, or excitement 128

apéritif: alcoholic drink taken before a
meal as an appetizer 232

apex: farthest point opposite the base,
as in a triangle or pyramid *67*

aphelion: farthest point from the sun
in the orbit of a planet or
comet *131*

apiary: place where bees are kept 53

aplomb: absolute confidence in oneself; poise 221

apnea: temporary cessation of
breathing 107

apogee: farthest point from earth in
the orbit of a heavenly body; highest point; culmination 65, 127

apostate: one who has forsaken the
faith, principles, or party he or she
supported earlier *260*

appellation: name 213

appendectomy: surgical removal of the
appendix 118

apprehend: seize or take into custody;
understand 175

apprehensive: fearful of what may
come 175

appropriate: take for oneself 212

approximate: nearly correct 83

apropos: by the way; incidentally 235

apropos: appropriate; relevant;
pertinent 235

aqueduct: artificial channel for conducting water from a distance 168

arbiter: a person having power to decide a dispute *88*

arbitrary: proceeding from a
whim or fancy; autocratic;
tyrannical 88

arbitrate: decide a dispute, acting as
arbiter (judge); submit a dispute to
an arbiter 88

arbitrator: judge *88*

archaic: no longer used, except in a
special context; old-fashioned 76

aria: melody; an elaborate, accompanied melody for a single voice in
an opera 247

aristocracy: class regarded as superior
in some respect *218*

aroma: pleasant odor 70

aromatic: sweet-scented; fragrant 70

arpeggio: production of the tones of a
chord in rapid succession and not
simultaneously; a chord thus
played 246

arrogant: haughty *93*

arroyo: watercourse; small, often dry,
gully 264

arthropod: any invertebrate (animal
having no backbone) with jointed
legs 119

ascetic: self-denying; person who
shuns pleasures 43

aseptic: free from or keeping away
disease-causing
microorganisms 107

asinine: like an ass or donkey; stupid,
silly 208

assertive: acting and speaking
boldly *171*

assuage: ease or lessen 211

astringent: drawing (the tissues)
tightly together; stern; substance
that shrinks tissues and checks flow
of blood by contracting blood
vessels 54, 146

asunder: apart 200

asymmetrical: not balanced in
arrangement *92*

asymptomatic: showing no symptoms
of disease 107

atheism: godlessness 107

atlas: book of maps 188

atom: smallest particle of an
element 118

atomizer: device for converting a liquid to a fine spray 118

atrophy: lack of growth from want of
nourishment or from disuse 107

attaché: member of the diplomatic staff of an ambassador or minister 218

attenuate: make thin; weaken 46

atypical: unlike the typical 107

au courant: well-informed; up-to-date 216

audiophile: one who is enthusiastic about high-fidelity sound reproduction 101

au revoir: good-bye till we meet again 222

auriferous: bearing or yielding gold 181

auroral: pertaining to or resembling the dawn; rosy 188

auspices: patronage and care *187*

austere: stern *146*

autarchy: rule by an absolute sovereign 126

autobiography: story of a person's life written by the person himself 116

avant-garde: experimentalists or innovators in any art 230

avarice: greed 213

averse: disinclined *65*

aversion: strong dislike 65, 177

avert: turn away; prevent 137, 177

aviary: place where birds are kept 53

avoirdupois: weight 235

axiom: self-evident truth; maxim 88

axiomatic: self-evident 88

bacchanalian: jovial or wild with drunkenness 188

bacchic: jovial or wild with drunkenness 188

bactericide: substance that kills bacteria 145

bacteriology: science dealing with the study of bacteria 114

badger: nag 53

baffle: bewilder 17

bagatelle: trifle 235

banter: playful teasing 58

baritone: male voice between bass and tenor 243

barrio: Spanish-speaking neighborhood 264

bas-relief: carving or sculpture in which the figures project only slightly from the background 230

bass: lowest male voice *230*

basso: lowest male voice 243

bathos: abrupt decline in dignity or importance at the end *67*

baton: stick with which a conductor beats time for an orchestra or band 230

beget: bring into life or into existence 211

begrime: make dirty 201

behest: command; order 204

beholden: bound in gratitude; indebted 204

behoove: be necessary for; be proper for 204

belittle: disparage 201

benediction: blessing 212

benighted: unenlightened; ignorant 201

benign: not dangerous; gentle 55

beset: attack on all sides; surround 201

besmirch: soil *82*

bête noire: object or person dreaded 224

betimes: early 204

bias: opinion formed before there are grounds for it; unthinking preference 88

bibliophile: lover of books 101

bibliophobe: one who strongly dislikes books 101

bigoted: narrow-minded 88

bigotry: views or behavior of a bigot 88

billet-doux: love letter 223

biochemistry: chemistry dealing with chemical compounds and processes in living plants and animals 117

biocidal: destructive to life 117

biocide: substance that destroys living microorganisms 145

biodegradable: decomposable into harmless substances by living microorganisms 117

biogenesis: development of life from preexisting life 117

biography: story of a person's life written by another person 117

biology: science dealing with the study of living organisms 115, 117

biometrics: statistical analysis of biologic data 117

biometry: statistical calculation of probable duration of human life 117

biopsy: diagnostic examination of a piece of tissue from the living body 117

biota: the living plants (flora) and living animals (fauna) of a region 117

biped: two-footed animal 173

blandishment: word or deed of mild flattery; enticement 47

blasé: tired of pleasures; bored 216

bliss: perfect happiness 41

blithe: merry; joyous; heedless 42

bluster: talk or act with noisy violence 189

boa constrictor: snake that crushes its prey in its coils 146

bodega: small grocery store 264

bolero: lively dance in ¾ time; the music for this dance; short, loose jacket 262

bombastic: using pompous language 180

bona fide: made or carried out in good faith 158

bonanza: accidental discovery of a rich mass of ore in a mine 262

bonbon: piece of candy 232

bon mot: clever saying 223

bouffant: full; puffed out 234

bouquet: pleasant odor 70

bourgeois: having to do with the middle class; lacking in culture or refinement 216

boutique: small shop specializing in fashionable clothes 234

bovine: cowlike or oxlike; sluggish and patient 208

bow: forward part of a ship 80

bowdlerize: remove objectionable material from a book 82

brava: (used to applaud a woman performer) well done 254

bravado: boastful behavior: pretense of bravery 262

bravo: (used to applaud a performance or male performer) well done 254

bravura: piece of music requiring skill and spirit in the performer; display of daring or brilliancy 247

brazen: shameless; made of brass or bronze; harsh-sounding 93

breach: a breaking gap; violation 67

brine: salty water; ocean 80

brisk: lively 245

brochure: pamphlet 223

bronco: half-wild pony 264

buffo: male singer who plays a comic role in an opera 251

bugbear: object of dread 224

buoy: keep afloat; raise the spirits of 42

buoyant: cheerful; able to float 42

burly: strongly and heavily built; husky 46

burro: small donkey used as a pack animal 264

buxom: plump and attractive 46

caballero: gentleman or gallant; horseman 259

cabana: beach shelter resembling a cabin 262

cajole: persuade by pleasing words 47

cajolery: persuasion by flattery; wheedling; coaxing 47

callow: young and inexperienced 76

calumnious: falsely and maliciously accusing 57

calumny: false and malicious accusation 57

cameo: gem carved with a design higher and different in color than its background; brief role by a prominent performer; exceptionally fine brief passage 249

campanile: bell tower 249

canard: false rumor 223

canine: doglike; one of four pointed teeth 208

concise: expressing much in a few words *190*

concur: agree; happen together 170

concurrent: running together; occurring at the same time 170

condescend: bow; stoop 211

conducive: tending to lead to 168

conduct: lead; guide 168

confidant(e): one to whom secrets are entrusted 158

confident: having faith in oneself 158

confidential: communicated in trust 158

confine: imprison 26

conflagration: fire 213

confrere: colleague; co-worker 218

congratulate: express pleasure at another's success 165

coniferous: bearing cones 181

conjectural: of the nature of a guess or assumption *123*

conjecture: a guess 176

connoisseur: expert 218

conquistador: conqueror 259

consecrate: bless 211

consecutive: following in order 169

consequence: result; importance 169

conserve: keep from waste; save 8

consign: hand over 35

consignee: person to whom something is shipped 35

consommé: clear soup; broth 232

constrict: bind; draw together; render narrower; shrink 146

consume: eat 211

consummate: perfect; superb 66

contact: touching or meeting; connection 174

contaminate: make impure by mixture 81

contemporary: of the same period 76

contemporary: person living at same time as another 76

contend: strive in opposition *170*

contiguous: touching; near 83, 174

contingent: dependent on something else; accidental 174

contort: twist out of shape *149*

contortionist: person who can twist or bend his or her body into odd postures 149

contour: outline of a figure 91

contralto: lowest female voice 243

contrariwise: on the contrary 202

contretemps: inopportune occurrence; embarrassing situation 225

contrite: showing regret for wrongdoing 44

contrition: regret for wrongdoing 44, 213

controversy: dispute 177

convalesce: recover health after illness 55

convalescent: person recovering from sickness 55

conventional: generally accepted *90*

convex: rounded like the exterior of a circle *91*

convict: prove guilty; person serving a prison sentence 150

conviction: state of having been judged guilty of an offense; strong belief 150

convince: persuade or show conclusively by argument or proof 150

convivial: fond of dining with friends; jovial 42, 148

corporal: bodily 167

corporation: body authorized by law to carry on an activity 167

corps: organized body of persons; branch of the military 167

corpse: dead body 167

corpulent: very fat 167

corpus: general collection of writings, laws, etc. 167

corpuscle: blood cell; minute particle 167

corpus delicti: facts proving a crime has been committed; body of the victim in a murder case 167

corroborate: confirm 211

corrupt: change from good to bad 144

corsage: small bouquet worn by a woman 234

coterie: set or circle of acquaintances 218

countermand: issue a contrary order 156

coup de grâce: merciful or decisive finishing stroke 235

coup d'état: sudden, violent, or illegal overthrow of a government   229

coy: pretending to be shy   93

cravat: necktie   234

credence: belief   157

credentials: documents, letters, references, etc., that inspire belief or trust   157

credible: believable   157

credit: trust   157

credulous: too ready to believe   157

creed (credo): summary of principles believed in or adhered to   157

crescendo: gradually increasing (or a gradual increase) in force or loudness   245

criminology: scientific study of crimes and criminals   115

criterion: standard   88

croissant: rich, flaky crescent-shaped roll   232

crone: withered old woman   76

crux: essential part   88

cuisine: style of cooking   232

cul-de-sac: blind alley   225

culmination: highest point   67

culpable: blamable   *173*

cumbersome: burdensome   202

cupola: rounded roof; small dome or tower on a roof   249

current: now in progress; a running or flowing, as of water   170

curriculum: specific course of study in a school or college   170

curry favor: seek to gain favor by flattery   47

cursive: running or flowing   170

cursory: running over hastily   170

deadlock: stoppage produced by the opposition of equally powerful persons or groups   *225*

debacle: collapse   225

debonair: affable and courteous   217

debut: formal entrance into society; first public appearance   *218*

debutante: young woman who has just made her debut   218

decade: period of ten years   26

decapitate: behead   211

deceptive: misleading   89

declivity: downward slope   67

decontaminate: rid of contamination   *81*

decrepit: weakened by old age   76

decrescendo: gradually decreasing (or a gradual decrease) in force or loudness   245

deduce: derive by reasoning   89

deduction: subtraction; reasoning from the general to the particular   168

defamatory: harming or destroying a reputation   *58*

defective: flawed; incomplete; imperfect   *174*

defile: make filthy   *82*

deflect: turn aside   153

defunct: dead; extinct   76

degrade: lower   *68*

dejected: sad; in low spirits   44, 176

delectable: very pleasing   42

demarche: course of action, especially one involving a change of policy   229

demise: death, especially of a monarch or other important person   179

demitasse: small cup for, or of, black coffee   233

demure: falsely modest or serious; grave   93

denouement: solution of the plot in a play, story, or complex situation   231

denunciation: public condemnation   *192*

dermatology: science dealing with the skin and its diseases   115

derogatory: expressing low esteem   58

desperado: bold, reckless criminal   259

despise: loathe   17

despotic: unjustly severe   *88*

détente: a relaxing, as of strained relations between nations   229

detention: act of keeping back or detaining   154

detonate: explode; cause to explode   27

detriment: damage; disadvantage   8

devotee: ardent adherent 218, *259*

devour: eat greedily or ravenously; seize upon and destroy 147, 211

diabolic(al): devilish; very cruel; wicked; fiendish 208

dichotomy: cutting or division into two 118

diffident: lacking self-confidence 93, 159

digressive: rambling *174*

dilemma: situation requiring a choice between two equally bad alternatives 89

dilettante: person who follows some art or science as an amusement or in a trifling way 251

dimorphous: occurring under two distinct forms 130

dipody: verse (line of poetry) consisting of two feet 119

dipsomania: abnormal, uncontrollable craving for alcohol 80

disconsolate: cheerless 44

discredit: cast doubt on; disgrace 157

discursive: wandering from one topic to another 171

disgruntled: in bad humor; discontented 44

disharmony: discord; lack of harmony *8*

disintegrate: break up 211

disrupt: break apart; cause disorder 144

distort: twist out of shape; change from the true meaning 91, 149

diva: principal female singer; prima donna 251

diversion: entertainment; amusement 177

divert: turn aside; amuse 177

docile: easily led *10, 168*

dogmatic: asserting opinions as if they were facts 89

dolce: soft; sweet 245

dolce far niente: delightful idleness 253

doldrums: calm, windless part of the ocean near the equator; listlessness 80

doleful: causing grief or sadness 44

dolorous: full of sorrow *44*

domicile: home 213

dour: gloomy *44*

Draconian: harsh 188

dregs: most worthless part; sediment at the bottom of a liquid 68

droll: odd and laughter-provoking 58

dross: waste; scum on the surface of melting metals 82

duckling: little duck 203

duct: tube or channel for conducting a liquid, air, etc. 168

ductile: able to be drawn out or hammered thin (said of a metal); easily led 168

duenna: elderly woman chaperon of a young lady; governess 260

duet: piece of music for two voices or instruments; two singers or players performing together 248

dysentery: inflammation of the large intestine 103

dysfunction: abnormal functioning, as of an organ of the body 103

dyslexia: impairment of ability to read 103

dyslogistic: expressing disapproval, uncomplimentary 103

dyspepsia: difficult digestion; indigestion 103

dysphagia: difficulty in swallowing 103

dysphasia: speech difficulty resulting from brain disease 103

dysphoria: sense of great unhappiness 103

dystopia: imaginary place where living conditions are dreadful 103

dystrophy: faulty nutrition 103

earthy: coarse, worldly 68

earldom: realm or dignity of an earl 202

ebullient: overflowing with enthusiasm 17

echolalia: automatic repetition of what others say 189

éclat: brilliancy of achievement 221

eclectic: choosing (ideas, methods, etc.) from various sources 89

ecology: science dealing with the relation of living things to their environment and to each other   115

ecstasy: state of overwhelming joy   42

ecstatic: in ecstasy; enraptured   42

effrontery: shameless boldness   35

egoism: excessive concern for oneself; selfishness   94

egress: exit   171

eject: throw out   176

élan: enthusiasm   221

elate: lift up with joy   66

elated: in high spirits   43

elite: group of individuals thought to be superior   218

elocution: art of speaking or reading effectively in public   180

eloquent: speaking with force and fluency   180

Elysian: blissful; heavenly   189

emaciated: abnormally lean because of starvation or illness   46

emancipate: free   211

émigré: refugee   219

eminence: high rank; lofty hill   66

eminent: standing out; notable; famous   66

emissary: person sent on a mission   179

emit: send out; give off   179

empathy: the complete understanding of another's feelings, motives, etc.   128

encomium: speech or writing of high praise; tribute; eulogy   57

encore: repetition of a performance; rendition of an additional selection   231

endocarditis: inflammation of the lining of the heart   125

endocrine: secreting internally   124

endoderm: membranelike tissue lining the greater part of the digestive tract   125

endogamy: marriage within the tribe, caste, or social group   124

endogenous: produced from within; due to internal causes   124

endomorphic: occurring within   130

endoparasite: parasite living in the internal organs of an animal   125

endophyte: plant growing within another plant   125

endoskeleton: internal skeleton or supporting framework in an animal   124

endosmosis: osmosis inward   124

ennui: boredom   221

en route: on the way   235

ensemble: complete costume of harmonious clothing and accessories   234

entente: understanding or agreement between governments   229

entourage: group of attendants accompanying a person   219

entrée: main dish at lunch or dinner   233

entre nous: between us   223

entrepreneur: one who assumes the risks and management of a business   219

environs: districts surrounding a place; suburbs   83

envoy: diplomatic agent; messenger   219

ephemeral: fleeting; short-lived   27

equanimity: evenness of mind   222

equine: of or like a horse   209

eristic: prone to controversy; argumentative   189

erupt: burst or break out   144

esprit de corps: feeling of union and common interest pervading a group   167, 221

ethereal: of the heavens; delicate   66

ethnology: science dealing with the races of mankind, their origin, distribution, culture, etc.   115

etiquette: conduct and manners of polite society   236

eugenics: science dealing with improving the hereditary qualities of the human race   104

eulogistic: expressing praise   57

eulogize: praise; extol; laud; glorify   57, 104

eupepsia: good digestion   104

euphemism: substitution of a "good" expression for an unpleasant one   104

euphonious: pleasing in sound   104

euphoria: sense of great happiness or well-being   104

euthanasia: illegal practice of painlessly putting to death a person suffering from an incurable, painfully distressing disease   104

euthenics: science dealing with improving living conditions   104

evict: expel   150

evince: show clearly   151

exaggerate: overstate   17

exalt: lift up with joy, pride, etc.; raise in rank, dignity, etc.   66

excoriate: flay, fleece, skin   211

excruciating: unbearably painful   35

exculpate: acquit   *34*

excursion: going out or forth; expedition   171

execrate: curse   211

execute: follow through to completion; put to death   169

exhort: urge   18

exhortation: urgent recommendation or advice   18

exocrine: secreting externally   124

exogamy: marriage outside the tribe, caste, or social group   124

exogenous: produced from without; due to external causes   124

exoskeleton: hard protective structure developed outside the body   124

exosmosis: osmosis outward   125

exoteric: external; readily understandable   125

exotic: introduced from a foreign country; excitingly strange   8, 125

expectorate: spit   211

expedite: accelerate or speed up; make easy   173

expertise: expertness   18

expurgate: remove objectionable material from a book; purify   82

extinct: no longer in existence   *76*

extol: praise   *57*

extort: wrest (money, promises, etc.) from a person by force   149

extraneous: not relevant; beside the point   *92*

extrovert: person more interested in what is going on around him than in his own thoughts and feelings   177

facade: face or front of a building, or of anything   236

facetious: in the habit of joking; said in jest without serious intent   59

facilitate: make easy   *173*

fait accompli: thing accomplished and presumably irrevocable   225

fallacious: based on an erroneous idea   89

fallacy: erroneous idea   *89*

fallible: liable to be mistaken   89

falsetto: unnaturally high-pitched male voice, artificial voice   244

farcical: exciting laughter   *60*

fatal: causing death   *166*

fathom: get to the bottom of; ascertain the depth of   *68*

fauna: animals of a particular region or period   189

faux pas: misstep or blunder in conduct, manners, speech, etc.   225

fawning: slavishly attentive   *48*

fealty: loyalty; faithfulness   *159*

feline: catlike; sly; stealthy   208

fester: form pus; rot   55

fete: to honor with a party; festival   236

fetid: ill-smelling   *70*

fiancé(e): person engaged to be married   219

fiasco: crash; complete or ridiculous failure   253

fidelity: faithfulness to a trust or vow; accuracy   159

fiduciary: held in trust; confidential   159

fiesta: saint's day; any festival or holiday   262

filament: thread   213

geography: study of the earth's surface, etc.   127

geology: science dealing with the earth's history as recorded in rocks   115, 127

geometry: mathematics dealing with lines, angles, surfaces, and solids   127

geomorphic: pertaining to the shape of the earth or the form of its surface   127

geophysics: science treating of the forces that modify the earth   127

geopolitics: study of government and its policies as affected by physical geography   127

geoponics: art or science of agriculture   127

georgic: agricultural; poem on husbandry (farming)   127

geotropism: response to earth's gravity, as the growing of roots downward in the ground   127

Germanophilia: admiration of Germany or the Germans   100

Germanophobe: one who dislikes Germany or the Germans   100

Germanophobia: dislike of Germany or the Germans   100

germicide: substance that kills germs   145

glee: joy   *59*

glum: gloomy   44

goatish: goatlike; coarse; lustful   209

gondola: boat used in the canals of Venice; cabin attached to the underpart of an airship   254

gosling: young goose   204

gourmand: person excessively fond of eating and drinking   219

gourmet: connoisseur in eating and drinking   219

gracious: courteous   165

gradation: a change by steps or stages   171

grade: step; stage   172

gradient: rate at which a road, railroad track, etc., rises; slope   172

gradual: by steps or degrees   172

graduate: complete all the steps of a course and receive a diploma or degree   172

graduated: arranged in regular steps, stages, or degrees   172

grandee: nobleman of the highest rank; person of eminence   260

grandiloquent: using lofty or pompous words   180

graphic: clear-cut and lifelike   *149*

grateful: thankful   165

gratify: give or be a source of pleasure or satisfaction   165

gratis: without charge or payment; free   165

gratitude: thankfulness   165

gratuitous: given freely; unwarranted   165

gratuity: present of money in return for a favor or service   165

grave: deserving serious attention   92

grave: slow (the slowest tempo in music)   244

grotto: cave   254

gruesome: horrifying and repulsive   *55*

gull: deceive; cheat   27

gullible: easily deceived   27

gusto: liking or taste; hearty enjoyment   253

habeas corpus: writ requiring a detained person to be brought before a court to investigate the legality of that person's detention   167

hacienda: large ranch; landed estate; country house   262

haggard: careworn   46

haggle: argue over a price   27

halcyon: calm   53

hamper: interfere with   35

harlequin: clown   58

harmony: peaceable relations   8

heath: tract of wasteland   204

hector: to bully; to bluster   189

herbicide: substance that kills plants   145

herbivore: plant-eating animal   147

herbivorous: dependent on plants as food   147

hypothesis: theory or supposition assumed as a basis for reasoning   123

hypothetical: pertaining to a supposition made as a basis for reasoning or research   89, 123

hypothyroid: marked by deficient activity of the thyroid gland   123

ignominy: shame   213

ignore: disregard   9

illusion: false impression   89

imbibe: drink   211

imbroglio: difficult situation, complicated disagreement   253

immaculate: absolutely clean   82

immerse: plunge into a liquid   27

immortal: not subject to death; imperishable   166

immortality: eternal life; lasting fame   166

immunity: resistance to a disease; freedom from an obligation   55

impasse: predicament affording no escape; impassable road   225

impede: hinder   173

impediment: hindrance; defect   9, 173

impertinent: inappropriate, rude   154

impregnability: strength; state of being unconquerable   213

impresario: organizer; manager; promoter   252

impudent: insolent   *93*

imputation: charge, esp. a false charge; insinuation; accusation   58

inadvertently: carelessly; unintentionally   177

inamorata: woman who loves or is loved   252

inamorato: man who loves or is loved   252

inane: silly; pointless   18

inanity: foolishness; shallowness   *18*

incense: substance yielding a pleasant odor when burned   70

incognito: with one's identity concealed; disguised state   253

incommunicado: deprived of communication with others; in solitary confinement   262

incomprehensible: not understandable   *175*

inconsequential: unimportant   169

incontrovertible: certain   177

incorporate: combine so as to form one body   167

incorruptible: incapable of being corrupted or bribed   144

incredible: not believable   158

incredulity: disbelief   158

incredulous: disbelieving; skeptical   *157*

incrustation: crust or coating   *250*

incur: meet with something undesirable; bring upon oneself   171

incursion: a rushing into; raid   171

indemnify: reimburse   18

indigo: plant yielding a blue dye; deep violet-blue   264

indisputable: too evident for doubt   *90*

indolent: lazy   9

indubitable: certain   90

induce: move by persuasion   168

induct: admit as a member   168

induction: ceremony by which one is made a member; initiation; reasoning from the particular to the general   168

inebriated: drunk   80

infallible: incapable of error   *89*

infanticide: act of killing (or killer of) an infant   145

infantile: of or like a very young child; babyish   77, 209

infer: derive by reasoning   *89*

inference: conclusion   *176*

infernal: pertaining to the realm of the dead; hellish   *194*

infidel: one who does not accept a particular faith   159

infidelity: faithlessness   *159*

inflection: change in the pitch or tone of a person's voice   153

inflexibility: rigidity   153

infraction: violation   151, 212

ingénue: naive young woman; actress playing such a role   219

ingenuous: artlessly frank   *217*

ingrate: ungrateful person   165

ingratiate: work (oneself) into another's favor   47, 165

ingratitude: ungratefulness   165

initiate: begin 211

inject: force or introduce a liquid, a re-mark, etc. 176

insatiable: incapable of being satisfied *148*

insecticide: preparation for killing insects 145

insectivorous: dependent on insects as food 147

insomnia: inability to sleep 26

insomniac: person suffering from insomnia 26

intact: kept or left whole 9, 174

intaglio: design engraved by making cuts in a surface 250

intangible: not capable of being touched 174

interject: throw in between 176

interlocutor: one who participates in a conversation; questioner 180

intermezzo: short musical or dramatic entertainment between the acts of a play; short musical composition be-tween the main divisions of an ex-tended musical work; a short, inde-pendent musical composition 248

intermittent: coming and going at intervals 179

interpose: place between *176*

interrupt: break into or between 144

intimidate: make fearful 211

intolerant: narrow-minded *88*

intoxicated: drunk *80*

intractable: hard to manage *152*

intricate: complicated *34, 190*

introvert: person more interested in his or her own thoughts than in what is going on around him or her 178

invalid: having no force; void 9

invalidate: make valueless 211

invert: turn upside down 178

inveterate: firmly established by age; habitual 77

invigorate: give vigor, life, or energy to 211

invincible: incapable of being conquered 151

involuntary: not done of one's own free will 65

iridescent: having colors like the rainbow 190

ironic(-al): containing or expressing irony 59

irony: type of humor whose intended meaning is the opposite of the words used 59

irrational: senseless *90*

irrelevant: not pertinent; inapplicable 92

jetsam: goods cast overboard to lighten a ship in distress 81

jettison: throw (goods) overboard to lighten a ship or plane; discard 81

jocose: given to jesting; playfully humorous 59

jocular: given to jesting; done as a joke *59*

jocund: merry 43

jovial: jolly 190

jubilation: rejoicing; exultation 43

junta: council for legislation or administration 260

junto: political faction; group of plotters 260

juvenile: of or for youth; immature 77

juxtapose: put side by side 83

juxtaposition: close or side-by-side position 83

kith and kin: friends and relatives 69

labyrinthine: full of confusing pas-sageways; complicated, like the Labyrinth 190

lackey: follower who carries out an-other's orders like a servant; toady 47

laconic: using words sparingly 190

laissez-faire: absence of government interference or regulation 229

lament: mourn; deplore 44

lamentable: pitiable 44

languid: lacking in vigor; weak *148*

lank: lean; ungracefully tall; lanky 47

lapse: cease being in force; become invalid 28

lapse: slip; error; interval 27

larceny: theft 213

largo: slow and dignified 244

Latino: Latin American 260

Latino: characteristic of Latinos 260
latter: later; second; last 8
laudable: praiseworthy 57
laudatory: expressing praise 57
lax: careless *179*
leeward: in the direction away from the wind 81
legato: smooth and connected 246
legerdemain: sleight of hand 221
legitimate: rightful; justifiable *88*
lento: slow 244
lesion: injury 55
lethargic: unnaturally drowsy; sluggish 190
lettre de cachet: sealed letter obtainable from the King of France (before the Revolution) ordering the imprisonment without trial of the person named in the letter 229
levity: lack of proper seriousness 60
liaison: bond; coordination of activities 225
libel: false and defamatory written or printed statement 58
libelous: injurious to reputation; defamatory 58
liberate: free 211
libretto: text or words of an opera or other long musical composition 248
lineage: descent in a line from a common ancestor *69*
lionize: treat as highly important 53
lissom(e): lithesome; nimble 203
lithe: slender and agile *47*
loath: disinclined 65
loathe: detest 65
lobotomy: type of brain surgery 118
longevity: long life; length of life 77
loquacious: talkative 180
Lucullan: luxurious 190
ludicrous: exciting laughter 60
lupine: of or like a wolf; ravenous 209

macho: overly assertive, domineering, virile male 260
macrocosm: great world; universe 105
macron: horizontal mark indicating that the vowel over which it is placed is long 105

macroscopic: large enough to be visible to the naked eye 105
maestro: eminent conductor, composer, or teacher of music; master in any art 252
maître d'hôtel: headwaiter 219
majolica: variety of enameled Italian pottery richly decorated in colors 250
maladroit: unskillful; clumsy 217
malaise: vague feeling of bodily discomfort or illness 221
malign: speak evil of 58
malignant: threatening to cause death; very evil 55
malleable: capable of being shaped by hammering; adaptable 91
malodorous: ill-smelling 70
mañana: tomorrow 264
mandate: authoritative command; a territory administered by a trustee (supervisory nation) 156
mandatory: required by command 156
mantilla: woman's light scarf or veil; cloak or cape 262
marathon: long-distance footrace 190
marine: of the sea or shipping 81
mariner: sailor; seaman 81
maritime: of the sea or shipping *81*
martial: pertaining to war; warlike 190
martinet: person who enforces very strict discipline 219
martyrdom: state of being a martyr 202
mastectomy: surgical removal of a breast 118
masticate: chew 211
matador: bullfighter appointed to kill the bull 266
maternal: motherly; inherited from or related to the mother's side 69, 207
matriarch: mother and ruler of a family 77
matriarchy: form of social organization in which the mother rules the family or tribe, descent being traced through the mother 126
matricide: act of killing (or killer of) one's own mother 145

mature: full-grown, carefully thought out 77

maudlin: weakly sentimental and tearful 44

mean: without distinction *68*

medley: mixture *225*

meekness: lack of nerve 18

melancholy: sad *45*

mélange: mixture 225

memento: keepsake; reminder *237*

menace: threat 213

menagerie: place where animals are kept 54

menial: low 68

mentor: wise and trusted advisor; athletic coach 191

mercurial: vivacious; changeable; crafty; eloquent 191

mesa: flat-topped rocky hill with steeply sloping sides 264

mestizo: person of mixed American Indian and European ancestry 260

metamorphosis: change of form 130

meteorology: science dealing with the atmosphere and weather 115

mettlesome: spirited 203

mezzanine: intermediate story in a theater between the main floor and the first balcony 250

mezzo-soprano: female voice between contralto and soprano 243

mezzotint: picture engraved on copper or steel by polishing or scraping away parts of a roughened surface 250

microbe: microscopic living animal or plant; microorganism 105, 117

microbicide: agent that destroys microbes 105

microcosm: little world; the world in miniature 105

microdont: having small teeth 105

microfilm: film of very small size 105

microgram: millionth of a gram 105

micrometer: millionth of a meter 105

microorganism: microscopic living animal or plant 106

microscopic: invisible to the naked eye *105*

microsecond: millionth of a second 106

microsurgery: surgery with microscopes and minute instruments or laser beams 106

microvolt: millionth of a volt 106

microwatt: millionth of a watt 106

microwave: very short electromagnetic wave; microwave oven 106

milieu: environment 236

militant: given to fighting *171*

millipede: wormlike animal with two pairs of legs on most of its segments 173

mirage: optical illusion 225

mirth: merriment *59*

misandry: hatred of males 102

misanthrope: hater of humanity 102

misanthropy: hatred of humanity 102

misconception: erroneous belief *89*

misogamy: hatred of marriage 102

misogyny: hatred of women 102

misology: hatred of argument or discussion 102

misoneism: hatred of anything new 102

missile: weapon propelled to hit a distant object 179

missive: letter 179

mocking: ridiculing *60*

moderato: in moderate time 245

modest: humble; decent *93*

modesty: freedom from conceit or vanity 93

molt: shed feathers, skin, hair, etc. 56

momentous: very important *92*

monarchy: state ruled over by a single person, as a king or queen 108, 126

monitor: regulate the operation of a machine or process 155

monochromatic: of one color 108

monocle: eyeglass for one eye 108

monogamy: marriage with but one mate at a time 108

monogram: two or more letters interwoven to represent a name 108

monograph: written account of a single thing or class of things 108

monolith: single stone of large size 108

monolog(ue): long speech by one person in a group 108

monomania: derangement of mind on one subject only 108

monomorphic: having a single form 109, 130

monophobia: fear of being alone 100

monosyllabic: having but one syllable 109

monotheism: belief that there is but one God 109

monotonous: continuing in an unchanging tone; wearying 109

morbid: having to do with disease; gruesome 55

moribund: near death 166

morose: ill-humoredly silent *45*

morphology: branch of biology dealing with the form and structure of animals and plants 115, 130

mortal: human being; person; individual; destined to die 166

mortality: death rate; mortal nature 166

mortician: undertaker 166

mortification: embarrassment 166

mortify: humiliate, embarrass 166

mortuary: funeral home; morgue 166

mot juste: the exactly right word 223

mountebank: quack; boastful pretender 252

mournful: full of sorrow *44*

musicale: social gathering, with music as the featured entertainment 231

mustang: bronco 264

musty: moldy or stale *70*

myrmidon: obedient and unquestioning follower 191

mythology: account or study of myths 115

nadir: lowest point 68

naive: simple; unsophisticated 217

narcissistic: in love with oneself 191

nautical: of the sea or shipping *81*

navigate: sail 211

necrology: register of persons who have died 115

nectar: something exceptionally delicious to drink 191

nemesis: due punishment for evil deeds; one who inflicts such punishment 192

nepotism: favoritism to relative to those in power 69

nettlesome: irritating 35

neurology: scientific study of the nervous system and its diseases 115

noblesse oblige: principle that persons of high rank or birth are obliged to act nobly 221

noisome: offensive to the sense of smell; unwholesome 70, 203

nom de plume: pen name; pseudonym 223

nonage: legal minority; period before maturity 77

nonagenarian: person in his 90's 77

nonbiodegradable: not readily decomposable by microorganisms *117*

noncarcinogenic: not cancer-producing 9

nonchalant: without concern or enthusiasm 217

nonpareil: person of unequalled excellence; paragon 220

nostalgia: homesickness; yearning for the past 45

notwithstanding: despite the fact that 201

nouveaux riches: persons newly rich 220

nowise: in no way 202

noxious: harmful *70*

nugatory: worthless 92

nuptials: wedding 213

nutriment: food 213

obese: extremely overweight; corpulent; portly 46

obesity: excessive body weight; corpulence 46

obligatory: required *156*

oblivion: condition of being forgotten or unknown 35

oblivious: forgetful 35

obloquy: a speaking against; public reproach 180

obsequious: showing excessive willingness to serve 48

obsolescent: going out of use 78

obsolete: no longer in use 78

obverse: front of a coin, medal, etc. 178

Occident: West 18

occidental: western 18

octogenarian: person in his or her 80's 77

odoriferous: yielding an odor, usually fragrant 181

odorous: having an odor, especially a sweet odor 70

odyssey: any long series of wanderings or travels 192

offal: waste parts of a butchered animal; refuse 82

officialdom: those having the authority of officials 202

olfactory: pertaining to the sense of smell 70

oligarchy: form of government in which a few people have the power 126

olio: mixture 262

Olympian (Olympic): majestic; godlike; lofty 192

omnibus: bus; book containing a variety of works by one author; covering many things at once 152

omnifarious: of all varieties, forms, or kinds 152

omnific: all-creating 152

omnipotent: unlimited in power 152

omnipresent: present everywhere at the same time 152

omniscient: knowing everything 152

omnivore: person or animal that eats everything 148

omnivorous: eating everything; fond of all kinds 148, 153

opera: play mostly sung, all costumes, scenery, action, and music 248

opinionated: unduly attached to one's own opinion 89

optional: not compulsory; discretionary 156

oratorio: musical composition, usually on a religious theme, for solo voices, chorus, and orchestra 248

ornate: elaborate 234

ornithology: study of birds 54

orthodox: conforming to accepted doctrines, especially in religion 90

ostentatious: done to impress others 93

osteopath: practitioner of osteopathy 129

osteopathy: treatment of diseases by manipulation of bones, muscles, nerves, etc. 129

oust: expel 150

overweening: thinking too highly of oneself 94

ovine: of or like a sheep 209

pacify: calm 211

paean: song or hymn of praise, joy, or triumph 192

paleontology: science dealing with life in the remote past as recorded in fossils 115

palette: thin board on which an artist lays and mixes colors 231

palladium: safeguard or protection 192

paltry: practically worthless 92

pampas: vast, treeless, grassy plains, especially in Argentina 264

panic: unreasoning, sudden fright that grips a multitude 192

paradox: self-contradictory statement which may nevertheless be true 90

paradoxical: self-contradictory, yet possibly true 90

paramount: chief 92

parasite: animal, plant, or person living on others 54

parasol: umbrella for protection against the sun 236

par excellence: above all others of the same sort 236

parody: humorous imitation of a serious writing 60

parrot: repeat mechanically, like a parrot 54

parsimonious: stingy 9

partiality: special taste or liking 88

parvenu(e): person suddenly risen to wealth or power who lacks the proper social qualifications 220

passé: old-fashioned; behind the times 236

pasta: wheat paste or dough 253

paternal: fatherly; inherited from or related to the father's side 69, 207

pathetic: arousing pity 45, 128

pathogenic: causing disease 129

pathological: due to disease 129

pathology: science dealing with the nature and causes of disease 115

pathos: quality in drama, speech, literature, music, or events that arouses pity or sadness 45, 128

patina: film or incrustation, usually green, on the surface of old bronze or copper 250

patio: paved outdoor dining or lounging area adjacent to a house 262

patriarch: venerable old man; father and ruler of a family or tribe; founder 78

patriarchy: form of social organization in which the father rules the family or tribe, descent being traced through the father 126

patricide: act of killing (or killer of) one's own father 145

peaceable: disposed to peace; not quarrelsome 151

peccadillo: slight offense 262

peculate: steal 211

pedal: lever acted on by the foot 173

pedestal: support or foot of a column or statue; foundation 173

pedestrian: foot traveler; commonplace 173

pedigree: an ancestral line 69

penitent: feeling regret for wrongdoing 44

pensive: thoughtful in a sad way 45

peon: common laborer; worker kept in service to repay a debt 260

perfidious: false to a trust; faithless 159

perfidy: violation of a trust 159

pericardium: membranous sac enclosing the heart 130

perigee: nearest point to the earth in the orbit of a man-made satellite or heavenly body 127, 130

perihelion: nearest point to the sun in the orbit of a planet or comet 131

perimeter: the whole outer boundary or measurement of a surface or figure 131

periodontics: branch of dentistry dealing with bone and gum diseases 131

peripheral: on the periphery (outside boundary) 131

periphery: outside boundary 131

periphrastic: expressed in a roundabout way 131

periscope: instrument permitting those in a submarine a view of the surface 131

peristalsis: wavelike contraction of the intestines which propels contents onward 131

peristyle: row of columns around a building or court; the space so enclosed 131

peritoneum: membrane lining the abdominal cavity and covering the organs 131

peritonitis: inflammation of the peritoneum 131

persistence: perseverance 154

pert: saucy 93

pertinacious: adhering firmly to a purpose or opinion 154

pertinent: bearing on the matter in hand 154

perusal: reading; study 17

peruse: read 19

perverse: turned away from what is right or good 178

pervert: turn away from right or truth; person who has turned from what is normal or natural 144, 178

pesticide: substance that kills rats, insects, bacteria, etc. 145

pestiferous: infected with or bearing disease; evil 181

pestilential: morally harmful; pertaining to a pestilence 56, 181

petrology: scientific study of rocks 115

petty: trifling 92

philanthropist: lover of mankind   101
philanthropy: love of mankind   101
philatelist: stamp collector   101
philately: collection and study of stamps   101
philharmonic: pertaining to a musical organization   101
philhellenism: support of Greece or the Greeks   101
philippic: bitter denunciation; tirade   192
philogyny: love of women   101
philology: study of language   101
philosopher: lover of wisdom   101
phlebotomy: opening of a vein for the purpose of diminishing the supply of blood   118
phobia: fear; dread; aversion   100
photophobia: morbid aversion to light   100
physiology: science dealing with the functions of living things or their organs   116
pianissimo: very soft   246
piano: soft   246
piazza: open square in an Italian town; veranda or porch   254
picador: horseman who irritates the bull with a lance at the beginning of a bullfight   260
picaro: adventurous rogue; vagabond   260
piddling: trifling   92
pièce de résistance: main dish; main item of any collection, series, program, etc.   233
pimento (pimiento): thick-fleshed pepper used for stuffing olives and as a source of paprika   263
pince-nez: eyeglasses clipped to the nose by a spring   236
pinnacle: highest point   65
piscine: of or like a fish   209
pizza: large, flat pie of bread dough spread with tomato pulp, etc.   253
pizzicato: direction to players of bowed instruments to pluck the strings instead of using the bow   247
plaudit: applause; enthusiastic praise   57

plausible: apparently trustworthy   90
pliable: easily bent or molded; capable of adaptation   153
plight: unfortunate state   45
plumb: get to the bottom of; ascertain the depth of   68
plutocratic: having great influence because of one's wealth   193
podiatrist: chiropodist   119
podium: dais; low wall serving as a foundation   119
poignant: painfully touching   45
politico: politician   252
pollute: make unclean   81
Pollyanna: irrepressible optimist   188
polyarchy: rule by many   109
polychromatic: showing a variety of colors   109
polygamy: marriage to several mates at the same time   109
polyglot: speaking several languages; person who speaks several languages   109
polygon: closed plane figure having many angles, and hence many sides   109
polymorphic: having various forms   109
polyphonic: having many sounds or voices   109
polysyllabic: having more than three syllables   109
polytechnic: dealing with many arts or sciences   109
polytheism: belief that there is a plurality of gods   109
poncho: large cloth, often waterproof, with a slit for the head   263
ponder: weigh in the mind   88
portfolio: briefcase; position or duties of a cabinet member or minister of state   254
porcine: of or like a pig   209
portico: roof supported by columns, forming a porch or a covered walk   250
portly: imposing, especially because of size   46
posthumous: published after the author's death; occurring after death   78

potpourri: mixture *225*
precipice: cliff 66
precipitous: steep as a precipice; hasty 66
précis: brief summary 223
precursor: forerunner 171
predecessor: one who precedes another *171*
predicament: unfortunate state *45, 89*
predilection: inclination to like or choose something *88*
preeminent: standing out above others 66
prehensile: adapted for seizing 175
prejudice: unreasonable preference or objection *88*
premier: prime minister 229
premiere: first performance 236
premonition: forewarning 156
premonitory: conveying a forewarning 156
preposterous: senseless 90
prestissimo: at a very rapid pace 245
presto: quick 245
presumptuous: taking undue liberties *94*
pretentious: done to impress others *94*
prevaricate: lie 211
prima donna: principal female singer, as in an opera; highstrung, vain, or extremely sensitive person 252
primeval: pertaining to the world's first ages *78*
primitive: characteristic of the original state of the world or of man *78*
primordial: existing at the very beginning; first in order 78
pristine: in original state; uncorrupted 78
probe: investigation 28
prober: investigator 28
procreate: beget 211
procrustean: cruel or inflexible in enforcing conformity 193
prodigious: enormous 35
prodigy: person of extraordinary talent or ability 35
profound: very deep 68
progenitor: forefather 69
progeny: children; descendants 69

progress: act of going from a worse to a better state 172
progressive: going forward to something better 172
projectile: object designed to be shot forward; anything thrown forward 176
proliferous: producing new growth rapidly and extensively 181
propinquity: kinship; nearness of place 83
prosecute: follow to the end or until finished; conduct legal proceedings against 169
prostrate: lie face down 211
protean: exceedingly variable; readily assuming different forms or shapes 193
protégé(e): person under the care and protection of another 220
prow: forward part of a ship *80*
proximity: nearness *83*
pseudopod: temporary extension of the protoplasm, as in the ameba, to enable the organism to move and take in food 119
psychology: science of the mind 116
psychopathic: pertaining to mental disease; insane 129
puberty: physical beginning of manhood (age 14) or womanhood (age 12) 78
pudgy: short and plump; chubby 46
pueblo: Indian village built of adobe and stone 263
puerile: foolish for a grown-up to say or do; childish 79, 207
pungent: sharp in smell or taste; biting 71
purge: cleanse; rid of undesired element or person 82
putrefy: rot *55*
putrid: stinking from decay; extremely bad 71
Pyrrhic: gained at too great a cost 193

qualm: misgiving *44*
queue: line of persons waiting their turn 237

raconteur: person who excels in telling stories, anecdotes, etc. 220

raillery: pleasantry touched with ridicule *58*

raison d'être: reason or justification for existing *237*

rancid: unpleasant to smell or taste from being spoiled or stale *71*

rank: having a strong, bad odor or taste; extreme *71*

rankle: cause inflammation *55*

rapport: relationship characterized by harmony, conformity, or affinity *222*

rapprochement: establishment or state of cordial relations; a coming together *229*

rapture: state of overwhelming joy *42*

rash: overhasty *66*

ratiocinate: reason *212*

rational: able to think clearly; based on reason *90*

rationalize: devise excuses for one's actions, desires, failures, etc. *90*

ravine: deep, narrow gorge worn by running water *68*

raze: demolish *10*

reactionary: resisting change; ultraconservative *172*

rebuff: snub; insult *28*

recuperate: recover health after illness *55*

recur: happen again *171*

reek: emit a strong, disagreeable smell; be permeated with *71*

reflect: throw back light, heat, sound, etc.; think *153*

reflex: involuntary response to a stimulus *154*

refract: bend a ray of light, heat, sound, etc., from a straight course *152*

refractory: hard to manage *152*

regicide: act of killing (or killer of) a king *145*

regime: system of government or rule *230*

regimen: set of rules to improve health *56*

regressive: disposed to move backward *172*

reimburse: indemnify *18*

reinvigorate: give new vigor to *36*

reject: refuse to take *176*

rejuvenate: make young again *36*

relevant: bearing upon the matter in hand *92*

reluctant: disinclined *65*

remand: send back; recommit *156*

remiss: negligent *179*

remission: period of lessening of the symptoms of a disease *179*

remit: send money due; forgive *179*

remorse: regret for wrongdoing *213*

render: deliver; give *28*

rendering: presentation; interpretation *28*

rendezvous: meeting place; appointment to meet at a fixed time and place *237*

renegade: deserter from a religion, party, etc.; traitor *260*

repartee: skill of replying quickly, cleverly, and humorously; witty reply *223*

repast: meal *28*

repentant: showing regret for wrongdoing *44*

repertoire: list of plays, operas, roles, compositions, etc., that a company or performer is prepared to perform *231*

replenish: refill *28*

reprehend: find fault with; rebuke *175*

reprehensible: blamable *175*

reproof: rebuke *155*

reprove: disapprove or criticize *155*

repugnance: strong dislike *65*

repulsive: offensive *47*

residual: remaining after a part is used or taken *36*

residue: remainder *36*

restrict: keep within limits *146*

résumé: summary *223*

retentive: able to retain or remember *154*

reticent: inclined to be silent *10*

retinue: group of followers accompanying a distinguished person *154*

retire: withdraw from active duty; go to bed 10

retort: reply quickly or sharply in kind; quick, sharp reply 10, 149

retrograde: going backward; becoming worse 172

retrogression: act of going from a better to a worse state 172

retrogressive: disposed to move backward *172*

revere: regard with reverence 212

reverse: back part of something *178*

revert: go back 178

revive: bring back to life 148

rialto: marketplace; theater district of a town 250

rift: crack or opening *67*

rigor mortis: stiffness of the body that sets in after death 166

riposte: quick retort or repartee; in fencing, quick return thrust after a parry 224

rogue: tricky, deceitful fellow *260*

rotund: rounded-out; full-toned 92

rotunda: round building, especially one with a dome or cupola; large, round room 250

rout: state of confusion *225*

rueful: pitiable *44*

rupture: break; hostility 144, 212

Russophobe: one who dislikes Russia or the Russians 100

salubrious: healthful 56

salutary: beneficial 36

salvo: simultaneous discharge of shots; burst of cheers 254

sangfroid: coolness of mind or composure in difficult circumstances 221

sanguinary: bloody 209

sanguine: having a ruddy color; confident 209

sarcasm: sneering language intended to hurt a person's feelings 60

sarcastic: expressing sarcasm 60

sardonic: bitterly sarcastic 60

satire: language or writing that exposes follies or abuses by holding them up to ridicule 60

satiric(-al): expressing satire 60

saturnine: gloomy 193

savoir faire: knowledge of just what to do 222

scavenger: animal or person removing refuse, decay, etc. 54

scent: smell; perfume 71

scent: get a suspicion of 71

scherzo: light or playful part of a sonata or symphony 248

scintillate: sparkle; twinkle 212

score: twenty 28

scrupulous: painstaking; careful; upright *179*

scrutinize: examine very closely 36

scrutiny: examination; inspection; review 36

scuffle: struggle; wrestle; grapple 19

sebaceous: greasy; secreting sebum (fatty matter) 56

sedate: of settled, quiet disposition *93*

seduction: act of leading astray into wrongdoing 169

senile: showing the weakness of age 79

señor: gentleman; Mr. or Sir 261

señora: lady; Mrs. or Madam 261

señorita: young lady; Miss 261

septuagenarian: person in his 70's 77

sequel: something that follows 169

sequence: the following of one thing after another 170

sequential: arranged in a sequence; serial 170

serpentine: winding in and out 92

servile: befitting a slave or servant *68*

sforzando: accented 246

shard: fragment *213*

sibling: one of two or more children of a family 70, 204

sierra: ridge of mountains with an irregular (saw-toothed) outline 264

siesta: short rest, especially at midday 263

silhouette: outline; shadow 237

simpatico (simpatica): likable; congenial 252

sinuous: bending in and out 92

siren: dangerous, attractive woman; woman who sings sweetly; apparatus for sounding loud warnings 193

skeptical: incredulous; disbelieving *157*

slander: false and defamatory spoken statement 58, *169*

slanderous: falsely and maliciously accusing *57*

slatternly: untidy 82

sloven: person habitually untidy, dirty, or careless in dress, habits, etc. 82

snub: insult; rebuff 28

sober: not drunk; free from excitement or exaggeration 80

sobriety: temperance; abstinence 80

sobriquet: nickname 237

sociology: study of the evolution, development, and functioning of human society 116

solo: piece of music for one voice or instrument; anything done without a partner 248

solon: legislator; wise man 194

sombrero: broad-rimmed, high-crowned hat 264

somniferous: inducing sleep 181

sonata: piece of music (for one or two instruments) having three or four movements in contrasted rhythms but related tonality 248

sophistry: clever but deceptive reasoning 90

soprano: highest singing voice in women and boys 243

sordid: filthy 82

sororicide: act of killing (or killer of) one's own sister 145

sot: drunkard *80*

sotto voce: in an undertone; privately 254

soup du jour: special soup served in a restaurant on a particular day 233

souvenir: keepsake 237

Spartan: marked by self-discipline, bravery, and ability to endure pain 194

specious: apparently reasonable, but not really so 90

speculate: reflect; buy or sell with the hope of profiting by price fluctuations 91

spurn: reject 19

squalid: filthy from neglect 82

squalor: filth; degradation 82

staccato: disconnected; with breaks between successive notes 247

staid: of settled, quiet disposition 93

starboard: right-hand side of a ship when one faces forward 81

starveling: one who is thin from lack of food 203

stentorian: very loud 194

stern: back part of a ship *80*

stigma: mark of disgrace 58

stigmatize: brand with a mark of disgrace 58

stipend: fixed pay for services 19

stricture: adverse criticism 146

stringent: strict 147

stripling: lad 204

stucco: plaster for covering exterior walls of buildings 250

Stygian: dark; gloomy; infernal 194

subject: force (someone) to undergo something unpleasant 176

sublimate: redirect the energy of a person's bad impulses into socially and morally higher channels; purify 66

sublime: uplifting 67

subservient: useful in an inferior capacity; servile *68*

subversion: sabotage; undermining 10

subvert: undermine 10

succession: the following of one thing after another: *170*

successive: following in order *169*

succumb: yield 212

suckling: child or animal that is nursed 203

suicide: act of killing one's self 146

sullen: resentfully silent; glum 45

sully: soil 82

summit: highest point 65

sumptuous: luxurious *190*

superannuated: retired on a pension; too old for work 79

supersede: force out of use; displace 36

supersensitive: excessively sensitive *123*

supplant: replace; supersede *36*

supposition: a guess *123, 176*

supreme: above all others *92*

surveillance: close watch 19

survive: remain alive after 148

suture: stitch 28

svelte: slender 47

sweltering: oppressively hot 36

sycophant: parasitic flatterer 48

symbiosis: the living together in mutually helpful association of two dissimilar organisms 117

symmetrical: balanced in arrangement 92

symmetry: balance; harmony 92

sympathy: a sharing of (''feeling with'') another's trouble 128

table d'hôte: describing a complete meal that bears a fixed price 233

taco: fried, folded tortilla stuffed with chopped meat, cheese, shredded lettuce, etc. 264

tact: sensitive mental perception of what is appropriate on a given occasion 174, *222*

tactful: having or showing tact 174

tactile: pertaining to the sense of touch; able to be touched 174

tangent: touching; line or surface meeting a curved line or surface at one point, but not intersecting it 174

tangential: merely touching 174

tangible: touchable 174

tantalize: excite a hope but prevent its fulfillment; tease 194

tarnish: soil or dull *82*

taurine: bullish 208

technology: use of science to achieve a practical purpose 116

tedium: boredom *221*

teetotaler: person who totally abstains from intoxicating beverages 80

telepathy: transference of the thoughts and feelings of one person to another with no apparent communication 128

temerity: insolence; effrontery 35

tempera: method of painting in which the colors are mixed with white of egg or other substances, instead of oil 250

temperate: moderate in eating and drinking *80*

tenable: capable of being maintained or defended 91

tenacious: inclined to hold fast *154*

tenacity: quality of holding fast 154

tenancy: period of a tenant's temporary holding of real estate 154

tenet: principle or doctrine generally held to be true 155

tenor: adult male voice between baritone and alto 243

tenure: period for which an office or position is held 155

tepid: lukewarm 19

tepidly: unenthusiastically; lukewarmly *19*

terpsichorean: pertaining to dancing 194

terra-cotta: kind of hard, brownish-red earthenware, used for vases, statuettes, etc.; dull brownish-red 250

terse: free of unnecessary words *190*

tête-à-tête: private conversation between two persons 224

theology: study of religion and religious ideas 116

theory: a supposition supported by considerable evidence *89*

therapeutic: curative 56

thespian: pertaining to the drama or acting 194

throes: pangs 45

titanic: of enormous strength, size, or power 194

tome: one volume of a work of several volumes; scholarly book 118

tonsillectomy: surgical removal of the tonsils 118

toreador: bullfighter, usually mounted 261

torero: bullfighter on foot 261

torrid: sweltering *36*

torsion: act of twisting; twisting of a body by two equal and opposite forces 149

torso: trunk or body of a statue without a head, arms, or legs; human trunk 250

tortilla: thin, flat, round corn cake 263

tortuous: full of twists or curves; tricky 150

torture: inflict severe pain upon 150

toupee: wig 234

tour de force: feat of strength, skill, or ingenuity 237

toxic: poisonous 56

tracheotomy: surgical operation of cutting into the windpipe 118

tractability: obedience 10

tractable: capable of being controlled 10, *146*

traduce: malign; slander; vilify 169

tranquillity: harmony *8*

transgress: step beyond the limits; break a law 172

transitory: fleeting; ephemeral *27*

travesty: imitation that makes a serious thing seem ridiculous 60

treatise: written account *223*

tremolo: rapid repetition of a tone or chord without apparent breaks, to express emotion 247

tribulation: suffering 45

tribute: speech or writing of high praise *57*

trio: piece of music for three voices or instruments; three singers or players performing together 248

tripod: utensil, stool, or caldron having three legs 119

truckle: submit servilely to a superior 48

turncoat: apostate *260*

tutti: all (direction for all to perform together) 248

tutti: section of musical composition performed by all the performers 248

tyrannicide: act of killing (or killer of) a tyrant 146

unfledged: without feathers; immature *76*

unflustered: calm *36*

unguent: ointment 56

unintentionally: unwittingly *28*

unipod: one-legged support *120*

unmanageable: unwieldy *36*

unrestricted: not confined within bounds; open to all 147

unruffled: not agitated 36

unsavory: unpleasant to taste or smell; morally offensive 71

untenable: incapable of being held or defended 155

unwieldy: bulky 36

unwittingly: inadvertently; by accident 28

ursine: bearish 208

utopia: imaginary place of ideal perfection *103*

vagabond: one who wanders from place to place, having no fixed dwelling *260*

vain: conceited; worthless 93

vainglorious: excessively proud or boastful 93

valet: manservant who attends to the personal needs of his employer 220

valid: logically correct *89*

vanity: condition of being too vain; conceit 93

vanquish: conquer 151

vaquero: cowboy 261

velocipede: child's tricycle 173

velocity: speed 213

vendetta: feud for blood revenge 253

venerable: worthy of respect because of advanced age, religious association, or historical importance 79

venerate: regard with reverence 212

veracity: truthfulness 213

verity: truth 213

versatile: having many aptitudes 178

verse: line of poetry   178

vertex: farthest point opposite the base, as in a triangle or pyramid; apex   67

vertigo: dizziness   178

veteran: person experienced in some occupation; ex-member of the armed forces   79

viaduct: bridge for conducting a road or railroad over a valley, river, etc.   169

vibrato: slightly throbbing or pulsating effect, adding warmth and beauty to the tone   247

victor: winner   151

vignette: a literary sketch; short verbal description   231

vile: unclean; hateful   *82*

vilification: defamation   213

vilify: speak evil of   57, 169

viral: caused by a virus   56

virile: having the physical capabilities of a male   208

virtuoso: one who exhibits great technical skill in an art, especially in playing a musical instrument   252

virulent: extremely poisonous; very bitter   56

virus: disease-causing organism; corruptive force   57

vis-à-vis: face to face; in comparison with; in relation to   237

vivace: spirited   245

vivacious: lively in temper or conduct   148, *191*

vivacity: liveliness of spirit   148

vivid: (used for things) having the vigor and spirit of life   149

vivify: enliven; make vivid   149

vivisection: operation on a living animal for scientific investigation   149

vociferous: producing a loud outcry   181

vogue: fashion   234

void: invalid   *9*

volition: will   65

voracious: greedy in eating; incapable of being satisfied   148

vulpine: like a fox; crafty; cunning   209

wager: bet   19

wane: decrease gradually in size   19, 204

warlock: sorcerer or wizard   204

warp: threads running lengthwise in the loom   204

wax: grow in size   205

wheedle: persuade by pleasing words   *47*

winsome: cheerful; merry   203

withal: with it all; as well   205

withdraw: take back; draw back   37, 201

withhold: hold back   201

withstand: stand against; resist   201

womanly: having the qualities considered desirable in a woman   208

woof: threads running from side to side in a woven fabric   205

wrangle: haggle; bargain   *27*

wrench: twist violently   *150*

wretched: sunk to a low condition   *67*

writ of mandamus: written order from a court to enforce the performance of some public duty   156

xenophobia: aversion to foreigners   100

yclept: named; called   205

yearling: one who is a year old   203

yore: long ago   79

zany: clown; buffoon   37

zany: mildly insane   37

zenith: highest point; point in the heavens directly overhead   67

PRONUNCIATION SYMBOLS

ə	banana, collide, abut
ˈə, ˌə	humdrum abut
ᵊ	immediately preceding \l\, \n\, \m\, \ŋ\, as in battle, mitten, eaten, and sometimes cap and bells \-ᵊm-\, lock and key \-ᵊŋ-\; immediately following \l\, \m\, \r\, as often in French table, prisme, titre
ər	operation, further, urger
ˈər-, ˈə-r	as in two different pronunciations of hurry \ˈhər-ē, ˈhə-rē\
a	mat, map, mad, gag, snap, patch
ā	day, fade, date, aorta, drape, cape
ä	bother, cot, and, with most American speakers, father, cart
à	father as pronounced by speakers who do not rhyme it with bother
au̇	now, loud, out
b	baby, rib
ch	chin, nature \ˈnā-chər\ (actually, this sound is \t\ + \sh\)
d	did, adder
e	bet, bed, peck
ˈē, ˌē	beat, nosebleed, evenly, easy
ē	easy, mealy
f	fifty, cuff
g	go, big, gift
h	hat, ahead

The system of indicating pronunciation is used by permission. From *M Webster's Collegiate Dictionary*, Tenth Edition, © 1993 by Merriam-Webster porated.

hw   whale as pronounced by those who do not have the same pronunciation for both *whale* and *wail*

i   tip, banish, active

ī   site, side, buy, tripe (actually, this sound is \ä\ + \i\, or \à\ + \i\)

j   job, gem, edge, join, judge (actually, this sound is \d\ + \zh\)

k   kin, cook, ache

k̲   German ich, Buch

l   lily, pool

m   murmur, dim, nymph

n   no, own

ⁿ   indicates that a preceding vowel or diphthong is pronounced with the nasal passages open, as in French *un bon vin blanc* \oeⁿ-bōⁿ-vaⁿ-bläⁿ\

ŋ   sing \'siŋ\, singer \'siŋ-ər\, finger \'fiŋ-gər\, ink \'iŋk\

ō   bone, know, beau

ȯ   saw, all, gnaw

oe   French boeuf, German Hölle

ȫ   French feu, German Höhle

coin, destroy, sawing

pepper, lip

car, rarity

less

something between, as in shy, mission, machine, special (actually, this is a single sound, not two); with a hyphen between, as in death's-head \'deths-ˌhed\

between, as in thin, ether (actually, this is a single sound); with a hyphen between, two sounds as in ...ud\

<u>th</u>   **th**en, ei**th**er, **th**is (actually, this is a single sound, not two)

ü   r**u**le, y**ou**th, union \\'yün-yən\\, few \\'fyü\\

u̇   p**u**ll, w**oo**d, b**oo**k, curable \\'kyu̇r-ə-bəl\\

ue   German f**ü**llen, h**ü**bsch

u̅e̅   French r**ue**, German f**üh**len

v   **v**i**v**id, gi**v**e

w   **w**e, a**w**ay; in some words having final \\(ˌ)ō\\ a variant \\ə-w\\ occurs before vowels, as in \\'fäl-ə-wiŋ\\, covered by the variant \\ə(-w)\\ at the entry word

y   **y**ard, **y**oung, cue \\'kyü\\, union \\'yün-yən\\

ʸ   indicates that during the articulation of the sound represented by the preceding character the front of the tongue has substantially the position it has for the articulation of the first sound of *yard*, as in French *digne* \\dēnʸ\\

yü   **you**th, **u**nion, c**ue**, f**ew**, m**u**te

yu̇   c**u**rable, f**u**ry

z   **z**one, rai**s**e

zh   with nothing between, as in vi**si**on, a**z**ure \\'azh-ər\\ (actually, this is a single sound, not two); with a hyphen between, two sounds as in ga**z**e**h**ound \\'gāz-ˌhau̇nd\\

\\   slant line used in pairs to mark the beginning and end of a transcription: \\'pen\\

ˈ   mark preceding a syllable with primary (strongest) stress: \\'pen-mən-ˌship\\

ˌ   mark preceding a syllable with secondary (next-strongest) stres \\'pen-mən-ˌship\\

-   mark of syllable division

( )   indicate that what is symbolized between is present in some u ances but not in others: *factory* \\'fak-t(ə-)rē\\